$E \varphi \, 30$

REASONS FOR JEWISH CUSTOMS

AND TRADITIONS

(*Taamei HaMinhagim*)

Reasons For Jewish Customs And Traditions

(Taamei HaMinhagim)

By

RABBI ABRAHAM ISAAC SPERLING

◆

Translated into English

By

Rabbi Abraham Matts

BLOCH PUBLISHING COMPANY

New York

Copyright © 1968 by Rabbi Abraham Matts
All Rights Reserved
Printed in the United States of America
Library of Congress Catalog Card Number: 68-31711
ISBN: 0-8197-0184-X

Preface

The original Hebrew edition of Taamei HaMinhagim (Reasons for our Customs), was published in 1890 by Rabbi Abraham Isaac Sperling, who was born in the city of Lvov in 1850 and died there in 1920.

This compendium is to this day regarded by students of Jewish thought and practice as the most popular of all books written on this complex subject.

To the English speaking reader, however, this significant work has virtually been a closed book. I have attempted this translation in the hope that it will stimulate interest in the entire area of Jewish customs and discussions of their meaning and their significance. This is especially important in this century of the "decline of man," when our inquisitive youth seems in danger of losing sight of his relationship not only with G-d but also with his fellow-man.

The entire cycle of human life, from birth until death with its ceremonials, rituals, customs and traditions, is outlined and explained on the basis of reasons given for them in Holy Writ, Codes of Law and many other authoritative sources, including many ingenious tales and parables of our sages.

These ceremonial acts of course, are but the means to an end, namely the religious life. If they fail to achieve that objective, they are useless. Hence, there is only one criterion for determining the usefulness and validity of a religious practice; that is, *its power to arouse or to deepen spiritual emotion!*

May this book bring to many readers a better understanding of the customs and traditions of our people. May its contents be vividly impressed upon their minds and upon their hearts and may it serve as a guide and counselor in their daily lives.

ABRAHAM MATTS

Table of Contents

Preface 7

Customs Upon Arising in the Morning 13

Customs Connected with Putting on Tzitzith 19

Laws Concerning Tefillin 26

Morning Prayers and Benedictions 29

The Shema 40

Customs Pertaining to the Eighteen Benedictions 44

Customs Pertaining to the Priestly Blessing 62

Customs Pertaining to Propitiatory Prayers 67

Customs Pertaining to the Reading of the Law 78

The Synagogue 83

The Breaking of Bread 86

The Grace after Meals 90

The Blessings over Fruits 99

Various Blessings 100

Customs Pertaining to the Afternoon Service 112

Customs Pertaining to the Evening Service 113

Customs Pertaining to Sabbath Observance 116

The Blessing of the New Moon 167

Passover Customs 175

Shavuoth Customs 202

Tisha B'av 206

Fast Days — Communal and Private 213

Rosh Hashanah Customs 216

Yom Kippur Customs 232

Sukkoth Customs 246

The "Four Species" 248

Shemini Atzereth Customs 254

Simhath Torah Customs 256

Hanukkah Customs 258

Four Important Scriptural Readings 263

Purim Customs 264

Circumcision 271

Pidyon Ha-Ben 277

Marriage and Divorce 278

Visiting the Sick 289

Mourning Customs 290

Bibliography and Index 306

To My Wife, CHAYE ELKE

and our daughters

STISHA YEHUDITH

and

BATHYA GOLDA

ושמרתם ועשיתם כי היא
חכמתכם ובינתכם לעיני העמים
אשר ישמעון את כל החקים
האלה ואמרו רק עם חכם ונבון
הגוי הגדול הזה.   (דברים ד':ו')

Observe therefore and do them;
for this is your wisdom and under-
standing in the sight of the peoples,
that, when they hear all these
statutes, shall say: "Surely this is
a wise and understanding people."

(DEUT. 4:6)

Customs Upon Arising in the Morning

1. QUESTION:

Why do we wash our hands immediately upon rising in the morning?

ANSWERS:

1. A man awakening in the morning is like a new creature, as it is written: "They (the souls) are new every morning" (Lam. 3:23). It is therefore incumbent upon every man to purify himself and wash his hands out of a vessel upon awakening.

(Beth Yosef, Ch. 4)

2. While man is asleep, the holy spirit departs from his body and he becomes impure. The impure spirit clings particularly to his hands. It is therefore a religious requirement to wash one's hands in the morning immediately upon arising.

(Zohar, Parshath VaYeshev)

3. According to Jewish law, no one is permitted to walk four cubits (one cubit being from 18-22 inches) without first having washed his hands. If the vessel of water happens to be some distance away from his bed and there is no one to bring it close to him — some sages say that one may obey the law by walking less than four cubits at a time in order to get at the vessel. This procedure is incorrect, however, for it is better to go at a fast pace and get to the water as quickly as possible, so as not to keep the impure spirit lingering on one's fingers.

(Shaarei Teshuva in name of Birke Yosef 1:2)

The author of *Atereth Z'kenim* (Ch. 4) says in the name of the Zohar:
One who walks four cubits in the morning before having washed his hands incurs the penalty of death.

The author of *Agra D'Pirka,* relates in the name of his grand-uncle, the *Meharmaz,* concerning the prohibition against walking four cubits in the morning without washing, "that one should be careful not to place his feet on the ground before washing, so as not to give the evil spirit the chance to wander over the entire body while it is in an upright position."

The author of *Shulhan Arukh HaRav* (4:2) writes: One should be very careful not to touch any kind of food or drink before washing, so as not to make the food unclean.

2. QUESTION:

Is it permissible to say the Blessing recited when washing your hands while the water in which you have just washed away your impurity is before you?

ANSWER:

The author of *Birke Yosef* maintains that the very observant do not pronounce any blessing or prayer while the water in which they just washed the impurity from their fingers is before them.

The author of *Avodat Hakodesh* suggests that the vessel containing the impure water be covered, for water defiled by impurity from the fingers is considered more impure than urine.

The author of *Kav Hayashar* (Ch. 3) writes: It is the custom of "men of good works" (Anshe Maaseh) to recite the following prayer immediately after the Blessing for washing the hands: "O G-d of all souls! May it be Thy Will, O L-rd, our G-d and G-d of our fathers, Abraham, Isaac and Jacob to stand us in good stead, and to free us and our children from all sin and transgression, so that we may fulfill the commandments of Thy Holy Torah undisturbed by alien thoughts. Purify our hearts to serve Thee in truth and sincerity, Amen!"

It is written in the Zohar (Vayeshev) that the waters in which the impurity of the fingers was washed away should not be kept in the house for any length of time.

3. QUESTION:
Why do we wash our hands three times?

ANSWER:

We presume the impure spirit has definitely left us after three washings. In other cases, however, one pouring of water over our hands is considered sufficient.

(Seder Hayom)

 4. QUESTION:
When must the hands be washed?

ANSWER:

On awakening from sleep; on leaving the lavatory or bath; on paring one's nails; after having cut one's hair; after having taken off one's shoes (with one's hands); after sexual intercourse; after having touched vermin; after having combed one's hair; after having touched the body in hairy places usually covered by clothing; after leaving a cemetery; after attending a funeral and on leaving a house where there is a corpse.

If he failed to wash his hands on one of the aforementioned occasions, his knowledge will leave him if he is a learned man, and if he is an ignorant man, he will become insane.

(Orakh Hayyim 4:18)

Eliyahu Rabbah states: The statement "he will become insane" implies that he will eventually transgress some law, for one does not commit a sin unless one has taken leave of his senses.

The author of *Magen Avraham* (4:17) holds that one need *not* wash three times after leaving the lavatory. In a later chapter (7:1), he states the view of the Zohar that one must wash three times also in this case, but he does not agree with this opinion.

The author of *Shaarei T'shuvah* (4:20) writes: The "venerable Rabbis" (Rabbanan keshishoei), did wash three times in the above-mentioned case, but only once after removing their leather shoes.

The author of *Kitzur SHeLaH,* in the name of the author of *Hechal HaKodesh,* also maintains that one must wash his hands three times upon leaving the lavatory.

(Magen Avraham 7:1)

5. QUESTION:

Why do we pronounce a Blessing (al netilat yadayim) when we wash our hands in the morning?

ANSWER:

A man rising in the morning is like a new creature. He must, therefore, after washing his hands, "praise G-d and render thanks unto Him." This washing which is an act of ritual purification, should be done out of a vessel, just as the Priests of the Holy Temple were accustomed to purify their hands daily out of the wash-basin prior to performing their functions in the Temple.

(*Magen Avraham* 4:1, *in name of Rabbi Solomon ben Abraham Adreth — RaSHBA*)

6. QUESTION:

When putting on our shoes, why must we put on the right shoe before the left?

ANSWER:

Certain precepts found in Biblical law imply that the Torah considers the right side of the body more important than the left. Thus, newly consecrated priests had the blood of the sacrificial ram sprinkled on "the thumb of the *right* hand and the toe of the *right* foot" (Lev. 8:23). P. 126

The right foot is used in the *halitzah* act (Yevamoth 104a).

NOTE: (*Halitzah* Ceremony by which a man is released from the obligation to marry his brother's childless widow. In this ceremony the woman must remove the shoe from the man's right foot as a token gesture of the contempt in which he should be held for not marrying her).

Therefore, the right side should be given precedence over the left in all matters, including the act of dressing.

If the shoes require lacing, the right shoe should be put on first but should not be laced until after the left shoe has been put on and laced, for in the act of fastening a knot, the left takes precedence over the right, since the knot of the *Tefillin* is fastened on the *left* hand.

However, when removing the shoes (regardless of whether or not they have laces), the left shoe should be removed first, for if the right shoe were to be removed while the left foot is still covered, it would be considered a slight to the right foot.

(*Levush* — *Rabbi Mordecai Jaffe*, 2:4)

7. QUESTION:

Prior to performing a Mitzvah it is customary to declare: L'Shem Yihud ... b'Shem kal Yisrael — "In the name of the Holy Unity ... in the name of all Israel I am prepared and ready to fulfill the command of my Creator." Why?

ANSWER:

Each and every Mitzvah bears within itself the entire Torah and embraces the whole of man. Hence, when we are about to perform a Mitzvah, we introduce it with the words "in the name of all Israel," to imply that we want our good deed to involve all our fellow-Jews.

(*Beth Aaron, by Aaron, Rebbe of Karlin,* Parshath Ekev)

The author of *Zerah Kodesh* Parshath Vayeshev) writes:

If one about to worship G-d prefaces his prayer with the declaration "In the name of the Holy Unity ... In the name of all Israel ..." — all the prayers he will recite thereafter will be accepted by G-d even though he may not be overly zealous in obeying all the laws of the Torah.

It is written in the Zohar (Parshath Thazria):

Rabbi Eliezer said: All the deeds of man must be *done for the sake* of the Holy Name of G-d. Therefore, the Holy Name of G-d should be mentioned before every good deed so that the evil spirit which is frequently within man will not prevail over the good deed he is about to perform.

8. QUESTION:

But why is "In the name of the Holy Unity..." not said before performing the mitzvah **of hospitality which is certainly a good deed of great magnitude?**

ANSWER:

The mitzvah to receive guests is even *greater* than waiting upon G-d Himself... It is therefore unnecessary to recite at that time, "In the name of the Holy Unity."

(Degel Machnei Ephraim)

The *Rachmei Ha-Av* relates the following test put to the father of the Baal Shem Tov.

Rabbi Eliezer, the father of the Baal Shem Tov, lived in a small village. His hospitality was as that of our father Abraham — in that he placed guards at the outskirts of the village and had them stop poor wayfarers and bring them to his house for food and shelter.

The heavenly bodies rejoiced at his doing, and once they decided to test him. Satan offered to put him to the test, but the prophet Elijah begged to be sent in his stead. Disguised as a poor wayfarer, carrying knapsack and staff, he came to Rabbi Eliezer's house on a Sabbath afternoon and greeted the Rabbi with a "Gut Shabbos." Not wishing to embarras him, the Rabbi did not reprimand the wayfarer for dishonoring the Sabbath by carrying a knapsack and staff, but invited him to the Sabbath meal and made him as comfortable as possible. He did not even utter a word of reproof the next morning when his guest was about to leave.

The prophet Elijah then revealed himself to Rabbi Eliezer and promised him a son who would cause the eyes of Israel to see the Light, and that son grew up to be, Israel ben Eliezer, Baal Shem Tov, the founder of Hassidism.

Customs Connected with
Putting on the *Tzitzith*

 9. QUESTION:
What is the reason for the custom of covering one's head with the Tallith?

ANSWER:

The act of covering one's head with the Tallith, humbles the heart of the man, so that he will fear the L-rd.

(Beth Yosef, Ch. 8)

Said the author of *Baer Hetev*: One should cover his head with his Tallith so that he may pray with fear and awe.

(8:3)

The author of *Eliyahu Rabbah* (8:4), says in the name of the author of Adei Zahav that one should cover his head with the Tallith from the beginning of the prayers until the end, and not just throw the Tallith over his shoulders as some people do after pronouncing the Blessing over the Tallith. It is to such people that the Biblical passage "And thou hast cast Me behind thy back" (I Kings 14:9) alludes.

It is written in the Zohar (Parshath Bamidbar): Spread over your head the blanket of *Mitzvah* (symbolized by the Tallith).

The *Magen Avraham* (8:3) however writes: The Gemara (Kiddushin 29b) teaches us that an unmarried man did not cover his head (with a Tallith), even if he was a scholar; on the other hand, neither did one who was not a scholar, even if he was married (Ibid. 8a).

10. QUESTION:
Why must the head be covered at all times?

ANSWER:

Says the author of the *Turei Zahav,* Rabbi David Halevy (8:3): Even when not praying, one should be very careful *not* to go bareheaded, especially since the nations of the world have accepted the head covering as a sign of disrespect so that they immediately remove their hats upon entering an abode, or when sitting down to a meal, and Israel, is not to imitate the other nations in manner of dress, etc., as it is written, "And in their customs ye shall not walk" (Lev. 18:3).

It is therefore incumbent upon man to keep his head covered at all times, so that "the fear of the L-rd may be upon him!"

(Sabbath 156b)

The Talmud (Kiddushin 33a) relates that Rabbina was sitting with Rabbi Jeremiah, when a bareheaded man passed by. Exclaimed Rabbi Jeremiah: "How insolent this man is!"

11. QUESTION:

Why must each of the ritual fringes (tzitzith) consist of eight threads?

ANSWER:

The Talmud (Menahoth 42a) states: It is written in the Torah, "Thou shalt make thyself twisted cords (*gedillim*) on the four corners of thy covering" (Deut. 22:12). Had the word for "cords" been in the singular (*gedil*), it would have meant that there needed to be only two threads (as one thread is doubled into two). The plural form indicates that four threads are required. When these four threads are drawn through the perforation in the garment and then doubled, the result is a total of eight threads.

(TaZ 11:13)

Rabbi Simon ben Zemach Duran, the TaSHBeTZ, writes:

The Tallith has four Tzitzith (fringes). Since each fringe consists of eight threads, each Tallith has a total of thirty-two threads in all, corresponding to the numerical value of the letters in the Hebrew word *Lev* (Heart — 32 — לב).

This implies that the Mitzvah of the ritual fringes is comparable to the entire Torah, for the Torah begins with the letter *Beth* (B're-shith — "In the beginning") (Gen. 1:1), and ends with the letter *Lamed* (L'enei kal yisrael — "In the sight of all Israel") (Deut. 34:12).

Together, the Lamed and the Beth form the word *Lev.*

12. QUESTION:

When should a child first begin to wear a Tallith **Katan?**

ANSWER:

The custom is to put a *tallith katan* on a child when he begins to talk, or at the age of three years. It is not done earlier because "man is as the tree of the field" (Deut. 20:19). Even as the fruit grown by a tree during its first three years may not be eaten (Lev. 19:23), so the child, too, is considered immature and unconsecrated until he reaches the age of three years.

(*Eliyahu Rabbah* 17:3)

13. QUESTION:

Why and how should one perform the commandment to "look" upon the Tzitzith (Num. 15:37-41)?

ANSWER:

A person should look at his tzitzith at every opportunity, for it is very good for his soul. Looking at the fringes will draw man away from sin.

(*Atereth Z'kenim, Ch.* 8)

The author of *Ktav Yosher* writes in the name of the Ari:

One should look at the Tzitzith every minute in the following manner: take the four tzitzith in your hand and look at them twice (once for each eye). This is most conducive to bringing down an abundance of sustenance (parnasa) from above, as it is written: "The *eyes* of all wait upon Thee; and Thou givest them their food in due season" (Psalms 145:15).

The author of *Kitzur SHeLaH* writes: One who brushes the Tzitzith over his eyes when reciting the Biblical passage relating to the laws of Tzitzith (Num. 15:37-41) can be sure that he will never go blind.

Said Rabbi Isaiah Horovitz, the Shelah HaKadosh:

The Hebrew letters in the word *Kanaf* — כנף (skirt or edge-tzitzith), has the same numerical value as the word *kaas*-anger.

From this we infer that one who is angry should grasp his tzitzith so that his anger will subside.

14. QUESTION:

Why are the ritual fringes called gedillim?

ANSWER:

The word *gedillim* is derived from *gadal*, the Hebrew for "growing." The custom is to make fringes even for a small child and to put them on him even before he is taught to perform any other precept.

The term *gedillim* implies that as the child *grows* with the tzitzith close to his body, the mitzvah of tzitzith grows along with him in that it becomes more meaningful to him as he grows older.

(*Rabbenu Tzvi Ha-Kohen of Rimanov*)

15. QUESTION:

Why must the Tzitzith be white?

ANSWER:

To emulate G-d. The Talmud tells us that G-d envelops Himself in His Tallith (Rosh Hashanah 17b). And this Tallith, with its Tzitzith, must be white, as it is written, "His raiment was as white snow" (Daniel 7:9).

(*Atereth Z'kenim, Ch. 9*)

The *atarah* or ornamental border adorning the *Tallith*, should also be white (Shaarei T'shuvah 9:2).

16. QUESTION:
Why is a thread or stripe of blue usually woven into
the Tallith or along its edges?

ANSWER:

In accordance with the Biblical passage: "that they put with
the fringe of each corner a thread of blue" (Num. 15:38).

(*P'ri Megaddim* 9:6)

17. QUESTION:
We coil the thread seven times in the first, eight
times in the second, eleven times in the third, and
thirteen times in the fourth. The fringes are thus
made up of a total of thirty-nine coils. What is the
symbolic significance of this procedure?

ANSWER:

Thirty-nine is the numerical value of the Hebrew letters ה-ו-ה-י
אחד, "The L-rd is One!"

(*Beth Yosef, Ch.* 11)

18. QUESTION:
Why must each fringe have five knots?

ANSWERS:

1. The five knots symbolize the Five Books of Moses.

2. The Hebrew letters in the word Tzitzith (ציצית) have a
total numerical value of 600. When 5 (for the five knots) and 8
(for the eight threads) are added to this number, we arrive at a total
of 613, corresponding to the 613 Commandments of the Torah.

(*Rashi, Commentary on Tractate Menahoth* 43b)

19. QUESTION:
Why must the Tallith Katan be worn all day long?

ANSWER:

So that one may remember the Commandments of G-d at all times.

(*Orakh Hayyim* 24:1)

20. QUESTION:

Why may the perforation into which the fringe is inserted not be more than three thumbs' breadths away from the edge of the garment?

ANSWER:

The pertinent Biblical law states that the fringes must be placed in "each corner." If they were placed more than three thumbs' breadths away from the garment's edge, they would not be in the "corners" of the garment but within the garment itself.

(*Ibid.* 11:9)

21. QUESTION:

Why is it customary not to use a knife for cutting the tzitzith, but to use the teeth instead, if necessary?

ANSWER:

This is in accordance with the Mishnah (Midoth 3:4) which states that "if iron touches a stone, the stone becomes unfit for use in the building of an altar" for "iron shortens life, whilst the altar prolongs it" (ibid.). The metal from which swords and other weapons are forged, is the symbol of strife, while the altar signifies peace and reconciliation between G-d and man and between man and his fellowman.

Accordingly, it would not be proper to build an altar with stones that have been cut with tools of iron.

The same principle is taken to apply to the tzitzith also, for the

Talmud says that "children die young because of the sin they commit in not wearing their *tzitzith*" (Tractate Sabbath 32b).

As a consequence, wearing tzitzith, like the altar, prolongs the life of man. Accordingly, it would not be proper to use a knife (which shortens life), to cut the tzitzith (which are meant to prolong life).

It is advisable therefore, to use one's teeth rather than a knife to cut the threads.

(Mesorat HaBrith)

22. QUESTION:

Why do we wrap ourselves in the Tallith before putting on the phylacteries (Tefillin)?

ANSWER:

The Mitzvah of Tzitzith is so important that the Scriptures equated its observance unto the observance of all the commandments in the Bible, as it is written: "That ye may look upon them (the tzitzith), and remember all the commandments of the L-rd" (Num. 15:39).

Furthermore, the donning of the Tallith is a "daily" Mitzvah, as it is observed every day, Sabbaths, Holidays and weekdays, whilst the Tefillin are worn on weekdays only, and it is an established rule that when the choice is "between the daily and the periodic, the daily is given precedence over the periodic."

(Levush 25:1)

Laws Concerning *Tefillin*

23. QUESTION:

What special honors are paid to the Tefillin?

ANSWER:

The Tefillin are called *pe-eir* or "glory," as it is written, *pe-eirkha havosh alekah* — "thy glory (Tefillin) bind around thy head" (Ezekiel 24:17).

(Moed Katan 15a)

Therefore one should take pride in the Tefillin, donning them as an ornament. When purchasing a new pair of Tefillin, one should buy only the best, and from a competent and G-d fearing man.

Likewise, the *retzuot* (the straps) as well as the *battim* (capsules) should be jet black and of the best quality, for one should not try to economize when buying objects to use in fulfilling a Divine precept.

From time to time, they should be blackened with black ink so that they will look fresh and new at all times. If the Tefillin should become unfit for use, a new pair should be bought.

(Seder Hayom)

24. QUESTION:

Why are the Tefillin put on the left hand rather than on the right hand?

ANSWER:

It is written (ידכה), "And it shall be for a sign upon thy hand" (Ex. 13:16). Say the Rabbis: The word *yad-chah* (thy hand), means *yad-keiha*, i.e., the "left hand," which is the weaker and feebler of the two.

(Menahoth 37a)

The author of Siddur Lev Same'akh writes:

I have heard many righteous sages say that "when they tied the knot of the Tefillin on their left hand, they were tying multitudes of Israelites to the Almighty G-d, blessed be He!"

25. QUESTION:

When should boys begin to put on Tefillin?

ANSWER:

There is a difference of opinion as to when a boy should begin to put on Tefillin. According to the ReMa, Rabbi Moses Isserles (37:3), he should begin when he reaches the age of thirteen years and one day.

The author of *Magen Avraham* (ad locum) says that it is the custom today to have the boy start putting on the Tefillin two or three months prior to his Bar Mitzvah.

The author of *Hadrath Kodesh* writes in the name of Rebbe Shalom of Belz, that it is best that the boy should begin to put on the Tefillin at the time prescribed by the Torah, i.e., at the age of thirteen years and a day, for he is then likely to be mature enough and spiritually ready to obey the Commandments of G-d.

He also writes that it is customary for an orphan to start putting on his Tefillin a few months prior to his Bar Mitzvah, perhaps in order that the child's act may bring comfort to the soul of his departed parent.

26. QUESTION:

Why is the arm phylactery strap wound around the arm seven times?

ANSWERS:

1. To recall the seven hand maidens who were chosen from the household of Ahasuerus to serve Queen Esther (Esther 2:9).

(Kitzur SHeLaH)

2. To recall the seven Angels: Michael, Gabriel, Raphael, Uriel, Tzadkiel, Yufiel and Raziel.

(Agra D'Pirka, in name of Zohar (Song of Songs)

3. The author of *Totzoath Hayyim* writes: The seven windings symbolize the Seven Benedictions which are recited at each marriage ceremony.

27. QUESTION:

Why should a pupil not remove his Tefillin while standing face to face with his teacher?

ANSWER:

It is considered a sign of disrespect to remove one's Tefillin in front of one's teacher. The proper thing for the pupil to do is to turn away from his teacher when he removes them.

(Levush — Rabbi Mordecai Jaffe 38:10)

It is written in the *Kitzur SHeLaH* that one should also not face the Holy Ark when removing the Tefillin, but should move away from the Ark.

It is customary that if Scrolls of the Law happen to be in a room, one must turn away from them when removing his Tefillin.

28. QUESTION:

The straps belonging to the Tefillin worn on the head, cannot be used as straps for the Tefillin worn on the arm. Why not?

ANSWER:

The Gemara (Menahoth 43b) says, "Holy vessels may be raised (in degree of sanctity) but not lowered." The phylactery worn on the head is considered more sacred than the phylactery worn on the arm, for it contains four passages from the Law and the letter *Shin* for *Shaddai*. As a consequence, straps belonging to the Tefillin for the head cannot be used for Tefillin worn on the arm.

29. QUESTION:

What other marks of respect should be accorded the Tefillin?

ANSWERS:

1. If one accidentally dropped his Tefillin so that they fell to the ground, he should fast all that day. If the Tefillin were in their bag when they fell, he should make a donation to charity.

(Eliyahu Rabbah 40:5)

2. If young students studying the Torah drop their Tefillin, they should study two or three hours longer than they had planned to do on that day.

(Responsa of MaHaRYE of Bruna)

Morning Prayers and Benedictions

30. QUESTION:

Why is the prayer Adon Olam recited at the beginning and again at the conclusion of morning prayers?

ANSWER:

It is an "advertisement," as it were, of G-d's attributes as implied in the appellations by which we refer to Him. The first two words, *Adon Olam* — "Master of the World" denote *Adonai,* the name of G-d implying His Creatorship of the Universe.

The verse, *V'hu haya, v'hu hove, v'hu yiyeh* — "He was, He is, He shall remain," denotes His mercy and compassion as implicit in the Tetragrammaton (YHWH).

The verse, *B'le Reshith* — "Without beginning, without an end" denotes that plenitude of might which comprehends all the forces of eternity and infinity and is implied by the designation *Elohim.*

(Rebbe of Apt)

The author of *Kitzur SHeLaH* states in the names of Rabbi Judah the Pious, Rav Hai Gaon, and Rav Sherira Gaon: "One who recites the *Adon Olam* prayer with true devotion, never permitting his mind to stray for a moment from the sublime message of the prayer, may be sure that the rest of his prayers, too, will be accepted on High, and the Adversary will not be able to nullify these prayers."

That is why *Adon Olam* is recited at the beginning and again at the conclusion of morning prayers.

31. QUESTION:

The Benediction recited over the Torah in the morn-ing prayers reads:

"Blessed art Thou, O L-rd our G-d, King of the Universe, who hast chosen us from all peoples and given us Thy Torah. Blessed art Thou, O L-rd, who gives [us] the Torah."

Why is the verb in the present tense?

ANSWER:

Because in fact, He gives us His Torah anew each day. If we study His Law without cease, we will continually discover new teachings and new insights which were veiled from our view before. Therefore, if one has the proper approach to the study of the law, he can experience the Revelation every day in his own life.

(Sefer Hassidim)

It is written in *Ma'or Vashemesh*: We find in the Holy Books, and I have heard it from my Rabbis, that the most important thing of all in the service of G-d is that man should reflect on his past and meditate on the improvement of his inner self before commencing the study of the Torah, or before carrying out a commandment of G-d.

Said Yakov Yitzchak, the Rebbe of Lublin: If a person does not repent before beginning to study the Torah — concerning such a person the Psalmist says, "To the wicked G-d says, What hast thou to do to declare My statutes" (Ps. 50:16).

If, however, one repents and *then* studies the Holy Torah, he is called a righteous man, for the Rabbis teach us in the Talmud: "One who has betrothed a wife unto himself with the understanding that he is a righteous man — his betrothal holds good even if he should be a sinner, for he may have in-between times repented" (Kiddushin 49b).

An unequalled method for retaining what one has learned is "to center all of one's self and all of one's thoughts on our Teacher Moses, peace be upon him. In that way, his soul will cleave to the soul of our Teacher Moses, who is the Source of the Torah."

(Mayim Rabbim, Genesis, in the name of Rabbi Moses Schreiber (Hatham Sofer))

32. QUESTION:

Why must at least one hundred benedictions be pronounced each day?

ANSWERS:

1. One hundred Jewish people died daily, and no one knew the cause thereof, until King David, through the Holy Spirit, came to understand that it was because the people were not giving thanks to G-d for all the goodness and kindness He had shown them. David therefore instituted the one hundred benedictions to offset the hundred deaths, and lo and behold, as soon as people began to recite the 100 Benedictions each day, the dying ceased.

An allusion to this event is made in 2 Sam. 23:1: "Thus says the man (David) who was raised *up on high* (Heb:*ol*). The numerical value of the letters in the Hebrew word *ol* (עֹל), is one hundred. From this we learn that David instituted the one hundred Benedictions.

(Tur, Ch. 46, in the name of Natronai Gaon; see Menahoth 43b)

2. To counteract the one hundred curses found in the Book of Deuteronomy: ninety-eight in Deut. 28:15-58, and two more in Deut. 28:61.

(Rokeach)

33. QUESTION:

Why do women pronounce the special Benediction, "Who hast made me according to Thy Will?"

ANSWERS:

1. To affirm her faith in the absolute and unfathomable justice of Providence, and her resignation to the decree of G-d, Who made her "according to His Will."

2. It is written in *Torath HaShem* Parshath Vayetze): The reason for the daily recital of the Benediction, "... who hast not made me a woman," recited by men, is that in Jewry the men have more commandments to observe than women, and so are considered to be in a more privileged position than women.

34. QUESTION:

The Blessings begin with the words baruch atah — "Blessed art Thou," which seems as if we were facing Him directly. Why do we then continue with melech ha-olam — "King of the Universe," which would imply that we are not personally face to face with Him?

ANSWERS:

1. It is written: "I have set the L-rd always before me" (Psalms 16:8). When we mention G-d's Name, i.e. "Blessed art thou, O L-rd," it should be as if the L-rd were always "before you," as the Psalm puts it.

But then we continue with — "King of the Universe," "to declare that He is not only *my* G-d facing *me,* but also the G-d and King of the entire Universe. It is this G-d Who has sanctified us by His Commandments and commanded us to observe them."

(*Abudraham*)

2. After saying, "Blessed art Thou, O L-rd, our G-d," we immediately continue with "King of the Universe," because Judaism believes in a living G-d who is at work in nature and history as

Creator, Ruler, Guide and Benefactor. He is the G-d not merely of one sect, people, race or land but of the spirit of all flesh — truly, "The King of the Universe."

(*Arvei Nahal, Parshath Balak*)

35. QUESTION:

Why do we respond Amen when hearing a Blessing recited?

ANSWER:

It is written: "For I will proclaim the name of the L-rd, Ascribe ye greatness unto our G-d" (Deut. 32:3).

Said Moses to Israel: "When I will recite a Blessing, you shall answer *Amen.*"

(*Abudraham*)

NOTE: *Amen* means "It is true." When responding *Amen,* we should bear in mind that the contents of the Benediction we have just heard are true, and that I implicitly believe in them.

We also deduce from the verse quoted above that, upon hearing the utterance of His Name (Adonai), which is always the third word of the blessing, one should respond — "Blessed be He and Blessed be His Name."

(*See Makhtzith HaShekel, Ch.* 192;
Yoma 37a; *Berakhoth* 21a *and* 45a)

The author of *Or Tzaddikim* writes: If one has not responded "Amen" upon hearing a Blessing, especially during the prayers recited by the Cantor — it is urgent that he repent. He also needs to do penance, if he has not responded with "Let his great Name be blessed forever and to all eternity."

As the Holy Zohar (Vayelech) puts it: "Even when one answers *Amen,* but without being properly aware of its meaning — it would have been better if he had not been born!"

Therefore, a man should repent of each "Amen" he failed to say with proper devotion, and very great is the reward of him who responds "Amen" and "Let His great Name be blessed..." in a loud and vigorous voice, for the L-rd will have compassion and mercy upon him.

Rabbi Shimon ben Lakish said: He who responds "Amen" with great fervor will have the gates of Eden opened for him, as it is written, "Open ye the gates, that there may enter the righteous nation, which guards the truth" (Is. 26:2). Read not *shomer emunim* (which guards the truth), but *she-omrim Amen* (which say *Amen*).

What is the meaning of *Amen?* Rabbi Haninah said: "The initials of *El Melekh Ne'eman* — 'G-d, faithful King.'" (אל מלך נאמן.)

(*Sabbath* 119b; see *Tur, Ch.* 124)

36. QUESTION:

According to law, the Morning Benedictions should be uttered as the occasion demands.

For instance, as soon as one arises from his sleep, he should say, "O my G-d, the soul which Thou gavest me is pure...," concluding with the words, "Blessed art Thou...Who restorest the souls unto the dead"; On hearing the rooster crow early in the morning, he should recite the blessing, "Who givest to the cock the understanding to distinguish between day and night"; On putting on his clothes, he should utter the Benediction, "Who clothes the naked," etc., etc. Why, then, are all the Morning Benedictions recited together nowadays one after the other?

ANSWERS:

1. In the days of old, when the Jews lived in purity and holiness even at night — their hands were always pure so that they were fit to pronounce the necessary Benedictions whenever the occasion arose.

Today, however, our hands are not always ritually clean, so that we cannot pronounce the Blessings at the proper time. Therefore we wash and cleanse ourselves in the morning and immediately thereafter recite all the Benedictions at one time.

2. Because of the illiterate who would not know which blessing to recite when the occasion arose. Therefore the Blessings were organized in their present form by the Great Synod, to be recited by the Cantor in the Synagogue. Then, by simply responding "Amen," even the illiterate could fulfill their obligations with regard to all the Blessings.

(Levush 46:2-3)

37. QUESTION:

We recite the prayer, "At all times let man revere G-d in private as well as in public . . ." Next, we recite the Shema, and then we conclude the Benediction with the words, "Who sanctifiest Thy name before the whole world."

Why, then, do we emphasize the private aspect of worship?

ANSWER:

According to medieval authorities, the aforementioned prayers were the agonizing cry of a generation passing through the fires of persecution at a time when Jewish public worship was forbidden, probably under the Persian ruler Yazdegerd II who, in the year 456 C.E., prohibited the observance of the Sabbath and the public reading of the *Shema.*

These prayers were meant to be an abridged version of the Morning Service. They begin with the exhortation to be G-d-fearing in private, then proceed to give thanks to G-d for the privilege of proclaiming the confession of faith with "Hear, O Israel," and end with a petition for the fulfillment of the Messianic prophecies of peace and deliverance.

Today they are an exhortation to man in an age of freedom and democracy, to be G-d-fearing not only in public but to revere G-d also in private.

38. QUESTION:

> Immediately after the reading of the Shema in the
> morning, we recite the prayer, "Thou wast the same
> ere the world was created..." What is the origin
> of this prayer?

ANSWER:

This prayer is taken from the Midrash Va'ethchanan, in the name
of Jerusalem Talmud Perek Ha-Roeh which states: "When the
Jews enter the Synagogues and recite the *Shema*, the Heavenly Hosts
join with Israel in antiphonal song proclaiming "Thou wast the
same ere the world was created..."

> (*Or Tzaddikim, by the Kabbalist Rabbi Meir Papirsh*)

This prayer emphasizes the absolute unity and eternity of G-d
in time and space; it is thus an extension of the declaration concerning G-d's Kingdom.

39. QUESTION:

> Why are the prayers and precepts concerning the
> daily sacrifices recited every day even now, when
> the Temple is no more?

ANSWER:

Says the Gemara (Taanith 27b): Abraham asked G-d: "When
the Temple is no more, what will become of the daily sacrifices?"

Said G-d to Abraham: "I have already set down the 'Order of
the Sacrifices' which will be given to your descendants, the children
of Israel.

As long as they will study and recite this code, I will deem it
as meritorious as if they had actually made the offerings, and I
will forgive them all their iniquities."

> (*Tur, Ch.* 48)

It is advisable to recite the Daily Sacrifices in the synagogue,
for the synagogue is considered a "smaller version of the Sanctuary"

(*bet mikdash me'at*). It is meant to replace, in a small measure, the Temple where the Sacrifices were offered. For the very same reason, the Order should be recited standing, for according to law, the person making the offering had to do so in a standing position.

(*Kitzur SHeLaH*)

40. QUESTION:
Why did the Rabbis institute the daily recital of Chapter 5 of Tractate Zebakhim from the Mishna?

ANSWER:
When we recite this Mishnaic text as part of our daily worship, we will have recited excerpts from all three divisions of our sacred Codes: Scripture, Mishna and Talmud.

(*Tur, Ch. 50*)

This is why we begin in the morning service with a Scriptural Reading (Num. 28), followed by a Mishnaic excerpt (Zebakhim Ch. 5), and by the Baraitha of Rabbi Ishmael which is actually part of the *Midrash* but is considered equivalent to the Talmud.

(*Abudraham*)

41. QUESTION:
Why was this particular Chapter from the Mishna chosen for recital in the Morning Service?

ANSWER:
This is the only Chapter in the Mishna which does not record controversy or differences of opinion among the Sages.

The recital of this Chapter symbolizes our desire for peace.

(*Beth Yosef, Ch. 50; see the Shulhan Arukh of
Rabbi Isaac Luria, known as the Ha-Ari*)

42. QUESTION:
What is the origin of the prayer "O give thanks unto the L-rd, call upon His Name..." (I Chron.

16:8-36) which is recited daily before the Ark of the Law?

ANSWER:

This anthem was first recited by King David when the Ark was brought in solemn procession to Zion.

(*Tur, Ch.* 51)

43. QUESTION:

What is the origin of the prayer "The L-rd is King; the L-rd was King; the L-rd shall be King for ever and ever" (I Chron. 16:31), which is recited as part of the P'sukei Dezimra, (Chants of Sabbath and Holidays), and why is it recited standing?

ANSWER:

To emulate the angels in Heaven. Tradition has it that each morning an angel *stands* in the midst of the Heavens and proclaims: "The L-rd is King; the L-rd was King; the L-rd shall be King for ever and ever."

The entire heavenly Hosts then repeat this sentence after him until they reach the verse "Bless ye the L-rd" (Barekhu).

It is customary among the Sephardim to recite this verse twice, the better to "proclaim the Unity of G-d's Kingdom."

(*Beth Yosef, Ch.* 50)

44. QUESTION:

Why is Psalm 145 (Tehilla Le David — "I will extol Thee, O King ..."), preceded by Ashre Yoshve Veisecha 'od yehallelukha — "Happy are they that dwell in Thy house, they shall yet praise Thee" (Psalms 84:5)?

ANSWER:

The Talmud explains that the verse "Happy are they that dwell in Thy House," bids us to betake ourselves to the synagogue and

recite preliminary devotions in order to attune our souls to participate in the Service and *then* we "will be praising Thee" (Berakhoth
32b). With that, we proceed to the Song of Praise written by King
David.

(See Tosfoth Berakhoth 32b, sub voce Kodem Tefillatho)

45. QUESTION:

Why do we recite Verse 18 of Psalm 115: (Va'a-
nachnu Nevareich Yah — "But we will bless the
L-rd now and evermore ... Hallelujah"), at the conclusion of the Ashrei prayer (Psalm 145)?

ANSWER:

Since we are told that one who recites *Ashrei* three times
daily is assured of his portion in the World to Come, we conclude
the *Ashrei* prayer with the hope that we will be found worthy to
praise G-d "now and evermore." i.e., in the World to Come.

(Beth Yosef, Ch. 51)

46. QUESTION:

Why is the final verse of Psalm 150 "Let everything
that has breath praise the L-rd, Hallelujah," repeated twice?

ANSWER:

Because this is the last verse of the Book of Psalms and also
marks the close of the *P'sukei Dezimrah,* the special Psalms recited
in the Morning Service.

(Tur, Ch. 5ʹ

47. QUESTION:

Why is the last verse of the "Song of Moses" (Ex.
14:30 - 15:18), "The L-rd shall reign for ever and
ever," repeated twice?

ANSWER:

To emphasize the message of this, the final verse of the Song which Moses sang in praise of the L-rd on the banks of the Red Sea.
(*Abudraham*)

The Shema

48. QUESTION:

Why is there no special benediction to be pronounced before reading the Shema?

ANSWER:

Since the *Shema* is part of the Torah, the Blessing recited at the beginning of the Morning Services concerning the study of the Torah "And commanded us to occupy ourselves with words of the Torah," is considered applicable also to the reading of the *Shema.*
(*P'ri Megaddim, Ch.* 239)

49. QUESTION:

In the first section of the Shema, it is written, "And thou shalt love the L-rd thy G-d with all thy heart, and with all thy soul, and with all thy might," whereas in the second section, the phrase "with all thy might" is omitted. Why?

ANSWER:

The Rabbis tell us (Berakhoth 54a) that the Hebrew word *me'odekha* — "all thy might," means that in proving our unquestioning loyalty to G-d we must not shrink from sacrificing whatever possessions He has allotted to us.

The first section which contains the words "with all thy might," is phrased in the singular — it is addressed to the individual, and there are some individuals who value money even more than they do their own lives. Therefore, the admonition that even such a man should be prepared to sacrifice to G-d his possessions which are dearer to him more than life itself.

The second section on the other hand, is in the second person plural — it is addressed to the people as a whole, and people in general do *not* value property above life. Therefore, the phrase, "with all thy might" is omitted there.

(Siddur Lev Sameiak, in the name of author's father-in-law, Sholom, Rebbe of Belz; also in Or HaHayyim, Parshath Ekev, sub voce, bekhol levavhem)

50. QUESTION:

Why does Jewish custom prescribe that a person should close his eyes or cover them with his hand when he recites the opening verse of the Shema?

ANSWERS:

1. In order to blot out all distractions so that one may concentrate entirely on *the thought of the Unity of G-d.*

For the same reason it is also customary to recite the first line of the *Shema* aloud.

(Levush 60:5)

2. The placing of the right hand over the eyes symbolizes the death of the pious. Hence, this gesture when reciting the opening verse of the *Shema* implies our willingness to sacrifice our very lives for G-d if He should require it.

(Menahem Mendel, Rebbe of Kassov)

51. QUESTION:

Why is it considered proper to remain seated while reciting the Shema?

ANSWER:

The Midrash relates the following incident in the life of Abraham:

On the third day after Abraham's circumcision, when the patriarch was still in great pain, G-d visited him while he was sitting by the door of his tent in the heat of the day. Seeing His Maker, Abraham attempted to rise from his seat, but G-d would not allow it. When Abraham protested that it was not proper that he should remain seated in the presence of the L-rd, G-d replied: "As thou livest, just as thou *art now sitting* and I am standing above you, so shall it be when thy children will enter their synagogues and read the *Shema in My honor* — they will be sitting while I will reside therein, as it is written, *Elohim nitzav baadath El* — "G-d standeth in the Congregation of G-d" (Psalms 82:1).

(Genesis Rabbah 48)

52. QUESTION:

Why is the response "Blessed be His Name, Whose glorious Kingdom is forever and ever," uttered immediately after the first line of the Shema?

ANSWER:

It is written in the Talmud: "Why do we add the verse "Blessed be His Name ...," etc., after the first sentence of the *Shema* [although Moses did not recite this sentence after he proclaimed the *Shema* in Deut. 6:4]?"

Rabbi Simon ben Lakish replies: "It is written, "And Jacob called unto his sons and said, etc." (Gen. 49:1). Jacob wanted to disclose to his children all that would happen to them in the future, but the Divine Glory departed from him at that moment and he grew afraid, saying, "Perhaps Heaven forfend, my children have some character defect like my grandfather Abraham, who begat Ishmael, or like Isaac, my father, who begat Esau."

Thereupon his children said to him in one voice "Hear, O Israel, the L-rd our G-d is One!" (Israel is also the other name of Jacob). In other words, they reassured him that they were of blameless character, saying, "Father! Just as there is but One G-d in your heart, so in our hearts, too, there is only One G-d."

Upon hearing this, Jacob cried out: "Blessed be His Name, Whose glorious Kingdom is forever and ever!"

(Pesahim 56a)

53. QUESTION:

Why are the tzitzith held in the left hand during the Reading of the Shema?

ANSWER:

So that the *tzitzith* should be closest to the heart, as it is written, "And these words which I command thee this day, shall be upon thine heart" (Deut. 6:6).

(*Levush* 24:2)

54. QUESTION:

Why does the Cantor repeat the last three words of the Shema: "The L-rd your G-d, is [the] true [G-d]" (Adonai Elohehem Emeth)?

ANSWER:

These three final words are repeated by the Cantor so that the total number of words in the *Shema* which actually has only 245 words should be 248, corresponding to the 248 limbs of the human body, all of which should praise the L-rd.

(*Tur, Ch.* 61)

55. QUESTION:

Why is it customary for the Rabbi to recite aloud the portion of the Shema referring to the tzitzith?

ANSWER:

This portion contains the remembrance of the liberation from Egypt, the beginning of Israel's life, and its corollary, the election of Israel.

The Rabbi recites it aloud in order to stress the importance of the message it contains and to direct the thoughts of the worshippers to the objective of the precept of *tzitzith,* namely, "to be holy unto your G-d."

(*Kerem Shlomo*)

Customs Pertaining to the Eighteen Benedictions

56. QUESTION:

Why are the two last words of the "Redemption" Prayer (recited just before the Eighteen Benedictions) in the past tense; i.e. "Who hast redeemed Israel" (go'al Yisrael), instead of in the present tense "The Redeemer of Israel" (go'el Yisrael)?

ANSWER:

Because the "Redemption Prayer" was meant to apply to the deliverances that G-d wrought for our people in the past .

(*Tur, Ch.* 111)

57. QUESTION:

Why, in the seventh of the Eighteen Benedictions, (Re-ei veanyenu), do we conclude in the present tense, i.e., "Blessed art Thou, O L-rd," the Redeemer of Israel" (go'el yisrael)?

ANSWER:

As opposed to the "Redemption Prayer" recited *before* the Eighteen Benedictions, this is a prayer for deliverance from affliction at all times, past, present and future.

(*See Rashi's Commentary to Megilla* 17b)

58. QUESTION:

Why did the Rabbis institute the Eighteen Benedictions?

ANSWER:

The Eighteen Benedictions were instituted as a permanent part of Jewish liturgy by the Great Assembly (the *Sanhedrin*).

The Benedictions composing this prayer date back to remote antiquity. The Great Assembly (*Sanhedrin*) merely put them together in the order in which we know and recite them today.

According to tradition the Eighteen Benedictions had their origins as follows:

First Benediction:

When Abraham was saved from the furnace of Kasdim, the angels declared: "Blessed art Thou, O L-rd, the Shield of Abraham," which today is the first of the Eighteen Benedictions.

Second Benediction:

When Isaac lay terror-stricken at the thought that he was about to be sacrificed, G-d sent His dew to revive him, whereupon the angels said, "Blessed art Thou, O L-rd, who quickenest the dead."

Third Benediction:

When Jacob arrived at the gates of heaven and proclaimed the holiness of G-d, the angels said, "Blessed art Thou, O L-rd, the Holy G-d."

Fourth Benediction:

When Pharaoh made Joseph ruler over all of Egypt, Joseph was not familiar with the seventy languages which a ruler of Egypt was required to know. But the Archangel Gabriel came and taught him those languages, whereupon the angels said: "Blessed art Thou, O L-rd, Who graciously bestowest knowledge."

Fifth Benediction:

When Reuben committed the sin against Jacob, his father, (Gen. 35:22), a death sentence went forth against him from heaven. But when he repented, he was given a reprieve, and the angels said: "Blessed art Thou, O L-rd, Who takest delight in repentance."

Sixth Benediction:

When Judah admitted the sin he had committed against Tamar,

he obtained forgiveness, whereupon the angels said: "Blessed art Thou, O L-rd, Who art ever forgiving."

Seventh Benediction:
When the children of Israel were enslaved by the Egyptians and G-d promised them that they would be liberated, the angels said: "Blessed art Thou, O L-rd, Who redeemest Israel."

Eighth Benediction:
When the Archangel Raphael came to Abraham to soothe the pain he suffered as a result of his circumcision, the angels said: "Blessed art Thou, O L-rd, Who healest the sick."

Ninth Benediction:
When Isaac's sowing in the land of the Philistines yielded an abundant harvest, the angels said: "Blessed art Thou, O L-rd, Who blessest the years."

Tenth Benediction:
When Jacob was reunited with his sons Joseph and Simon in Egypt, the angels said: "Blessed art Thou, O L-rd, Who gatherest the dispersed of Thy people Israel."

Eleventh Benediction:
When G-d communicated the laws of the Torah to Moses, the angels said: "Blessed art Thou, O L-rd, Who lovest righteousness and justice."

Twelfth Benediction:
When the Egyptians were drowned in the Red Sea, the angels said: "Blessed art Thou, O L-rd, Who shatterest the enemy and humiliatest the presumptuous."

Thirteenth Benediction:
When Joseph laid his hands on the eyes of his father Jacob when he passed away, the angels said: "Blessed art Thou, O L-rd, Who art the support and stay of the pious."

Fourteenth Benediction:
When King Solomon built the Temple, the angels said: "Blessed art Thou, O L-rd, Who buildest Jerusalem."

Fifteenth Benediction:
When the Children of Israel passed through the Red Sea singing hymns of praise to G-d, the angels said: "Blessed art Thou, O L-rd, Who causest salvation to sprout forth."

Sixteenth Benediction:
When G-d answered the prayers of the suffering Israelites in Egypt, the angels said: "Blessed art Thou, O L-rd, Who hearest our prayer."

Seventeenth Benediction:
When the Divine Presence descended on the Tabernacle between the Cherubim, the angels said: "Blessed art Thou, O L-rd, Who wilt restore thy Divine Presence to Jerusalem."

Eighteenth Benediction:
When Solomon dedicated the First Temple, the angels said: "Blessed art Thou, O L-rd, Whose Name is worthy of praise."

Nineteenth Benediction:
When Israel entered the Holy Land, the angels said: "Blessed art Thou, O L-rd, Who blessest this people Israel with peace."

(*Shibalei Ha-Lekett*)

NOTE:
The "Eighteen" Benedictions are really nineteen, the one that is twelfth in the order of recitation having been added at a later date to help counteract the disturbing agitation carried on by so-called heretics (in Hebrew: *Minim*), and other schismatic sects which departed from some of the basic tenets of Judaism.

59. QUESTION:
Why must one wear a belt (Hassidim wear a black woven belt known in Yiddish as gartel) when reciting the Eighteen Benedictions?

ANSWER:
The verse "Prepare to meet thy G-d, O Israel" (Amos 4:12) is taken to apply particularly to this prayer. Part of the preparation for worship is to separate the heart from the baser passions. This

is done symbolically by the belt which separates the upper part from the lower portion of the body.

(*Tur, Ch.* 91; *see Beth Yosef and Levush, ad locum*)

 60. QUESTION:

> Why is it considered improper to stand on an elevated place when praying, and why is it deemed important to make a point of standing in a low place instead?

ANSWERS:

1. It is written: *"Out of the depths* have I called Thee, O L-rd" (Psalms 130:1; Berakhoth 10a).

2. When one prays standing in an elevated place it would seem as if he were trying to reach up to Heaven to communicate with G-d, when in fact, "the whole earth is full of His Glory" (Isaiah 6:3).

This too, is the message conveyed by the words "Out of the depths have I called Thee, O L-rd."

(*Levush* 90:1)

61. QUESTION:

> Why must we stand with our feet close together when reciting the Eighteen Benedictions?

ANSWER:

To indicate that we have no desire to "lift our feet" to run elsewhere. Rather it is our high resolve to stand straight and erect turning all our thoughts and desires toward Him.

For this very same reason one should not lean against any object when reciting the Eighteen Benedictions, for that would be a sign of laziness and disrespect. When praying, one should always remember that he is standing before the Divine Presence.

(*Kitzur SHeLaH*)

62. QUESTION:

Why should the Eighteen Benedictions be recited in an undertone, audible to no one else in the Congregation?

ANSWERS:

1. So as not to embarrass the sinner when he recites the confession of sins "Forgive us, our Father, for we have sinned...," as part of the Eighteen Benedictions.

On Rosh Hashanah and Yom Kippur, on the other hand, it is customary to recite one's prayers aloud, for on these Holy Days the entire Congregation confesses its sins in unison in alphabetical order. Since this is a Public Confession and no individual is put to shame, it is only proper that it should be recited aloud.

(*Sotah, Ch. Elu Ne'emarin; see Orakh Hayyim* 101:3)

2. If one were to recite the Eighteen Benedictions aloud, it would seem as if his belief in G-d were not very firm, for it would make it appear that he does not think G-d could hear him unless he spoke to Him in a loud voice.

(*Sefer HaGan VeDerekh Moshe*)

63. QUESTION:

The opening verse of the Eighteen Benedictions begins with the words "Blessed art Thou, O L-rd our G-d and G-d of our fathers, G-d of Abraham, G-d of Isaac and G-d of Jacob."
Would it not have been simpler to say merely: "G-d of Abraham, Isaac and Jacob?"

ANSWER:

If we were to say "G-d of Abraham, Isaac and Jacob," the Name of G-d would be joined only with that of Abraham who was the first man to recognize the True G-d. This could be taken to imply that Isaac and Jacob merely followed the beliefs laid down by their fathers without personal conviction.

We join His Name to "each of the Patriarchs" to teach us that each Patriarch found the One G-d in the true Jewish way, not by blind adherence to the word of his ancestors but through his own reasoning and convictions.

(Responsa Panim Me'iroth, Part 1, Ch. 39)

64. QUESTION:

Why was the prayer for Rain, which is recited on Sukkoth, incorporated into the Benediction relating to the Revival of the Dead?

ANSWER:

To imply that just as G-d will give new life to the dead in their graves, He will also cause rain to fall, to give life to the seeds slumbering in the soil.

65. QUESTION:

Why was the Havdalah, which is recited at the end of the Sabbath, incorporated into the Benediction relative to Understanding?

ANSWER:

Because it is only through understanding and wisdom that we are able to fulfill our duties in the proper spirit, and to understand the difference between the workdays of the week and the Sabbath, our Holy Day of Rest.

(Rabbenu Yonah, Berakhoth, Ch. 5)

66. QUESTION:

Could not the Benediction "Heal us, O L-rd," have stood without the concluding phrase "and we shall be healed?"

Is not the latter part of the sentence superfluous?

ANSWER:

This Blessing is meant to convey the thought that we can be fully healed forevermore only if the L-rd heals us.

(*B'nei Yisashar*)

It is written in the *Sefer Hassidim*: (Book of the Pious, a 13th century Hebrew book on Jewish morals and ethics. Its authorship is attributed in large part to Rabbi Judah ben Samuel of Ratisbon (d. 1217) usually referred to as Rabbi Judah Hehasid (the Pious).

Do not rush through the reading of the Eighteen Benedictions. When you are in need of sustenance, do not concentrate exclusively on the Ninth Benediction, which asks for freedom from want, nor exclusively on the Eight Benediction, the prayer for healing when there is a sick person in your home. For if you will do that, it may be considered Above that you are in need of this one blessing only and need none of the other Divine favors.

67. QUESTION:

Why was the prayer known as Ya'ale Veyavo ("May our prayers arise") which is recited on Rosh Hodesh, inserted in the Seventeenth Benediction which speaks of the restoration of the Temple Service?

ANSWER:

In the *Ya'ale Veyavo* prayer we also ask G-d to restore Jerusalem and the Temple to the people of Israel.

(*Tosfoth Sabbath* 24a, *sub voce, Bevone*)

68. QUESTION:

What is the origin of the prayer beginning with Sim Shalom ("Grant peace"), which is recited in the Morning Service?

ANSWER:

It is generally deemed proper that whenever the Scroll of the Law is read, we must recite *Sim Shalom* in the Eighteen Benedictions,

(*Haazinu* — the Song of Moses, Deut. Ch. 32, was recited each morning in the Temple) for it contains the following words, "For by the light of Thy countenance Thou hast given us, O L-rd our G-d, the Torah of Life," and only that peace has abiding value which is the fruit of common gratitude and common devotion to His Torah.

(*Rabbi Simon ben Zemach Duran,*
known as the TaSHBeTZ)

69. QUESTION:

At the conclusion of the Eighteen Benedictions we recite "He Who makes peace..., and say ye: Amen."

To whom does "ye" refer?

ANSWER:

It refers to the angels who accompany each person, as it is written, "He will give His angels charge over you, to guard you in all your ways" (Psalms 91:11).

(*Kitzur SHeLaH*)

70. QUESTION:

What is the reason for the custom instituted by the Rabbis that one should recite a sentence which begins and ends with his name, (or one containing the letters of his name) at the conclusion of the Eighteen Benedictions?

ANSWER:

The name of each man signifies his individuality, in that "in each and every soul in Israel, there is contained a part of the Holy One, Blessed be He." Mentioning one's name at the conclusion of of the Eighteen Benedictions, therefore, implies a wish to associate his name with the holiness of the Holy One, blessed be He.

(*Zera Kodesh*)

71. QUESTION:

Why do we take three steps backwards before reciting the prayer beginning with Yehi ratzon — "May it be Thy Will ... that the Temple be speedily rebuilt in our days ... ?"

ANSWER:

"Nebuchadnezer *ran three steps* to honor G-d" (see Sanhedrin 96a), and therefore became king of Babylonia. Eventually, however, he was to destroy the Temple.

Therefore, at the conclusion of our prayers, we too take *three steps backwards,* to show our respect for G-d (as is the custom when leaving the presence of a superior), as if to say, "O G-d, may it be Thy Will that the three steps which I have taken in Your Honor, may nullify the three steps taken by the wicked Nebuchadnezer, and may the Temple be speedily rebuilt in our days, Amen."

(*Igeret HaTiyul, by the brother of Rabbi Lowe of Prague*)

72. QUESTION:

In the concluding meditation of the Shemona Esrei (Elohai netzor), we recite: "O my G-d! guard my tongue from evil ... Let my soul be unto all as dust." What is the meaning of this passage?

ANSWER:

According to Tosfoth Berakhoth 17 this means "that just as dust endures forever, so may it be Thy Will, O G-d, that my children (who represent the very soul of each man) should endure forever," as G-d promised Abraham, "And I will make thy seed as the dust of the earth" (Gen. 13:16); i.e., as the dust of the earth spreads from one end of the world to the other, so will thy seed be dispersed throughout all lands, and as the dust causes even metals to decay but itself endures, so will the idolaters perish, but Israel will endure forever (Midrash).

Rabbi Solomon Luria, the MaHaRSHaL, interprets the aforementioned as follows: "Just as the dust of the earth is stepped upon by all, but in the end the earth will cover all those who stepped upon it, so shall it be with those who vex me."

Said the prophet Isaiah: "Awake and sing, ye who *dwell* in the dust" (Is. 26:19). The author of *Torath Ha-Adam* paraphrased this verse as follows: "Today I am *on* the earth, but the very next minute I may be *in* it. I am therefore a neighbor to the dust of the earth."

The author of *Daath Moshe* writes in the name of Rebbe Zusia of Anipol: "Ah, Earth, you are better than I! I do not understand why I tread upon you, for the time will come when I will rest beneath you!"

73. QUESTION:

Why is the first of the three steps back taken with the left foot?

ANSWER:

As a rule, the first step is usually taken with the right foot. On this occasion, however, we take the first step with the left, to make it appear as though we found it very difficult to leave the presence of the L-rd.

(*Magen Avraham* 123:10)

74. QUESTION:

Why do the Rabbis compare one who returns to his place immediately after retreating the three steps — to a dog who returns to the food he has vomited? (See Alfasi, end of fifth Chapter in Berakhoth).

ANSWERS:

1. Once one has sincerely and truly repented from his sins, he should feel as pure as if he had never sinned at all. For the Rabbis insist that G-d will not reject any person whose contrition is genuine.

By renouncing his sins, man is restored to the Divine Presence and completely forgiven.

Therefore, once a man has completed his prayer and retreated three steps, he should remain standing there, with his feet close together, and believe in his mind and heart that his sincere prayer has been accepted on High and that he had been completely forgiven. If he were to return to his place immediately, it would seem as if he were rushing back to ask forgiveness for the sins he may commit "in the future," and this is comparable to a dog who vomits his food and then returns to it to eat it again.

(*Rabbi Jacob Molin-MaHaRIL BeLikuttim; TaZ* 123:3)

2. The three steps backward imply that he has concluded his prayers and is taking leave of the Almighty, like a servant humbly retreating from the presence of his master. If he were to return to his place immediately, it would look as if he were not leaving the presence of his master, but had just made some jerky motion.

Therefore, when taking the three steps backwards, one should remain standing until the Cantor has come to the *Kedusha*, or at least until the Cantor begins his repetition of the Eighteen Blessings.

(*Levush* 123:3-4)

75. QUESTION:

Why does the Cantor repeat the Eighteen Benedictions aloud after the Congregation has finished reciting them in an undertone?

ANSWER:

For the benefit of the unlettered members of his Congregation, for an illiterate cannot pray properly by himself.

(*Rosh Hashanah* 34b)

76. QUESTION:

Why is the one who chants the prayers called Hazzan in Hebrew?

ANSWER:

The Hebrew word *Hazzan* connotes "watching or overseeing." The *Hazzan* (the Cantor), is meant to be the official "watchman" of the Congregation, as he is the one who leads the entire Congregation in prayer.

(Abudraham)

The Rebbe of Berdichev once asked a Cantor why he was hoarse. — "It's quite obvious," the Cantor replied. "I just finished praying before the *Amud* (Reader's desk)!"

"Aha!" exclaimed the Berdichever. "Had you been praying before G-d, you would not have become hoarse."

(Zichron Tov, in the name of the Rebbe of Neschitz)

77. QUESTION:

When the Cantor repeats the Eighteen Benedictions aloud, he begins (as he did in the silent prayer), with the introductory verse, "O L-rd, open Thou my lips, and my mouth shall declare Thy praise" (Psalm 51:17).

At the conclusion of the Prayer, however, he should not say "Let the words of my mouth and the meditation of my heart be acceptable before Thee, O L-rd, my Rock and my Redeemer" (ibid. 19:15). Why not?

ANSWER:

The opening sentence, "O L-rd, open Thou my lips...," should be repeated by the Cantor so that G-d might enable him to pray properly on behalf of all his congregants. On the other hand, since this repetition of the Eighteen Benedictions is not the Cantor's personal prayer but his prayers on behalf of the congregation, it would not be proper for him to repeat the final passage "Let the words of my mouth and the meditation of my heart be acceptable before Thee..."

(TaZ 123:9)

78. QUESTION:

Why is it proper for the Cantor to wait until the Rabbi has concluded his prayer before beginning the repetition of the Eighteen Benedictions?

ANSWERS:

1. While most people recite their prayers quickly, there may be a few who do so slowly, enunciating each word with the proper thoughtfulness and devotion. It is only proper for the Cantor to wait for these people, so that they may be able to join in the *Kedusha* with the rest of the congregation. Since it may be safely assumed that the Rabbi is one of those who prays with particular devotion, the Cantor must wait for him to complete his prayer before starting the Repetition.

(Magen Avraham 124:7)

2. To accustom the congregation not to pray too quickly, since they must wait for the Rabbi to finish his prayers before proceeding to the Cantor's repetition.

The Rabbi, on the other hand, should not take too long over his prayers, as we read in the Talmud (Berakhoth 31a), "that Rabbi Akiba, when praying together with the Congregation, did not tarry too long over the Eighteen Benedictions."

(ad locum)

79. QUESTION:

What do the Scholars of the Law say regarding the spirit that should guide genuine prayer?

ANSWERS:

1. The author of *Yesh Nochlin* writes: When reciting the Eighteen Benedictions, one should do so with the proper concentration of heart and mind, and one should know the meaning of each and every word; one should not even meditate on matters pertaining to the Torah while praying, for prayer should be an outpouring of the soul, a veritable cry out of the depths of our hearts to our Father in Heaven.

2. The *Zohar* compares the effect of prayer on the human spirit with that of fire on coals.

"As the flame clothes the black sooty clod in a garment of fire and releases the heat imprisoned therein, so does prayer clothe a

man in a garment of holiness, evoking the light and fire implanted
within him by His Maker, illuminating his whole being and uniting
the world Above with that Below."

80. QUESTION:
   Why is it customary for the congregation to sway
   to and fro when reciting the Kedusha?

ANSWER:
   It is written, "And [even] the posts of the door were moved
by the voice of those who called" (Isaiah 6:4).
   If even the stone posts of the door were moved before the L-rd,
how much more should we tremble and sway in fear of Him.
                                        (Beth Yosef, Ch. 125)

81. QUESTION:
   Why are the prayers and supplications called Tefill-
   loth in Hebrew?

ANSWER:
   Tefillah is the Hebrew for "judgment." Prayer is the worshipper's
appeal to G-d to judge him with mercy and compassion.
                                        (Abudraham)

82. QUESTION:
   When the Cantor bows and recites "We give thanks
   to Thee..." (Modim anakhnu lakh), the Congregation does not join with him but recites the "Little
   Modim of the Rabbis" (Modim deRabbanan) in an
   undertone. Why?

ANSWER:
   It is not proper for a servant to send a messenger to express his
thanks to his master for all the kindness he has shown him.
   Each person must take upon himself the yoke of G-d and with
his own lips, give thanks to Him for having preserved Him in life,
etc.

Therefore, while the Cantor repeats the Modim aloud, each individual in the congregation recites in an undertone: "We give thanks unto Thee, for Thou art the L-rd our G-d and the G-d of our fathers, the G-d of all flesh, our Creator and the Creator of all things in the beginning. Blessings and thanksgivings be to Thy great and holy Name, because Thou hast kept us in life and hast preserved us: so mayest Thou continue to keep us in life and to preserve us. O gather our exiles to Thy holy courts to observe Thy statutes: to do Thy will, and to serve Thee with a perfect heart; seeing that we give thanks unto Thee. Blessed be the G-d to Whom thanksgivings are due."

(Abudraham)

83. QUESTION:

What is the origin of the term "Modim of the Rabbis" (Modim deRabbanan)?

ANSWER:

The "Little *Modim*" which is said by the entire Congregation in an undertone is an abstract of several prayers which were composed by the Rabbis.

(Sotah 40a; Tur Orakh Hayyim, Ch. 127)

84. QUESTION:

Why do the Rabbis refer to the Cantor as "one who passes before the Ark?"

ANSWER:

The prayers of the Cantor bring to the people an abundance of good from Heaven. Hence the Cantor is what might be called the congregation's "channel of influence" to Heaven.

In other words, through the prayers of the Cantor, "there pass the favors from Heaven which man requires."

(Ahavat Shalom, by Menachem Mendel, Rebbe of Kassov, Parshath Pinchas)

85. QUESTION:

Why was it formerly the custom of the Cantors to cover the sides of their faces with their hands when praying?

ANSWER:

So that the Cantor might not look around while praying, or be distracted from his thoughts, as the Cantor must always have his eyes on his prayerbook, for he must always remember before Whom he is standing.

The Cantor should not seek to impress his listeners with his beautiful voice and melodies, for these are alien thoughts and an abomination to the L-rd. Rather, his prayers should be an outpouring of the soul, to our Father in Heaven.

(*Mateh Moshe*)

In *Zera Kodesh* (Parshath Vayyera), the Rebbe of Ropshitz writes:

One should be very careful that no alien thoughts obtrude upon his mind while he is performing a mitzvah; nor should he say "What a wonderful deed I am about to perform; nor should he boast of his virtues after he has completed the good deed."

He also relates that when Rabbi Israel ben Eliezer Baal Shem Tov was about to depart from this world, his disciples heard him pray without cease "to be freed from alien thoughts."

In *Notzer Hessed* (Abot, Ch. 24) the Rebbe of Komorn writes:

The last words of Rabbi Israel ben Eliezer Baal Shem Tov were: *Ribbon kal ha-olomim,* "My G-d! Sovereign of all worlds! Let not the foot of pride overtake me" (Psalms 36:12).

When his soul was about to depart from his body, Rabbenu Isaac Luria (*Ha-Ari Hakadosh*) was heard praying: "O G-d, save me from the hands of pride!"

It is told by the author of *Divrei Yehezkel* (Parshath Ekev), that in the days of Rabbi Israel ben Eliezer Baal Shem Tov, there lived a man who had a reputation for extraordinary piety. The Hassidim of "the Baal Shem Tov" asked permission to go and visit this holy man to find out whether he really was as pious as he was reputed to be.

When the Baal Shem Tov consented, they asked him: "How will we be able to tell whether he is truly righteous or not?"

Replied the Baal Shem Tov: "Ask him to advise you how to fight off 'alien thoughts.' If he will offer you a clear-cut formula to keep alien thoughts away, you can rest assured that his good reputation is unfounded, for one has to struggle until one's very last breath, to keep alien thoughts out of his mind. This is the one task of man in this world: to engage in battle with one's thoughts to persuade them to do all things for the sake of His Name, Blessed be He!"

86. QUESTION:

The Rabbis say that the prayers of a congregation among whom there is not even one sinner are not accepted by G-d. What does this mean?

ANSWER:

When a righteous man is rapt in his prayers he will think only of G-d and no one else. He will therefore not be able to tear himself away from his thoughts long enough to cause an abundance of good to be sent from Heaven above to the people below.

However, when he knows that there is a sinner in the congregation, the righteous man will turn his attention also to the needs of the world and then the prayer of the righteous man will be heard and the needs of the people will be supplied.

(*Noam Elimelekh, Parshath Vayyera*)

Customs Pertaining to the Priestly Blessing

 QUESTION:

Why is it customary for the Cantor to recite the Priestly Blessing when repeating the Eighteen Benedictions?

ANSWER:

To recall the Priestly Blessing which was pronounced in the Holy Temple every morning and evening, after the offering of the daily sacrifices. This was one of the most impressive ceremonies in the daily service.

(*Kol Bo*)

 QUESTION:

Why is the Priestly Blessing recited by the Cantor after the "Blessing of Thanksgiving" (Modim)?

ANSWER:

To recall that Aaron too, blessed the people after having worshipped and given thanks to G-d. Cf. "And Aaron lifted up his hands toward the people and blessed them; and he came down from offering the sin-offering, and the burnt-offering, and the peace-offerings" (Lev. 9:22).

(*Ibid.*)

 QUESTION:

When the Cantor recites the Priestly Blessing, the congregation should respond not with "Amen" but with "Ken Yehi Ratzon — So may it be His will." Why?

ANSWER:

The Priestly Blessing is not a Benediction (Barukh Ata) but a prayer for peace. Hence *Ken Yehi Ratzon* is considered a more appropriate response than *Amen*.

(Abudraham)

 90. QUESTION:

Why do the Priests remove their shoes before ascending the platform to bless the congregation?

ANSWER:

To protect individual Priests from being wrongly exposed to public humiliation. If the Priests were permitted to wear their shoes when ascending the platform, it might happen that one of the Priests might find his shoelaces undone and remain in his seat to lace his shoes.

Meanwhile, the other Priests might have ascended the platform and begun the Blessing without him. This in turn would give rise to rumors to the effect that this one man had to remain in his seat because he was not qualified to give the Priestly Blessing because his mother had been a divorcée or had taken *halitzah* before marrying his father.

Marriages to women in these two categories are forbidden to descendants of Aaron. Accordingly, a person thought to be the son of such a union would be an object of ridicule, and the Priest in his seat would be exposed to humiliation without just cause.

(Levush, Ch. 128; see Sotah 40a)

 91. QUESTION:

Why must the Priests wash their hands before ascending the platform?

ANSWER:

In the days of the Temple, the Priests would wash their hands before the service, as it is written: "Lift up (i.e. wash) your hands in holiness and bless the L-rd" (Psalms 134:2).

(Levush 128:6-7)

92. QUESTION:

Before pronouncing the Blessing, the Priests recite the following Benediction: "Blessed art Thou, O L-rd our G-d, King of the Universe, Who hast sanctified us with the sanctity of Aaron, and hast commanded us to bless Thy people Israel in love."

Why were these last two words added?

ANSWER:

It is written in the *Zohar*: "If the Priest is not beloved by the congregation, or vice versa, he should not lift up his hands to bless the people."

(*Magen Avraham* 128:18)

93. QUESTION:

Why do the Priests hold their fingers spread while reciting the Priestly Blessing?

ANSWERS:

1. It is written in Song of Songs (2:9): "He peereth through the lattice." The Hebrew word *ha-Kharakim* (the lattice) is interpreted as referring to the five openings which G-d peers through to protect His people Israel (Rashi, ad locum).

(*Tur, Ch.* 128)

2. The movements involved in spreading the fingers make it appear as if the hands of the Priests were trembling in fear of G-d.

(*Shibalei HaLeket*)

94. QUESTION:

What is the explanation for the custom of the Priests to allow the folds of their Tallethim to drop over their faces and hands while they recite the Blessing?

ANSWER:

To keep from looking on the congregation; the better to concentrate on the significance of the act they are performing, and at the same time to keep the congregation from looking at them and thereby being distracted from the solemnity of the ceremony.

(*Beth Yosef, Ch.* 128)

95. QUESTION:

What is the text of the Priestly Blessing?

ANSWER:

The Priestly Blessing consists of three distinct parts:

1. "May the L-rd bless thee and keep thee."
2. "May the L-rd make His face to shine upon thee, and be gracious unto thee."
3. "May the L-rd lift up His countenance upon thee, and give thee peace" (Num. 6:24-26).

After the Cantor has chanted the first sentence, it is customary for the congregation to respond with the words: "May it be Thy will for the sake of our Father Abraham."

After the second sentence: "May it be Thy will for the sake of our Father Isaac."

After the third sentence: "May it be Thy will for the sake of our Father Jacob."

The *Baal HaTurim,* Rabbenu Jacob ben Asher, explains this custom as follows: The first word of the first sentence, *Yevarekhekha* (May the L-rd bless thee), alludes to Abraham, of whom it is written, "And I will bless those who bless thee" (Gen. 12:3).

The first word of the second sentence *Ya'er* (May the L-rd make His face to shine), alludes to Isaac, who is described as Olath Riyah — a "shining sacrifice" (Pirkei deRabbi Eliezer).

The first word of the third sentence *Yisa* (May the L-rd lift up), alludes to Jacob, of whom it is written, "And Jacob lifted up his feet" (Gen. 29:1).

(*See Baal HaTurim on Numbers* 6:24-26)

The *Kol Bo* gives the following comments on the Priestly Blessing: King Solomon instituted the custom to recite the Priestly Blessing in the Eighteen Benedictions.

The first sentence contains three words, (*Yevarekhekha Adonai V'Yishmerekha*), symbolizing the three Patriarchs, Abraham, Isaac and Jacob, symbolizing our prayer G-d might remember His Covenant with our Fathers.

The second sentence of five words, *Ya'er Adonai Panav Elekha Vikhuneka,* symbolizes the Five books of Moses which were given to us because of the merits of our Fathers.

The third sentence of seven words, (*Yisa Adonai Panav Elekha Veyasem Lekha Shalom*), alludes to the "seven heavens."

Thus, to our prayer that the One Who dwells in the Seven Heavens may bless us.

This also explains the sentence הנה מטתו שלשלמה ששים גבורים סביב לה — "Behold, it is the litter of Solomon; There are threescore mighty men around it, of the mighty men of Israel" (Song of Songs, 3:7).

The "three score mighty guardsmen" were the sixty letters spelling out the Priestly Blessing which were engraved on his bedstead.

96. QUESTION:
> After the Priests have completed the last words of the first and second parts of the Blessings, the congregation recites the prayer:
> "Sovereign of the Universe!
> I am Thine and my dreams are Thine; I have dreamed a dream, but know not what it portends. May it be acceptable in Thy presence..." What is the meaning of this prayer?

ANSWER:
It is written in *Torath Hayim*: Evil dreams are nullified by the Priestly Blessing because the Blessing contains sixty letters.

A dream is one-sixtieth of prophecy. Since the Priestly Blessing is complete prophecy, it can nullify dreams.

(*Midrash Talpiyoth, Letter Heth*)

97. QUESTION:

Why is the ceremony of the Priestly Blessing performed only on Festivals?

ANSWER:

Blessings should be given only by those who are joyous of heart, and such rejoicing comes only on Festivals.

(*ReMa* 128:44)

98. QUESTION:

Why is the Priestly Blessing not given in the Afternoon (Mincha Service)?

ANSWER:

By that time of the Feast Day, the Priests may be unfit to give the Blessing due to overindulgence in strong drink.

(*Taanith* 26b; *Orakh Hayim* 129:1)

Customs Pertaining to Propitiatory Prayers

99. QUESTION:

Why is Tahanun omitted on the Eve of Festivals but not on Fridays?

ANSWER:

The Eves of Festivals total only a very few days in the calendar. But to eliminate the *Tahanun* prayer each Friday morning would mean not reciting these prayers for nearly half the year, and this would not be proper.

(*Abudraham*)

100. QUESTION:

Why is the Tahanun omitted in the Mincha service on the Eves of Festivals, of Hanukkah, Purim and of Rosh Hodesh?

ANSWER:

To remind the worshipper to recite the *Yaale ve-yavo* prayer in the Eighteen Benedictions on Rosh Hodesh, or the *Al Hanissim* prayer on Hanukkah and Purim, etc.

101. QUESTION:

Why is Tahanun not recited in the house of a mourner, in the house of a bridegroom, or in the synagogue service when there is a bridegroom in the congregation or when a circumcision is held?

ANSWER:

In the house of a mourner, the "stern judgment" has already taken place and we do not add to it. As for bridegrooms and the participants in circumcision festivities, they are in that state of rejoicing which is deemed a time of "mercy," comparable to Sabbaths and Festivals, at which *Tahanun* is not recited.

(*Levush* 131:4)

102. QUESTION:

Why is Tahanun omitted in the synagogue service when there is a bridegroom in the congregation but not when there is a mourner present?

ANSWER:

Bridegrooms are in a state of rejoicing in which they may be likened to kings whose wishes and needs all must defer. Accordingly, the entire congregation omits *Tahanun*.

Mourners, on the other hand, are not in this category so that we need not defer to their wishes. *Tahanun* is therefore said, in accordance with the desire of the majority of the congregation, who are not in mourning.

(*Baer Hetev* 131:11)

103. QUESTION:

Why is the "Long" Ve-Hu Rahum ("And He, being merciful"), recited on Mondays and Thursdays?

ANSWER:

A boat loaded with Jews from Jerusalem landed in a place ruled by a wicked governor.

"Where are you from?" asked the governor.

"From Jerusalem," the Jews replied.

"Then I will put you to the test as Chananya, Mishael and Azaria were tested in the fire" (Daniel Ch. 3).

The Jews asked for thirty days grace. They immediately began a fast, and whoever had a dream would report to the others the next morning.

At the end of the thirty days, one of the old men who was very G-d-fearing but unlearned, told that he had seen in his dream, over and over again, a verse which contained the word *ki* (when) twice, and the word *lo* (not) three times.

One of the wise men present volunteered that the verse must have been Isaiah 43:2: כִּי תַעֲבֹר בַּמַּיִם אִתְּךָ אָנִי, וּבַנְּהָרוֹת לֹא יִשְׁטְפוּךְ, כִּי תֵלֵךְ בְּמוֹ אֵשׁ לֹא תִכָּוֶה, וְלֶהָבָה לֹא תִבְעַר בָּךְ. "*When* thou passest through the waters, I will be with thee, and through the rivers, they shall *not* overflow thee; *when* thou walkest through the fire, thou shalt *not* be burned, *neither* shall the flame kindle upon thee."

"The verse you saw in your dream," the wise man explained, portends that you will be saved from the fire, for you have implicit faith in the promise it contains."

When the governor had a fire lit in the market place, the old man walked into the flames and lo and behold, the fire broke up into three parts, and three righteous men were seen entering these parts to welcome the old man.

The three righteous ones then began to praise G-d. The first one chanted from *"Ve-Hu rahum"* to *"Ana melekh..."* The second took up the refrain, chanting from *"Ana melekh"* to *"En kamocha,"* and the third one took up the refrain from there, and so on until the end of the entire prayer.

The Rabbis then instituted that the *Ve-Hu Rahum* should be recited on Mondays and Thursdays which are days of judgment, when we plead with G-d for mercy!

(Kol Bo)

104. QUESTION:

Why do we conclude the Ve-Hu Rahum with the prayer, "As for us, we know not what to do; but our eyes are upon Thee...?"

ANSWER:

We did as our teacher Moses who, upon ascending the Mount to receive the Torah, prayed, sitting, standing and prostrating himself.

And now that we have done so, "we cry out that we do not know what to do next."

(Abudraham)

(Cf. Deuteronomy, Ch. 9, verse 9: "Then I *sat* in the mount"; Verse 18: "And I *fell down* before the L-rd"; Chapter 10:10: "And I *stood* on the mount...").

In our own prayers, we *sat* during the *P'sukei de-zimra,* stood during the Eighteen Benedictions, and *fell upon our faces* in the *Tahanun.*

105. QUESTION:

Why is the prayer "O G-d, slow to anger," which is said on Mondays and Thursdays before opening the Ark, recited standing?

ANSWER:

Because it contains the words "We have sinned against Thee, O L-rd," which form the basic Confession of Sins (Yoma 36b).

(Mateh Moshe)

106. QUESTION:

What is the origin of the custom of fasting on Mondays and Thursdays?

ANSWER:

The day on which Moses ascended Mount Sinai to bring down a new set of Tablets of the Law after the Israelites had worshipped the Golden Calf, was a Thursday, and the day on which he returned to the Children of Israel — forty days later — with the new Tablets was a Monday.

Accordingly, the Rabbis instituted Mondays and Thursdays as days of fasting and atonement.

(*Midrash Tanhuma on Gen.* 19:24 (*"Then the L-rd caused to rain upon Sodom..."*); see *Tosfoth Baba Kama* 82a, *sub voce,* Kedei)

107. QUESTION:

Why are the prayer "G-d slow to anger" and Psalm 20, not recited on Rosh Hodesh, Hanukkah, Purim?

ANSWER:

Because Rosh Hodesh is considered a Festival since Half-Hallel is chanted on it (Levush 418:1).

The foregoing applies also to Hanukkah, on which Hallel is chanted (ibid. 131:6; 683:1), and to Purim which is a day of festivity and merrymaking.

(*Beth Yosef, Ch.* 697)

108. QUESTION:

In Psalm 20, it is stated that "the name of the G-d of Jacob set thee up on high" (Verse 2). Why is there no mention of the other two Patriarchs, Abraham and Isaac?

ANSWER:

The verse quoted above begins with the words: "May the L-rd answer thee in the day of trouble." This wish is taken to refer to Jacob, for no other righteous man in our history saw so much trouble and suffering as our father Jacob. He had trouble with his brother Esau and his uncle Laban; he suffered the tragic loss of his wife Rachel; his sons fought to defend the honor of their sister Dinah; and he spent almost two decades mourning his son Joseph, whom he believed to be dead.

It was therefore considered appropriate to make special and exclusive mention of Jacob in a prayer of this nature.

(*Kad Hakemah*)

109. QUESTION:

The prayer Uva Letzion, "And a redeemer shall come to Zion," is followed by the "Sanctification" (Kadosh, Kadosh, Kadosh).
Why did the Rabbis place the Sanctification, or Kedusha, next to the "Prayer of Redemption?"

ANSWER:

The "Sanctification" or *Kedusha* was repeated at the conclusion of the services for the benefit of the ignorant, who usually arrive late for the services, and therefore missed the Kedusha of the Eighteen Benedictions (Sotah 49a).

In this individual recital of the Kedusha (Kedusha De-Sidra), a translation into Aramaic — the vernacular of the time was added, so that even those ignorant of Hebrew would be able to understand the prayer.

(*Abudraham*)

The original Kedusha contained only the two verses of the Prophets — Isaiah 6:3 and Ezekiel 3:12 which describe the adoration of G-d by the heavenly beings (*Kadosh, Kadosh, Kadosh* and *Baruch Kevod*).

The *Shema* was added in the days of the Byzantine Empire,

when Jews were persecuted and forbidden to recite the *Shema,* since it contradicted the doctrine of the Trinity.

As a consequence, the Rabbis inserted the opening and closing words of the *Shema* into the *Uva Letzion* prayer, at the conclusion of the service, where it was least conspicuous.

(*Levush, Ch.* 132)

The Shulchan Arukh Ha-Rav, by Rabbi Shneur Zalman of Ladi — Lubavitch) (Ch. 7), says in the name of Rabbi Amram Gaon: It is forbidden to leave the synagogue before the *Kedusha DeSidra* (the Kedusha in *Uva letzion*), and it is incumbent upon each and every worshipper to accept the yoke of G-d, with fear and awe, before His majesty, as the Rabbis say in the Talmud: "On what merit does the world exist? Upon the merit of the recital of the *Kedusha De-Sidra,* and of answering *Amen, Yehei Shmei Rabba Mevarach...,* ("Amen, May His great Name be blessed") (Sotah 49a).

110. QUESTION:

On what basis were the "Psalms of the Day" selected?

ANSWER:

On the first day of the week, we recite Psalm 24 which contains the words, "The earth is the L-rd's and the fullness thereof...," because when the L-rd first brought the world into being, He took possession of the Universe and gave His creatures life and became the Sovereign of the World.

On the second day of the week, we recite Psalm 48 which contains the words, "Great is the L-rd and greatly to be praised...," because on the Second Day of Creation He divided His works (the heavens from the earth) and reigned over them.

On the third day of the week, we recite Psalm 82 which contains the words, "G-d standeth in the congregation of the mighty...," because on the Third Day of Creation He, in His infinite wisdom, caused the earth to be revealed and the world to be prepared for its future occupants.

On the fourth day of the week, we recite Psalm 94 which begins, "O L-rd, to whom retribution belongeth...," to remind us of the punishment that will be meted out to anyone worshipping the sun and the moon, which were made on the Fourth Day of Creation.

On the fifth day, we recite Psalm 51 which contains the verse, "Sing aloud unto G-d, our strength...," because on the Fifth Day of Creation He made the fish and the birds, which praise His Name each day.

On the sixth day, we recite Psalm 93 which contains the verse, "The L-rd reigneth, He is clothed in majesty...," because on the Sixth Day of Creation He completed His works and reigned over them.

On the Sabbath, we recite Psalm 92 which contains the verse, "A Psalm, a song, for the Sabbath day...," because the Sabbath was the day on which the L-rd rested after having completed the work of Creation.

(*Rosh HaShanah* 31a)

111. QUESTION:

Why are En Kelohenu ("Who is like Our G-d") and Pitum HaKtoreth (the description of the incense offerings) not recited on weekdays?

ANSWER:

The omission of any of the prescribed ingredients in the preparation of the incense was a crime subject to the death penalty.

The recital of *Pitum Haktoreth* is considered tantamount to an actual offering. Therefore, if we were to omit mention of any of the "eleven spice compounds" to be used in the making of the incense, this omission, too, would be a crime punishable by death. Since in our hurry to get to work on weekdays, we might become guilty of such an omission, we prefer to omit the recital of this portion altogether.

(*Levush, Ch.* 133)

112. QUESTION:

Why are the following three verses recited before leaving the synagogue?

1. "Be not afraid of sudden terror . . ." (Prov. 3:25).

2. "Take counsel together . . ." (Isaiah 8:10).

3. "And even to your old age I am He . . ." (Isaiah 46:4) (Al Tira MiPahad Pithom).

ANSWER:

When the evil Haman departed triumphantly from the presence of King Ahasuerus, bearing in his hands the document authorizing him to do away with the Jews, he met three Jewish children going home from Hebrew school. Perversely, he asked the children to quote one of the verses from the Bible which they had studied at the academy that day.

One of the children recited the verse: "Be not afraid of sudden terror, neither of the destruction of the wicked when it comes."

The second child quoted the verse: "Take counsel together, and it shall be brought to naught; speak the word and it shall not stand; for G-d is with us."

The third child quoted the verse: "Even to old age I am the same, and even to hoary hair will I carry you; I have made, and I will bear; Yea, I will carry, and will deliver."

When Haman heard these verses, his smile vanished. Mordecai, on the other hand, became exceedingly happy, for these words conveyed to him the message that he had no cause to fear his mortal enemy Haman, and that G-d would redeem the Jewish people from Haman's evil scheme.

Therefore the Rabbis ordained that these three verses should be recited before leaving the synagogue, to remind G-d of His love for Israel so that He may have compassion upon us and redeem us as speedily as possible (Amen).

(Or Tzaddikim)

113. QUESTION:

Why is a quorom of ten adult males (minyan) required for the recital of any prayer sanctifying the L-rd?

ANSWER:

Because it is written: "Bless ye G-d in full assemblies" (Psalms 68:27). The total numerical value of the letters in במקהלת, the Hebrew for "assemblies" is equal to that of בעשרה, the Hebrew for "with ten."

The Gemara (Berakhoth 21b) says: Said Rabbi bar Ahada: "Whence do we learn that an individual cannot recite the *Kedusha* alone?"

— It is written: "So that I may be sanctified *amidst* the children of Israel" (Lev. 22:32). Therefore a prayer containing a sanctification should be recited by no less than ten men.

What is the proof thereof? asks the Gemara.

Rabbinai, the brother of Rabbi Chiya bar Abba, explained it. We deduce this from the word *tokh* ("amidst").

It is written (Lev. 22:32), "So that I may be sanctified *amidst* the children of Israel." It is written (Num. 16:21), *"Separate yourselves from the midst of* the congregation."

How do we know that the word "congregation" refers to ten men? It is written (Num. 14:27), "How long shall indulgence be given to this evil congregation."

This passage refers to the ten spies (excluding Joshua and Caleb) whom Moses sent out to explore the land of Canaan.

(*Agra de-Kallah — Korah*)

In ascertaining whether the required quorom is present, we must be careful not to count the heads of the people, for the Gemara says: "Israel must not be counted, not even for religious purposes" (Yoma 22b).

It is customary therefore, to count the people present by means of a Biblical verse containing ten Hebrew words; namely, *Hoshia eth amekha, uvarekh eth nahalasekha, ureim venaseim ad ha-olam —* "Save Thy people, and bless Thine inheritance; sustain them, and tend them for ever" (Psalms 28:9).

(*Kitzur Shulhan Arukh* 15:3)

Another Biblical verse that may be used for this purpose is the sentence in the *Ma Tovu* prayer, which is recited on entering the synagogue, namely, *Va-ani berov hasdekha avo vesecha eshtakhaveh el hekhal kadshekha beyirasekha* — "As for me, in the abundance of Thy lovingkindness will I come into Thy house" (Psalm 5:8).

(Sefer Ho-Orah)

General rules concerning the Reading of the Law.

When the Scroll of the Law is removed from the Ark, the entire congregation should rise and remain standing until the Scroll has been placed on the Reading table. The people close to the pulpit or the procession, press forward to see the Sefer Torah and to kiss its mantle.

It is for this reason that little bells are placed on the Torah ornaments. On hearing the tinkling of the bells, the congregation will know when to rise and pay their respects (Shaarei Ephraim 10:3).

One who is going up to read from the Torah, should go straight to the Reading Desk without making any stops, but should take a roundabout way back to his seat when he has completed the reading. Or at least he should go up to the Reading Desk from the right-hand side of the room and return to his seat by way of the left side (Levush 141:7).

It is not permissible to lean against the Reading Desk, as both the Reader and the one who is called up to the Torah must stand upright in awe and respect. An exception is made in the case of very heavy individuals who require a support to lean upon (Orakh Hayyim 141:1; see Tosfoth Megilla 31b, last line on page).

The TaZ (146:1) says that the MaHaRaM, Rabbi Meir of Rothenburg, would remain standing throughout the Reading of the Law.

One should definitely stand up when the individual called up to the Law recites *Barekhu*, for "any prayer which contains holiness (*Kedusha*), should be recited standing."

It was the custom of the Ha-*Ari*, Rabbenu Yitzhak Luria Ashkenazi, to remain seated through the Reading of the Law, to arise for the Half-Kaddish, and then to sit down again and remain seated for the rest of the reading. It was his custom also to remain standing during the recital of all the *Kaddeshim* read after the Eighteen Benedictions of the Morning, Afternoon and Evening services.

Customs Pertaining to the Reading of the Law

 114. QUESTION:

Why do we read portions in the Torah on Saturdays, Mondays and Thursdays?

ANSWER:

So as not to be without Torah for three days in succession, for it is written: "And they went three days in the wilderness, and found no water" (Ex. 15:22). From this verse we deduce the fact that three days must not go by without Torah (for the Torah is often referred to as "living waters").

(*See Baba Kama* 82a)

 115. QUESTION:

What is the origin of the saying that if the Torah is read on three consecutive days there will be rain?

ANSWER:

Since the Torah is referred to as "living waters," (see preceding question), it follows that if the Law is read on three consecutive days, rain is sure to come.

(*Ibid.*)

The Sefer HaBrith and the Sefer HaOlamoth both list the signs of imminent rain:

In human beings: A feeling of heaviness in the head or severe headaches, skin eruptions are apt to become worse; the pains of sick persons become more severe.

In animals: The cat combs its hair, the fowl parts its feathers, the rooster crows, the hen wallows in the dust, the peacock cries bitterly, the geese and other water-birds flock towards the shore flapping their wings back and forth and screaming wildly; all the creeping things which swarm over the earth come forth from their dung-hills and rubbish-heaps; the frog stops jumping and remains quiet and the bees stay in the beehive and do not go out.

In plants: The leaves of the trees will sway back and forth even when there is no wind.

In inanimate objects: Stones will prespire, salt becomes moist and cakes, and bubbles rise on the surface of the waters.

In the sun: If the morning sun will be a reddish light with a mixture of colors, if the skies will be encircled by heavy clouds, and if the sun will emit its rays towards the north while it will be dark in the south, there will be wind and rain. If the skies will be white in the east or the west; if, in the east or the west, close to the sun, there will be seen a round circle of clear white, there will be rain or winds.

If the early morning sun is clear white, there will be hail. If its rays are clear and red at sunset, the night will be clear and bright, but if the sun is turbid it will rain. If the skies are red at nightfall, the night will be clear, if the skies are red in the morning, the clouds will disperse and the day will be clear: likewise, if the morning skies will be dotted with small scattered clouds, or if the sun will turn red in the west, after the rain, it will be a very clear day.

In the moon: If the moon will look larger than usual, or if on the third day of the birth of the New Moon there will be gusts of wind, then it will rain on the following day; if on the sixteenth day after the birth of the New Moon, the moon will seem as if it were aflame, heavy storms will follow. If the moon looks whitish, there will be rain; if it is reddish, there will be wind.

Clouds which tend to be green and blackish in color indicate hail. Mist or black clouds, coming from above down below, will clear up the skies; clouds becoming reddish when the sun rises will bring rain in the evening. If, on the other hand, they become red at sunset, the next day will be very clear.

A rainbow in the morning is a sign of imminent rain.

A rainbow in the evening signifies a clear day.

A rainbow in the west will bring thunder.

A rainbow in the east — that depends on the time of the day:

If it appears in the morning, there will be wind; if it appears in the afternoon, there will be rain, and if it should appear in clear weather, there will be a storm.

116. QUESTION:

It is customary for a Priest (Kohen) to be called to the Reading of the Law before all others. Even if he should be an ignorant person, he is given priority over non-Kohanite sages.

He is not permitted to waive his right to his rabbi or any other important person.

What is the reason for this arrangement and what rules govern the procedure?

ANSWER:

To prevent bickering for the honor of being "called up" first (Gittin 59b).

If, there should be no Kohanite in the congregation, the most learned man present, regardless of whether he happens to be a Levite or an ordinary Yisrael, is called to the Torah first.

(Mateh Moshe)

117. QUESTION:

Why did the Rabbis rule that a portion of the Law to be read from by three individuals must contain at least ten verses?

ANSWER:

A Torah reading of less than ten verses would not be considered adequate. The portion containing the account of the Amalekite attack on the children of Israel, which is read at Purim time, is an exception to this rule for it contains only nine verses. The Rabbis did not see fit to add a verse to it because Amalek was the cause of a "lessening" of G-d's Name and Throne, as it is written, "The hand (Amalek) upon the throne of the L-rd" (Ex. 17:16).

Said the Rabbis: "Since Amalek caused a "lessening" of G-d's Throne, let the verses in the account of Amalek be decreased likewise."

(Levush 137:2; *see Tosfoth Megilla* 21b, *sub voce En, also* 22a, *sub voce En)*

118. QUESTION:

Why are no more than three persons called up to the Reading of the Law on Mondays and Thursdays and at Mincha services Saturday afternoon?

ANSWER:

On weekdays, people must go to work, and calling up more than three people would prolong the service unduly.

At Mincha services on Saturday afternoon, we also call up only three people, so that the service may be completed before dark.

(Rashi, Megilla 21a)

119. QUESTION:

On days when the reading is done from two Scrolls of the Law, both Scrolls are taken out at the same time. Why?

ANSWER:

Out of consideration for the congregants, so that they need not be kept waiting while the second Scroll is taken out.

(Yeshuoth Yaakov 147:5; *see Magen Avraham* 147:11)

120. QUESTION:

Why are the Scrolls of the Law written without vowels or punctuation?

ANSWER:

To enable scholars to expound the Torah in various ways, extracting all the ideas and teachings implicit in each verse.

(D'vash L'fi, in the name of Bachya ibn Pakudah)

121. QUESTION:

> On completing the last verse of the Book of Deuter-
> onomy ("... l'eynei b'nei yisrael"), we immediately
> start the Scriptural cycle over again with the first
> verse of the Book of Genesis (B'reshith). What is
> the message conveyed by this procedure?

ANSWER:

Read together, the last letter of the Book of Deuteronomy and
the first letter of the Book of Genesis spell *Lev* — the Hebrew
word for "heart." This should remind us that as the heart is to
the body, so is the Torah to the universe.

(Divre Emeth)

122. QUESTION:

> What is the reason for the ruling of Rabbi Ashi
> that in the Scroll of the Law, the last verse of the
> Book of Deuteronomy should end in the middle of
> the line?

ANSWER:

To teach us that we are still "in the middle" of studying the
Torah, and have not yet fathomed all its depths.

(Agra DePirka)

123. QUESTION:

> What is the origin of davenen, the Yiddish term
> for the daily prayers?

ANSWER:

The *notrikun* (stenography) of the word *da-ven-nen*, signifies
De-Avoth-Inun, i.e., "of our fathers," implying that the daily prayers
were instituted by our Fathers, Abraham, Isaac and Jacob.

(Magid Taalumah)

The Synagogue

124. QUESTION:

What is the basis for the view of the Rabbis that each synagogue should have twelve windows?

ANSWER:

The twelve windows correspond to the "twelve tribes of Israel." Each tribe has a "window in heaven" in character with its own distinct spirit and soul (neshama). Accordingly, twelve angels have been appointed over all the synagogues corresponding to the twelve tribes represented in the congregation. Each angel bears the prayers of his own tribe through his particular window, out of the synagogue and directly to the Throne of G-d.

(Sifsei Tzedek, Ch. 31)

125. QUESTION:

What forms of art or design must not be used in synagogue decoration?

ANSWER:

Many Gaonim prohibited paintings and drawings on the upper lintel, and in or around the Ark. Some Gaonim also vigorously objected to representations of animals like leopards, eagles, harts and lions.

(Orchoth Hayim, Ch. 150, in the name of Shaddai Hemed, and Rabbi Yom Tov Lipman Heller, et al; see also Birke Yosef, 141:6 and Baer Hetev 141:23; also Pishei T'shuva, 141:7 in the name of Ya'aroth D'vash, Part I, Lecture 2, where we are admonished not to have pictures engraved on synagogue walls or panels)

It is told that when the *Haham Tzvi,* Rabbi Tzvi Hirsh Ashkenazi, accepted the position in Amsterdam (1710), he refused to sit for a portrait. However, one artist managed to make a sketch of the Rabbis face without his knowledge, and this sketch served as the original for many copies.

(*Yad Ephraim, Ch.* 141, *in name of the Responsa of Rabbi Yaakov ben Tzvi* (*Yaavetz*), *son of the Haham Tzvi, Part I, Ch.* 170)

126. QUESTION:

In a bygone age, the beadle of the synagogue would rise up early in the morning to make the rounds of the homes of the congregants, knocking at their windows to awaken them for morning services.

Why would he knock three times?

ANSWER:

The Rabbis tell us that each person consists of three "partners," — his father, his mother and G-d.

The three knocks call on all three parts of the personality to come and offer praises and glory to the Creator of the World, blessed be He!

(*Geulath Yisrael*)

127. QUESTION:

Why did the beadle use a hammer to knock on the doors of the congregants?

ANSWER:

The consonants H, M and R, in Hebrew (המ"ר), are the initials of the words הירחק מ'שכן ר'ע "Keep thee away from an evil neighbor" (Ethics of the Fathers 1:7).

Rabbi Levi said, "Whoever has a synagogue in his town and does not go there to pray, is to be considered an evil neighbor."

The knock of the hammer on the window was supposed to remind the congregant that the beadle is awakening him to make sure he will not be called an "evil neighbor" because of non-attendance at synagogue services.

(Geulath Yisrael)

The Sefer HaGan VeDerech Moshe writes: One should always make an effort to pray only in the synagogue, even if there is no quorum (minyan) present; even if one must pray by oneself, he should do so in the synagogue if at all possible, for the angels of destruction waylay those prayers which are not recited at a House of Sanctity, and the only way to ward off these angels of evil is to take unto oneself "watchers," that is to pray together with a minyan, for a congregation united in the proclamation of the Unity and Holiness of G-d is justified in its conviction that its prayers will be answered.

One should select a G-d-fearing synagogue in which to pray, and take a permanent place (preferably near the wall) in which to stand for prayer, for then the Almighty will cause His Shekhina to descend upon that particular place.

I have come, the author continues, to warn those living in smaller communities where there is no minyan, to do the following:

As soon as you have moved into your home, choose one nice, clean room in the house and declare aloud: "I am hereby designating this room as my place of worship, to pray to the Almighty in the name of all of Israel. My family and I have chosen this place for prayer, for ourselves and for anyone who may enter my abode, and may it be the will of G-d to cause His Shekhina to dwell in this place even as His Glory rests in the synagogues of Israel, Amen."

If one will do this with sincerity and humility, the site chosen in the home will become holy like a synagogue, and his prayers will be accepted on High.

128.   QUESTION:

Why do the Rabbis urge us to light candles in the synagogue?

ANSWER:

Cf. ד' כבדו באורים כן על "Therefore glorify ye the L-rd in the regions of light" (Isaiah 24:15).

A brightly lit place of worship gives pleasure and at the same time inspires the worshipper with the sense of awe he should feel when he enters the synagogue.

(*Kad HaKemah*)

The Breaking of Bread

129. QUESTION:
The blessing recited over bread is: hamotzi lechem min HA-ARETZ — "Blessed art thou, O L-rd our G-d, King of the Universe, who bringest forth bread from the earth."
Why is the blessing not: borei peri ha-ADAMA — "who createst the fruit of the earth," or borei peri ha-CHITA — "who createst the fruit of the wheat?"

ANSWER:

The text of the blessing recited over bread is based on Psalm 104:14: *lehotzi lechem min ha-ARETZ* — "To bring forth bread out of the earth." The other blessings, like those recited over fruits of the earth are also based on Biblical texts, like *hine hevethi eth reshith peri ha-ADAMA* — "I have brought the first fruit of the land" (Deut. 26:10).

(*Abudraham*)

130. QUESTION:
Why must the bread be dipped in salt?

ANSWER:

Because the table represents the Sacrificial Altar, and the partaking of food symbolizes the Offering (the Karban), as it is written: *all kal karbancha takriv melach* — "With all thine offerings thou shalt offer salt" (Lev. 2:13).

(*ReMa* 167:5)

Another reason why it is good to have salt on the table is that while the company at table waits for the others to wash their hands, they must sit in silence and hence cannot perform any *mitzvot* during this time. Accordingly, Satan is ready with his accusations. But the 'bond of salt' (B'rith Melach), shielding Israel from harm, protects us from Satan as well.

(*Tosfoth, Berakhoth* 40a, *sub voce, Havei melach*)

It is also proper to keep the salt on the table until after Grace has been recited.

(*Kitzur SHeLaH*)

Writes the Kitzur SHeLaH: I have found it written in the name of a great Rabbi, that in Italy it was customary for those who had no time to study the Torah at table or those who were not learned in the Law, to recite at least three verses from the Pentateuch, three from the Prophets, and three from the Holy Writings as follows.

From the Pentateuch:

1. "Then said the L-rd unto Moses: Behold I will cause to rain bread from heaven for you; and the people shall go out and gather a day's portion every day, that I may prove them, whether they will walk in my law, or not" (Exodus 16:4).

2. "And ye shall serve the L-rd your G-d, and He will bless thy bread, and thy water; and I will take sickness away from the midst of thee" (Ibid. 23:25).

3. "And He afflicted thee, and suffered thee to hunger, and fed thee with manna, which thou knowest not, neither did thy father's know; that He might make thee know that man doth not live by bread only, but by everything that proceedeth out of the mouth of the L-rd doth man live" (Deut. 8:3).

From the Prophets:

1. "He shall dwell on high; His place of defence shall be the munitions of rocks; His bread shall be given, His waters shall be sure" (Isaiah 33:16).

2. "Wherefore do ye spend money for that which is not bread? And your gain for that which satisfieth not?
Hearken diligently unto Me, and eat ye that which is good, And let your soul delight itself in fatness' (ibid. 55:2).

3. "Is it not to deal thy bread to the hungry, and that thou bring the poor that are cast out to thy house? When thou seest the naked, that thou cover him, And that thou hide not thyself from thine own flesh?" (Ibid. 58:7).

And from the Holy Writings:

1. "And wine that maketh glad the heart of man, Making the face brighter than oil, And bread that stayeth man's heart" (Psalms 104:15).

2. "He hath given food unto them that fear Him;
He will ever be mindful of His covenant" (Ibid. 111:5).

3. "Who executed justice for the oppressed;
Who giveth bread to the hungry,
The L-rd looseth the prisoners" (Ibid. 146:7).

The Kitzur SHeLaH also writes:

I have before me the Mishnayot printed in Amsterdam, according to which the following verses should be recited after completing the study of a holy book, and also before the recital of the Grace after Meals.

These verses are very important, since whoever will recite them diligently is promised throughout his lifetime an abundance of food.

The verses to be recited are:

1. "To thank, praise, laud, glorify, extol, honor, bless, exalt and acclaim Thee, even beyond all the words of song and adoration of David the son of Jesse, thy anointed servant" — (Sabbath Morning Service).

2. "Thou wilt guide me with Thy counsel, and afterward receive me with glory" (Psalms 73:24).

3. "But He, being full of compassion, forgiveth iniquity, and destroyeth not, yea, many a time does He turn His anger away, and doth not stir up all His wrath" (Psalms 78:38).

4. "Happy is the man whom Thou chastenest, O L-rd, and teachest out of Thy Torah" (Psalms 94:12).

5. "And as for me, I have trusted in Thy lovingkindness;
My heart shall be glad in Thy salvation; I will sing unto the
L-rd, because He has dealt bountifully with me" (Psalms 13:6).

6. "I will greatly rejoice in the L-rd,
My soul shall be joyful in my G-d;
For He hath clothed me with the garment of salvation,
He hath covered me with the robe of victory,
As a bridegroom putteth on a priestly diadem,
And as a bride adorneth herself with her jewels" (Isaiah 61:10).

7. "And they that know Thy name will put their trust in Thee;
For Thou, L-rd, hast not forsaken them that seek Thee"
(Psalms 9:11).

8. "Be glad in the L-rd, and rejoice, ye righteous;
And shout for joy, all ye that are upright in heart" (Psalms
32:11).

9. "Thy word is a lamp unto my feet,
and a light unto my path" (Psalms 119:105).

10. "I will give thanks unto Thee, for Thou hast answered me,
And art become my salvation" (Psalms 118:21).

11. "The conclusion should be with the "Psalm for the Day,"
i.e. the Psalm which is meant to be recited on that particular
day of the week.

The Grace after Meals

131. QUESTION:

Why should all knives be removed from the table before Grace is recited?

ANSWER:

The table is compared to the sacrificial altar of old, concerning which it is written: "Thou shalt not lift up any iron upon them" (Deut. 27:5). Iron shortens the life of man, while the altar helps prolong his days. It is therefore considered improper that iron, the element which shortens life, should be raised on the "altar" which is intended to prolong life.

(*Shulḥan Arba*)

The *Kav Hayashar* (Ch. 64), writes in the name of Rabbenu Shelomo Lurie, that no 'empty vessels' should be left on the table while the Grace after Meals is being recited. The vessels should be full, or at least not entirely empty.

It is written in the *Zohar Hakadosh*: If a man or woman must go on a very important errand, and upon setting out from home comes upon an empty vessel, he or she should put off the errand, for blessings never come on empty space.

Elisha said to the wife of Obadiah: "What hast thou in the house?" And she answered... "A pot of oil!" To this the prophet said, "Good! Now the blessing of G-d will come upon you..." This implies that the blessing of G-d can only fall on some concrete object, and not on a vacuum (2 Kings, 4:2-7).

It is for this reason that all empty vessels should be removed from the table when the Blessings after Meals are recited.

132. QUESTION:

Why should the Grace after Meals be recited with a cup of wine in one's hand?

ANSWER:

Since wine is the most important of all beverages, it is only proper to bless G-d with a cup of wine in one's hand.

If no wine is available, or if it is too expensive, beer, mead or brandy can be substituted in localities where these beverages are commonly used. Water, however, may not be used, since water is neither a true beverage, nor a stimulant, but only quenches thirst.

(*Levush* 182:2; *TaZ* 182:1; *Magen Avraham* 182:2)

133. QUESTION:

Why are three men eating together, duty-bound under Jewish law, to join together in reciting the 'Introduction to Grace after Meals'?

ANSWER:

This rule is inferred from a Scriptural text: *Gadlu lashem itti, unromemah shemo yachdav* — "Magnify the L-rd with me, and let us exalt His Name together" (Psalms 34:4).

The imperative GADLU ('magnify'), is written in the second person plural. Hence, it cannot be used when only one other person besides the one leading the Grace is present. It can be used only when the leader has more than one person at the table to address. Therefore, when less than three men have eaten at the table, the 'Introduction to Grace' cannot be recited.

(*Berakhoth* 45a)

The Introduction to the Grace after Meals when three or more adult males have eaten together, is as follows: The one leading the Grace says aloud: "Let us say Grace. (In Hebrew: Rabbothai nevarech; Yiddish: Rabbosai, mir vellen benshen)."

The company responds: "Blessed be the Name of the L-rd from this time forth and forever."

The leader proceeds: "With the permission of those present, we will bless *Him* of whose bounty we have partaken."

The others respond: "Blessed be *He* of whose bounty we have partaken, and through whose goodness we live."

The leader replies: "Blessed be *He* of whose bounty we have partaken, and through whose goodness we live."

Note that the name of G-d is nowhere explicitly mentioned in this ritual.

It is only when the company consists of ten or more males that the word "Elohenu" (G-d) is used rather than "He." The Name of G-d may properly be mentioned only when a quorom of ten men above the age of thirteen are present (kal davar shebikdusha lo yehei ella beyud anashim gedolim uvnei chorin).

Therefore the name of G-d (ELOHENU), is mentioned in the Grace when ten men are present.

(Beth Yosef, Ch. 199)

 134. QUESTION:

> **Why is the Introduction to Grace not recited after partaking of fruit or of bread in the form of pastry like pies, etc.?**

ANSWER:

These foods are not considered a true "meal" since they are not associated with any set mealtime.

(TaZ 196:1)

135. QUESTION:

> **The blessing recited over the Torah is: "Barchu eth ADONAI hamevorach" — ("Bless ye the L-rd, who is to be blessed"), whereas in the blessing in the Grace after Meals it is "Nevarech ELOHENU" — ("Let us bless our G-d").**
>
> **What is the reason for this difference?**

ANSWER:

The Rabbis find a clear distinction in the use of these two terms for the Deity. ADONAI (LORD), describes the Deity in terms of His loving kindness, His acts of mercy and Divine revelation to mankind; while ELOHIM (G-d), emphasizes His Kingship and justice.

Since He created us in His own honor, it is only proper, and fitting and just that He should give us the physical sustenance we require. It is to emphasize this aspect of His nature that we employ the term *Elohenu* in the Grace after Meals.

The Torah, on the other hand is not our natural privilege. G-d gave it to us out of grace and compassion to reveal to us His mysteries and the proper way in which to live. Hence, when we are called up to the *Torah,* we use the word ADONAI, to stress this facet of His nature.

In view of the above, we can readily see why we should adhere scrupulously to the tradition handed down to us by our fathers (*minhag avosenu Torah hu*), "to eat dairy products on Shevuoth, the day of the Giving of our Torah": 'milk' being white and pure, is a symbol of hessed — the grace and Kindness of G-d Himself.

(*Bnei Yisaschar*)

136.   QUESTION:

It is customary to say Grace over a cup of wine. The Blessing over the wine is said at the conclusion of the Grace. In Kiddush and Havdalah, on the other hand, the Blessing over the wine precedes the main body of the Kiddush and Havdalah prayers. Why?

ANSWER:

The recital of Grace signifies the conclusion of the meal and all that has taken place at the table. Hence, if the Blessing over the wine were to be made before the Grace, the Grace would be considered not as a final act but as an interruption between the Blessing over the wine and the drinking thereof.

(*Tosfoth, Berakhoth 52 a,* sub voce, *verabee*)

It is customary to cover the bread while reciting Grace, so that the bread be not put to shame seeing that the cup of wine is held high in the hand of the person leading the Grace.

(*Magen Avraham* 180:4)

137. QUESTION:

The special prayer YAALE VEYAVO ("May our prayers ascend") is added on Rosh Hodesh and Festivals.

In the Grace after Meals, it is inserted prior to the prayer for the 'rebuilding of Jerusalem.'

Whereas, in the Shemona Esre it is inserted before the prayer of 'thanksgiving' (Modim). Why the difference?

ANSWER:

The *Yaale Veyavo* prayer added on Rosh Hodesh and Festivals is a *prayer* asking G-d on these days which He gave to us for festivity and joy to remember us and the entire household of Israel for goodness and blessings, so that we may able to celebrate these Festivals in a spirit of joy and gladness. It is therefore 'a prayer *and* a petition.'

In the Grace, it was inserted prior to the *petition* for the 'rebuilding of Jerusalem,' whereas in the Eighteen Benedictions, it was inserted in the 'Thanksgiving Prayer' which is actually, a *prayer* to return the children of Israel to Jerusalem.

(*Tosfoth Shabbat* 24a, sub voce *Bevonei*)

138. QUESTION:

If Rosh Hodesh falls on a Sunday, (i.e., it begins on Saturday night at sunset), and one was still eating at his table as the Sabbath ended — he says the prayer RETZEI which is inserted in the Grace after Meals on the Sabbath. But he must also recite Yaale Veyavo, which is recited on Rosh Hodesh (see TaZ 188:7).

On the other hand, when Hanukah or Purim fall on a Sunday and the Sabbath ended, and Hanukah or Purim set in while one was still eating at his table, he does recite RETZEI, the added Sabbath prayer in the Grace, but not the AL HANISSIM prayer which is added on Hanukah and Purim. Why not?

ANSWER:

The observance of Rosh Hodesh is based on the Torah. The festivals marked by the AL HANISSIM prayer, on the other hand, were not of Biblical origin but were only instituted by the Rabbis.

(Shabbat 24 a; see Magen Avraham 188:13 and 188:18; see Shulhan Aruch Harav 188:17)

139. QUESTION:

If one forgot to recite Yaale Veyavo in the Grace after Meals, he need not repeat the Grace from the beginning. On the other hand, if he forgot to recite Yaale Veyavo in the 'Eighteen Benedictions,' he must repeat the entire Eighteen Benedictions from the start. Why?

ANSWER:

Although true fasting on Rosh Hodesh or Hol Hamoed is forbidden, one is not required to eat a full meal on these days, as he can sustain himself with fruits or the like. In other words, he is not required to say the Grace if he has not had a full meal. Therefore, one who forgot to recite the Yaale Veyavo during the Grace after Meals, need not repeat the Grace.

On the other hand, man is explicitly commanded 'to pray daily.' Hence, one who forgot to recite the Yaale Veyavo on Rosh Hodesh or on Hol Hamoed, must repeat the entire Shemona Esrei.

(Berakhoth 49 b; see Kol Bo)

140. QUESTION:

One who forgets to recite RETZEI on Shabbas — but realized the omission before he came to the words "the good King who does good" — should say: "Blessed art Thou, O L-rd our G-d, King of the Universe, who hast given the Sabbaths for days of rest to Thy people Israel with love, for a sign and for a covenant. Blessed art Thou, O L-rd, who hallowest the Sabbath."

Likewise, one who forgot to recite the Yaale Veyavo prayer, but realized the omission before he came to the words "who is good and does good," should say: "Blessed art Thou, O L-rd our G-d, King of the Universe, who hast given Festivals to Israel for gladness and joy, this holiday of ————. Blessed art Thou, O L-rd, who hallowest Israel and the Festive Seasons."

But one who forgot to recite Yaale Veyavo on Rosh Hodesh, and he realized his omission before he came to the words "who is good and does good," need say only: "Blessed art Thou, O L-rd, our G-d, King of the Universe, who hast assigned unto us the beginning of months for a remembrance" (this Blessing is not concluded with Baruch).

Why need he say nothing more?

ANSWER:

Because on Rosh Hodesh one is not obligated to eat a regular meal necessitating the recital of Grace.

(*Levush* 188:6-7)

141. QUESTION:

Why does the Blessing "Blessed art Thou, O Lord, who in Thy compassion rebuildest Jerusalem. Amen" end with Amen, when no other blessing recited by an individual alone is given that ending?

ANSWER:

AMEN is said in order to make a distinction between the first three blessings in the Grace after Meals which are based on Biblical law, on the one hand, and the fourth blessing "who is good and does good," which was instituted later on by Rabbinical authority, on the other.

(*Tur, Ch.* 188)

142.　QUESTION:

What is the origin of the 'Fourth Blessing' in the
Grace after Meals "Who is good and does good..."?

ANSWER:

This fourth blessing was instituted in memory of the thousands
of Jews slain at Bethar in the year 135 C.E. The town of Bethar
had five hundred Jewish schools, of which each had five hundred
teachers to instruct the students. In addition, there were sixty-
thousand ordinary working people. During the reign of the Roman
emperor Hadrian (132-35 C.E.), Bethar, under the command of
Bar Kochba, was captured by Julius Severus, and all its inhabitants,
both young and old, were put to death.

The tyrant commanded that the dead should be left unburied.
The bodies of the dead were piled high in a large vineyard outside
the city limits and remained there throughout the last twenty-five
years of Hadrian's life. By miracle, the bodies did not decompose.
After the death of Hadrian, the bodies were buried in this same
vineyard.

On the day the dead of Bethar could at least be given a proper
burial, the Rabbis in Yavne ordained that the blessing "Who is
good and causest good to happen," should henceforth be recited in
the Grace after Meals. HATOV — "Who is good," refers to the
miraculous preservation of the bodies throughout the years that had
passed, and VEHAMETIV — "Who does good," to the fact that at
last, the time had come when the bodies could be given a proper
burial.

(*Midrash Echa Rabthi, Chpt's 2 and 4;
Berakhoth 48 b; Taanith 31 a; Baba Bathra 121 b*)

143.　QUESTION:

**The prayer recited by the master of the house
involving G-d's blessing on his wife, his children,
and the rest of his company at his table, ends with
the words, VENOMAR AMEN — "And let us say,
Amen, but the Grace ends with the words VE-IMRU
AMEN — "And say ye, Amen." Why?**

ANSWER:

When the master of the house invokes G-d's blessing on his own household, it would be improper for him to call on the others present to say AMEN in support of his personal wishes. The final verse of the Grace "He who maketh peace in His high places..." (Oseh Shalom) on the other hand, is not a prayer for personal favor but one of praise.

Since everyone is obliged to praise G-d, it is only right that the master of the house should turn to the guests at his table and say to them, "AND SAY YE, AMEN."

(*Magen Avraham* 189:1)

144. QUESTION:

When drinking from the Kiddush cup or from the cup used when reciting the Grace after Meals, it is customary to give a sip from 'this cup of Blessing,' to all those present at the table.

A few drops of fresh wine is added first into the cup. Why?

ANSWER:

It is the proper thing to do, as by adding a few drops anew into the cup, it would seem as if the cup had been fully refilled and regained its full measure.

(*Hagaoth Maimaniyoth, Laws of Sabbath, Ch.* 29)

It is customary for the wife to drink from 'this cup of Blessing,' so that she may be blessed by G-d.

(*Eliyahu Rabbah* 183:10)

The Blessings over Fruits

145. QUESTION:

Why are all the benedictions worded in the 'present tense.'

E.g. "Who CREATEST the fruit of the tree..."
"Who CREATEST the fruit of the wine?"

ANSWER:

The benedictions are all worded in the present tense to show that all things are in constant process of creation, as we recite in our prayers, "In His goodness He continually renews the act of Creation every day" (Daily Prayers). G-d is the prime cause of the Universe and without Him there would be no life. As Creator of the Universe, He is constantly at work creating and re-creating in accordance with His Will.

(*Sifte Emeth, by the Rebbe of Brezan*)

On partaking of meat, fish eggs, cheese, etc., or when drinking any liquid (except wine), we recite the benediction "by Whose Word *all things exist*" (Shehakol).

After partaking of these foods we pronounce the blessing "Who createst innumerable living beings WITH THEIR WANTS" (Bore nefashot).

According to *Divrat Shelomo* (Vayeshev), this means that those who fear the L-rd do not lack for anything, for everything in nature has been created for the benefit of man.

Since G-d is omnipresent in nature, the Divine Presence, the Shekhina, is clothed in an infinite variety of garments to provide for the needs of the G-d-fearing, and whatever man is lacking for his spiritual and physical needs, is provided for by G-d either directly or indirectly.

Man may have to leave his own country and kinfolk and move to another town to secure whatever he may be lacking spiritually or physically, as the Rabbis say, "he who lacks sustenance in one city should try another city" (Baba Metzia 75 b).

One might ask why he should have to pull up stakes and move to another town to seek his livelihood. Could not G-d sustain him and supply his needs in his own home town?

The answer lies in the fact that there may be 'some needed action, some good deed, or some sanctification of His Name in some form or other,' to be accomplished by you, and it is for 'that reason,' that you were sent to 'that particular spot' to carry out the action. It therefore behooves you to understand that while your own needs are to be supplied in that particular town, it is also His Will that you should proclaim His Name in that particular new locality, and that is the reason why 'your feet have brought you there!'

Various Blessings

146. QUESTION:

Why does wine require a benediction of its own, rather than the benediction generally recited over fruit?

ANSWERS:

1) It is the change from grape juice to wine that makes this fruit important, for wine gladdens the heart.

(*Berakhoth* 35b)

2) All other fruits lose their original properties and tend to deteriorate when they go through a change like fermentation. As long as the fruits have their original *form and taste*, the blessing recited for them as a rule is usually, BOREI PERI HA-ETZ — "Who createst the fruit of the tree." But when they have been changed beyond recognition, the proper blessing is SHE-HAKOL. In the case of corn and grapes on the other hand, the change is generally for the better, for the corn is remade into bread and the

grapes are turned into wine, and bread and wine are more important than the original materials from which they were created.

Therefore there are special blessings to be recited over bread and wine.

(Benei Yisaschar)

3) There is a distinct blessing over wine as there are many occasions when wine is used specifically, as for Kiddush and Havdalah, at engagements and at weddings.

(Rokeach — Rabbi Eliezer ben Judah)

147. QUESTION:

If — the guests at a meal have already drunk one kind of wine (over which they recited the blessing borei peri hagafen), and then another kind of wine is served, the blessing ha-tov veha-metiv ("who art good and doest good") must be recited.

Why this change in blessings in the case of wine but not in the case of bread or meat?

ANSWERS:

1) A change in wine requires this change in blessings because wine has two important properties — it makes people happy and stimulates the heart.

(Tosfoth Berakhoth 59 b, sub voce, Hatov)

2) Another reason is that we find 'praises' (shirah) mentioned only with regard to wine and not with regard to other foods.

Since wine, has a special blessing of its own, being a liquid that enjoys universal esteem, it is also proper that a change in wine should be accompanied by a change in blessings.

3) The *Iyun Tefillah* relates that on several occasions, when he was the guest of the Gaon of Buczacz, his host would honor him by asking him to recite a blessing. The Gaon would do this in the following way: He would place before him two cups of wine — the first cup containing red wine, and the second cup containing white wine. Then, "the Gaon directed me to pronounce, first, the

usual blessing 'Borei peri hagafen' over the red wine, and then, the blessing *'Hatov vehametiv'* over the white wine."

"I then said to the Gaon: Is it not written in the Shulhan Arukh that if both kinds of wine are on the table at one and the same time, the blessing *borei peri hagafen* is recited over the superior wine (the white wine), which then is taken to be applicable to the inferior wine as well?"

"His answer was: The law to which you refer is applicable only when you are at your own table and using your own wine. Here, however, you are my guest, and the wine is mine! I have given into your possession 'first the red wine,' and then the white wine!"

The *Iyun Tefillah* concludes his account by relating that the Gaon would reply to his blessing AMEN and would add, HU HETIV, HU METIV, HU YETIV LANU ("He has done good, He does good and He will do good unto us").

4) The blessing HATOV VEHAMETIV is recited when a different kind of wine is brought in because at festive gatherings, it is customary to place a variety of wines before the guest, and this makes for excessive enjoyment which is forbidden in this world, as it is written, "And rejoice with trembling" (Psalms 2:11).

The blessing "Who art good and doest good," is therefore recited, to inject a sombre note, for this is the blessing that is customarily recited at houses of mourning.

(*Kol Bo*)

148. QUESTION:

After a Bar Mitzvah has been called to the Reading of the Torah, and has concluded the blessing recited before beginning to read — his father says: Baruch sheptorani meansho shelazeh — "Blessed be He who hath freed me from the responsibility of this child." Why does this blessing contain no mention of the Name of G-d?

ANSWERS:

1) The Name of G-d is not mentioned because this blessing is not among those mentioned in the Talmud.

(*Eliyahu Rabba Ch. 225, in the name of Lehem Hamudoth*)

2) The author of the treatise Levush (225:2) maintains that this blessing is meant to be pronounced not by the father but by 'the son,' i.e., by the Bar Mitzvah himself who, now that he has come of age, will no longer be punished for the sins of his father.

149. QUESTION:

Why is the blessing "Who has freed me from the responsibility of this child," not pronounced by the father of a girl who has attained the age of Bas Mitzvah (twelve years and a day, the age of maturity for a girl)?

ANSWER:

This blessing is not pronounced by the father over a girl since a father is not commanded to teach his daughter as he is to teach his son.

(*Nazir* 29a; *Magen Avraham* 343:1-3; *P'ri Megadim* 225:5)

150. QUESTION:

When wine is drunk and the blessing borei peri hagafen recited over the wine, no other blessing need be recited over any other beverages served with the meal, providing that the other beverages were served at the time when the benediction over the wine was made. Why?

ANSWER:

Wine is an important beverage for which a distinct benediction of its own has been prescribed. There are many occasions when one must pronounce a benediction over wine, even if he has no desire to drink it, e.g. for Kiddush, Havdalah, the marriage ceremony, etc. Therefore all other beverages served after wine are considered of less importance, and do not require the recital of a new blessing.

(*Berakhoth* 41 *b;* *Levush* 174:4;
TdZ and Magen Avraham 174:1-2)

151. QUESTION:

Why is the benediction Sheheheyanu which is recited over food eaten the first time in a year, not recited over a "new" vegetable?

ANSWERS:

1)   Since vegetables remain in the earth throughout the year, what may seem to be a "new" vegetable may actually be a vegetable of the previous year's growth. Since this justifiable doubt exists, we do not recite the blessing over "new" food in that case, lest we be guilty of reciting a blessing "in vain."

(*SHeLaH*)

When a new vegetable would be served on a Sabbath to the Gaon of Buczacz, he would ask three of the people present whether this vegetable was "new," and only if the answer was in the affirmative would he pronounce the *Sheheheyanu* over the vegetable.

2)   Because vegetables are plentiful and therefore not considered rare delicacies.

(*Chaye Adam* 62:9)

3)   Another reason for not reciting *Sheheheyanu* over new vegetables is that they are in the ground all year long so that one can tear them out whenever one so desires. In other words, they do not have a definite season.

(*Levush* 225:6)

The proper recital of a blessing requires concentration and devotion, particularly when pronouncing 'the Name of G-d,' for His Name must be mentioned only with awe and reverence.

Rabbi Ber of Nadvorno relates that one of the very pious disciples of his late grandfather, Rebbe Aaron Leib, pleaded with his Rabbi to let him behold the Prophet Elijah if not in the flesh then at least in a dream.

The Rabbi consented, and Elijah appeared to him in a dream. In this dream the disciple set before Elijah a tasty dish and said to him: "Will my honored guest pronounce a blessing over the dish?" Whereat, Elijah became very angry and said, "Do you think that I would dare mention the Holy Name of G-d over a trifling matter such as this?"

The disciple then awoke, and his whole body would tremble with awe and reverence whenever he would have to mention the Name of the L-rd.

(Rachmei-ha-Av)

152. QUESTION:
There is a blessing to be recited after partaking of food, but none to be said after the study of the Torah. Why not?

ANSWER:

The study of Torah has no set time. Torah must be studied morning, noon and night, and we are not free to turn from it for even one minute. Accordingly, a "concluding prayer" after the study of Torah would not be in place, for we can never really "conclude" the study of the Law.

(Orchoth Hayim, Ch. 47, in the name of Beth Yosef)

153. QUESTION:
Why need no blessing be recited when smelling snuff?

ANSWER:

Because snuff does not have a pleasant aroma. The same is true also of tasteless tobacco.

(see Eshel Avraham Ch. 216; Baer Hetev 216:13)

154. QUESTION:
Why need no blessing be recited before smoking a cigarette, cigar or pipe?

ANSWER:

In Talmudical times there was no smoking as we know it today (cigarettes, cigars, pipe). But had smoking been known at that time, the Rabbis would most likely have formulated a blessing to be recited over it.

(Mishna Berura Ch. 210)

Sholom, Rabbi of Belz, gave up smoking a pipe because of the following incident: "In my younger days," he said, "while I was studying in the House of Study, I noticed a student emptying, cleaning and refilling his pipe in the midst of his studies. During the time it took him to do this, I studied one full page of the Talmud. I therefore said to myself: If a pipe requires me to waste so much time, it shall not even enter my mouth again. And it never did."

(Rachmei ha-Av)

155. QUESTION:

Why need no blessing be recited when performing an act of charity?

ANSWERS:

1) Charity should be given with joy and gladness. But since most people do not perform acts of charity with joy in their hearts, it is not considered mandatory to recite a blessing before doing so.

(Ma-or va-Shamesh, Parsha Pinhas, in the name
of Rabbi Menachem Mendel of Pristik)

2) Another reason why a blessing is not recited when performing an act of charity, is that the poor man may have a change of heart and refuse to accept the money offered, in which case your blessing would have been recited in vain.

(Eshel Avraham Ch. 223)

3) The reason we do not recite a blessing when giving charity to a fund rather than directly to a specified needy individual, is that the Mitzvah of charity is consummated only at moment when the needy individual actually receives the money.

(Orchoth Hayim, Ch. 92)

It is related that the Rebbe of Sassov once gave a sum of money to a man of evil repute. His disciples asked him: "Rabbi, How could you give your last penny to an evil man like this?" Replied the Rabbi:

"Know that I am also a good-for-nothing. But if I give charity to another good-for-nothing, G-d will deal with me 'measure for measure,' and He will give me sustenance, too."

(Ha-Maor Ha-Gadol)

In his early life, Rabbi Yechiel Michel, the Maggid of Zlochuv, lived in great poverty, but his faith and good courage never deserted him. His disciples once asked him: "Rebbe! how can you say in your prayers morning after morning, 'Blessed art Thou who hast supplied my every want?' Surely you lack everything a man needs?"

Replied the Maggid: "In all likelihood what I happen to need is poverty, and this the L-rd has supplied to me in ample measure."

(Ha-Maor ha-Gadol)

---

156. QUESTION:

Why is the blessing of SHEHEHEYANU not recited over a fragrant odor?

ANSWER:

It is the soul rather than the senses that derives pleasure from a pleasant odor, and since the soul is eternal, the Sheheheyanu blessing is not appropriate in this instance.

(Kerem Shlomo, in the name of Bigdei Yeshah)

---

157. QUESTION:

Why is there no blessing recited after enjoying fragrant scent?

ANSWERS:

1) Once one has ceased inhaling the fragrance, the pleasure has ceased. It is like food which is already digested.

(Rashi, Niddah 52 a, line 1)

2) Another reason is that the body has derived no benefit therefrom, i.e. the scent has not entered into the body.

(Kol Bo)

158. QUESTION:

There is no blessing to be recited when listening to vocal music or orchestral.

What makes the enjoyment of music different from that of a fragrant scent or good tidings?

ANSWER:

The author of *Machze Avraham* (Bereshith) asks: "Why do we not recite a blessing in the morning to thank G-d for giving us the ability to hear, when we do recite one in gratitude for having been given sight?" ("Who openest the eyes of the blind?").

His answer was: "The reason we do not recite a blessing for our ability to hear, is that the ability to hear proved to be Adam's downfall. When Adam listened to the words of his wife and ate the forbidden fruit the whole world became corrupt. We do not recite a blessing over something which brought harm to the world."

159. QUESTION:

Why is there no blessing recited when performing the commandment to honor one's father and mother?

ANSWER:

Honoring one's father and mother is a positive commandment, which is nullified if the father should not want the honor due him.

Accordingly, no blessing is recited when carrying out this commandment.

(*Shiyurei Beracha, Ch. 240, in the name of the RaSHBA*)

160. QUESTION:

Why is there no blessing to be recited by the Shohet when he tests his knife prior to performing the act of shehita (ritual slaughter?).

ANSWER:

If, after he has tested his knife, the shohet should decide not to slaughter the animal, the blessing would have been recited in vain.

(*Baer Hetev* 18:6)

161. QUESTION:

Why is there no blessing recited when examining the lung of an animal that has been slaughtered?

ANSWER:

If the lung is found to have an organic defect and is therefore *trefe*, the entire animal becomes unfit for consumption in keeping with the commandment of "thou shalt not eat *trefe;* ye shall cast it to the dogs (Ex. 22:30), a negative precept.

The examination of the lung, therefore, is not the performance of a positive commandment but an act to prevent the transgression of a negative commandment, and there are no blessings to be recited when observing a negative commandment.

(*see Rosh Ephraim* 39:19)

162. QUESTION:

Why are we not scrupulous in the matter of observing the law that the blessing Sheheheyanu is to be recited when one meets a good friend whom one has not seen for thirty days?

ANSWER:

Because a man has very few true friends. However, one should be punctilious about reciting the blessing on seeing a close relative like a brother, a sister, and especially one's son or daughter, or father or mother, where the rejoicing is greater than in the case of a mere friend.

On being reunited with such close relatives after a separation of twelve months, the benediction to be recited is: "Blessed art Thou, O L-rd, our G-d, who revivest the dead."

(*Yosef Ometz*)

163. QUESTION:

"And they shall judge the people with righteous judgment" (Deut. 16:18) is a positive commandment. Why, then, is there no blessing to be recited when one judges a case?

ANSWER:

The litigants may either refuse to accept the judgment or they may decide to drop the case. In either eventuality, the decision handed down by the judge would not be enforced and the blessing would have been one recited in vain.

(*Abudraham*)

The same rule applies to the performance of any of the positive commandments: "Helping your fellowman with his burden (Ex. 23:5); freeing slaves and presenting them with gifts (ibid. Ch. 21; Deut. 15:12-18); rising when a teacher of the law enters (Lev. 19:32); honoring and fearing one's father and mother (Ex. 19:3); loaning money to the poor (ibid. 22:24); returning a lost article (Deut. 22:1-3); rejoicing with the widow, orphan and stranger (ibid. 16:11); visiting the sick (Sotah 14a; Baba Metzia 30b); and comforting the mourners (Sotah 14a; Job 29:25)."

Any of these deeds of kindness may be refused by the intended recipient, and the blessing might therefore turn out to have been recited in vain.

(*Abudraham*)

164.   QUESTION:

Why is no blessing recited when returning a stolen article and when returning interest taken?

ANSWER:

Because they were necessitated by a sinful act performed sometime before. Had you not stolen it, you would not have had to return the article; had you not taken interest in the first place, you would not have had to return it.

(*Abudraham*)

165.   QUESTION:

Why is there no blessing recited when one performs the positive commandment to rebuke his neighbor if he is in need of it? (Lev. 19:17).

ANSWER:

The Rabbis say: I wonder whether there is anyone in this generation who will readily accept rebuke — whether there *is* one to accept it; and who is the one who knows really 'how to rebuke!' (Archin 16 b).

Accordingly, the blessing might well then turn out to have been recited in vain.

(*Abudraham*)

166. QUESTION:

Upon seeing 'a king of Israel,' the blessing "Who has imparted of His glory to flesh and blood," should be recited.

Upon seeing 'a king of any other nation,' the blessing, "Who has given of His glory to flesh and blood," is recited.

Why the difference in wording?

ANSWER:

Unlike the other nations, Israel is a part of Him and we cleave to Him; hence *imparted* is used.

(*Magen Avraham* 224:4)

167. QUESTION:

When seeing goodly trees or beautiful creatures, we are not in the habit of reciting the blessing, "...Who hast such as this in His world."

Likewise, when seeing a dwarf, an elephant or an ape, we are not in the habit of reciting the blessing, "...Who varies the forms of His creatures." Why not?

ANSWER:

These Benedictions are uttered only on *"first"* seeing, since only the first impression is striking. After that, the sight is an "accustomed" one, which does not call for the recital of a blessing.

(*Shulhan Arukh, Ch.* 225)

Customs Pertaining to the Afternoon Service

168. QUESTION:

Why is the Afternoon worship referred to in Hebrew, as the Mincha service?

ANSWER:

Mincha is the Hebrew term for "offering" or "gift." The afternoon service is, actually, a "gift" we send to G-d without being obliged by law to do so.

In the morning we must give thanks to G-d for returning our souls to us, and for all the good He has done for us; for the bright sunshine and so forth.

In the evening, we must beseech Him to watch over our soul during the night and to return it to us safely in the morning.

In the afternoon, however, there is nothing in particular for which we must pray, or render thanks. Still, we recite a prayer as a free-will offering to G-d. Hence, the designation *mincha* for the Afternoon Service.

(*Kedushath Levi, Parshath Hayye Sarah*)

Customs Pertaining to the Evening Service

169. QUESTION:

Why is Psalm 134 recited in some synagogues before the Ma'ariv service?

ANSWER:

To comply with the Talmudic precept (Berakhoth 4b) that "a man coming from the field in the evening should enter the synagogue [a little before the evening service begins]. If he is accustomed to reading from the Scripture, let him do so; if he is able to study the Law, let him do that. [Only] thereafter should he read the *Shema* and recite his prayers." The reason for this is that prayer should follow immediately after the study of Torah.

The Rabbis chose Psalm 134 as the Scriptural selection to be recited before the Ma'ariv service because it contains the verse "who stand in the House of the L-rd in the nights," which is taken to refer to those who study the Law during the night.

When the Ma'ariv is recited immediately after the *Mincha* service, Psalm 134 is not said, since the *Ashrei* prayer recited at the *Mincha* service already constitutes a *Scriptural* passage.

(*Eliyahu Rabbah, Chapters* 54:4 *and* 237:4;

see Makhtzith HaShekel 237:1)

170. QUESTION:

What are some of the rules pertaining to the proper time for reciting the Shema of the Evening Service?

ANSWER:

The Shulhan Arukh Ha-Rav writes: Many people are accustomed to recite Ma'ariv and the *Shema* before the stars are visible in the sky. But this is not right, because the law prohibits the reading of the Evening Service before three stars can be seen in the sky.

The *Terumath Ha-Deshen* (Ch. 1) writes: In certain places it is customary, in the summer, when the days are long, to read the *Shema* of Ma'ariv and to recite the Evening Service several hours before the stars appear in the sky.

This undesirable practice has come into vogue because recent generations have become weaker, and most of the people are hungry for supper on a long summer day. If these people were to sit down to their meal before Mincha, they would linger at the table and it would become very difficult to get them to come to the synagogue. In certain places, it therefore became the custom to have Ma'ariv follow immediately upon *Mincha* even while it was still day, to enable the people to have their meal after services.

The same author also writes: In the Yeshiva, I heard of an erudite Rabbi who had heard that one of the great Sages of old, who lived in the Ukraine, would read the *Shema* and the Ma'ariv service on Friday afternoons while it was still day. He would then have his Sabbath meal, and thereafter he and his flock would stroll above the banks of the Dnieper, returning home before it turned dark.

It is written in the *Zohar Hai* (Behukhothai) that the Rebbe Reb Elimelech would not speak at all after the Ma'ariv service until he retired for the night.

171. QUESTION:

Why is the prayer VeHu Rahum ("He, being merciful, forgives iniquity...,") recited before the Ma'ariv service?

ANSWERS:

1. Because tradition has it that sinners receive their punishment between *Mincha* and Ma'ariv.

(Sefer HaManhig)

2. Because, the evening service, unlike the morning and afternoon services, was not accompanied by a daily offering to atone for sin.

(Pardes, Ch. 2, in the name of Rabbi Eliezer ha-Gadol)

172. QUESTION:
What is the origin of the prayer "Blessed be the L-rd for evermore...," in the Ma'ariv Service, just before the Eighteen Benedictions?

ANSWER:

In ancient times, the synagogues would be out in the fields where there was no human habitation far and wide. As a consequence, many people were afraid to stay in the synagogue until after the Eighteen Benedictions were recited, because they did not want to walk home through the deserted fields so late.

The Rabbis therefore instituted prayer which is a condensation of the Eighteen Benedictions and to which the Name of G-d is mentioned eighteen times.

This prayer would take the place of the full *Shemona-Esrei*. Kaddish would then be recited, and the people were ready to leave for home.

We still observe this custom today because one should not abolish practices sanctified by long-time observance.

(*Tur, Ch.* 236; *see Tosfoth Berakhoth* 4b, *sub voce, de-amar Rabbi Yahanan*)

173. QUESTION:
Why does the Reader not repeat the Eighteen Benedictions aloud in the Ma'ariv service?

ANSWER:

Because Ma'ariv which was not accompanied by a sacrifice in the days of the Temple, is not a compulsory ritual. On the other hand, the *Shulhan Arukh Ha-Rav* writes in the name of Rabbenu Shelomo: "When our Rabbis point out that 'Ma'ariv is not obligatory' — they mean only referring to *Tefillah* — *the Eighteen Benedictions*."

The *Shema* is obligatory, and must be recited in the evening, with the blessings that precede and follow it, for this is a Biblical injunction. Cf. "And thou shalt talk of them (the *Shema*)...*when thou liest down* and when thou risest up" (Deut. 6:7).

Today, it is universally accepted that Ma'ariv is indeed obligatory, as Rabbi Yohanan was accustomed to say: "Who is sure to have a share in the world to come? He who recites the Eighteen Benedictions at the Evening service immediately after the benediction giving thanks to G-d for redemption (go'al Yisrael)."

(*Berakhoth* 4b; *see Tosfoth, ibid., sub voce, de-amar*)

Customs Pertaining to
Sabbath Observance

 174. QUESTION:

> In Hassidic circles, the custom is to bake twelve challot (Sabbath loaves) for the Sabbath. What is the origin thereof?

ANSWER:

To recall the "Show-Bread." (The twelve loaves of bread which were arranged in two rows on a special table in the Temple). Each week fresh loaves were prepared and set out on the Sabbath. The loaves from the week before were eaten by the Priests (Lev. 24:5-9).

This procedure was followed even when the Sabbath coincided with a Festival.

(*See Shaarei T'shuvah, Ch. 274; also Mateh Ephraim 624:50*)

 175. QUESTION:

> Why should one make sure to change clothes in honor of the Sabbath?

ANSWER:

Rabbi Hayim Yosef David Azulai said: Woe to those who do not change into their Sabbath garments on Friday night, but pray in their weekday clothes, changing into their Sabbath clothes only the next morning, and so mar the beauty and splendor of Friday night!

We read in *Toldoth Aaron* (Kee Tissa): Just as every man must review his deeds on the Eve of Yom Kippur, which is the end of the year, so, too, should he take stock of himself on Friday which is the end of the six days of Creation.

It is therefore fitting that a man should confess his sins and repent of them on Friday, and assume holiness and purity so that he may enter into the Holy Sabbath in purity, gird himself with the fear of heaven and never, not even for a moment, forget the holiness of the Sabbath.

It is written in *Or LeShamayim*, in the name of Rebbe Elimelekh, that the Eve of the Sabbath is in the same category, as Yom Kippur Eve.

176. QUESTION:

Why is it customary to place the Challot on the table on Friday afternoon, before lighting the Sabbath candles [which are also placed on that table]?

ANSWER:

If the lighted Sabbath candles were to be placed on the table first, one could no longer move the table, since candles, being *muktzeh,* must not be touched or moved on the Sabbath.

However, when the Challot, which are not *muktzeh* are placed on the table first, the Challot, being *non-muktzeh,* take precedence over the *muktzeh* objects, since they are required for the Sabbath meal. Therefore, in that case, the table may then be moved even though it bears a *muktzeh* object.

(*Likhutei Hilkhoth Shabbatt, No. 67*)

177. QUESTION:

Why are loaves of bread baked in honor of the Shabbos referred to as Challos?

ANSWER:

To remind the housewives of their duty to set aside a portion of the dough (to take *Challa*), as prescribed by Biblical law (Num. 15:17-21).

(*Eshel Avraham, Ch.* 260)

 178.   QUESTION:

> Why are at least two candles lit in honor of the Sabbath, and why is this ritual usually considered the duty of the woman rather than of the man in the house?

ANSWER:

To symbolize the two-fold command of Sabbath observance: "*Remember* (*zachor*) the Sabbath day to keep it holy" (Ex. 20:8), and *observe* (*shamor*) the Sabbath day to keep it holy" (Deut. 5:12).

Maimonides says: It is the women who should light the Sabbath candles, because they are usually at home at the time attending to the household (Maimonides, Sabbath Laws 5:3).

(*See Tur, Ch.* 263)

The two lights kindled on the Festivals, are meant to symbolize husband and wife.

(*Ibid., Eliyahu Rabbah*)

It is customary to cover all tables in the home with a fresh tablecloth for the Sabbath, even those tables which will not be used for Sabbath meals.

(*Eliyahu Rabbah* 262:3)

 179.   QUESTION:

> Why is the candle lighting ritual the time when the mother of the house should recite a prayer of her own for the happiness of her family and for sons who will "shine in the Torah?"

ANSWER:
Because prayers are more readily accepted when they are recited during the performance of a *mitzvah,* an act commanded by Jewish law.

(Rabbenu Bachya ibn Pakudah, Yithro)

The mother of Rabbi Shmuel Koidanover (the author of a number of noted Rabbinic Commentaries) could not read Hebrew, or pray in that language. Therefore when she would light the Sabbath candles, she would pray in Russian: "May it be the will of G-d, that my son Shmuel become a scholar in the Law!" And lo, her prayers were heard.

(Daat Moshe — Maggid of Koznitz — Terumah)

180. QUESTION:
After she lights the candles, the woman spreads out her hands or covers her eyes to keep from seeing the lights until she has pronounced the blessing. What is the reason for this procedure?

ANSWER:
Because the Rabbis have ruled that the blessing must be recited not before, but after the candles are lit.

Since no enjoyment may be derived from the lights until the blessing has been recited, the woman must not "see" them before.

(ReMa 263:5)

The reason for the ruling that the blessing must be said after, and not before the act of kindling is that if the blessing were to be recited first, it would seem as if the woman had already "inaugurated" the Sabbath. In that case, she could no longer light the candles, since the kindling of lights on the Sabbath is forbidden.

(Magen Avraham 263:5 and 263:12)

181. QUESTION:
Why is it customary to inaugurate the Sabbath with Six Psalms (beginning with Psalm 95 and continuing with Psalms 96, 97, 98, 99 and 29)?

ANSWER:
The Six Psalms correspond to the six days of the workday week.

(*Yaavetz*)

182. QUESTION:
What is the origin of the custom observed in certain places to distribute aromatic herbs on Friday?

ANSWER:
The herbs are intended for the pleasure of the *neshama yethera*, the "additional soul" which, according to the Talmud (Betzah 16a) comes to every Jew on Friday night, remaining with him until the end of the Sabbath.

(*Maateh Ephraim* 625:36)

183. QUESTION:
What is the purpose of the neshama yethera?

ANSWER:
To enable each Jew to enjoy to the full the Sabbath's gift of freedom from workday toil and care. That is why people who are small eaters the rest of the week are able to consume an abundance of food on the Sabbath.

It is told of the holy Rabbi Abraham Ha-Cohen of Amsterdam that he fasted for forty years, breaking his fast only on Sabbaths to partake of a sumptuous meal in honor of the Day of Rest.

(*Divrei Shaul, Part I, Betzah* 16)

184. QUESTION:
Why do we face west when reciting the last verse of the Lekha Dodi (i.e. Bo-ee ve-Shalom — "Come thou in peace")?

ANSWERS:
1. Because the *Shekhina,* the Glory of G-d, is in the west (TaZ 3:3).

2. To comfort the mourners in the congregation.

Mourners remain outside the auditorium until the congregation are about to "receive officially" the Sabbath with the Psalm for the Sabbath Day (*Mizmor Shir Le-Yom HaShabbos*) following the *Lekha Dodi.*

When the worshippers turn to the West, they face the rear door, behind which the mourners wait. In this manner they will find out which of their fellow-congregants are in mourning and in need of comfort.

(*Toldoth Menahem*)

185. QUESTION:

Why are bridegrooms honored by being seated in the front of the congregation at the Friday evening service?

ANSWER:

So that the whole congregation will know that there is a bridegroom in their midst, in whose happiness they can rejoice.

(*Toldoth Menahem*)

186. QUESTION:

On weekdays, Ve-Hu Rahum — "And He, being merciful ...," is recited before the Ma'ariv service.

Why is it not also recited before the Evening service on Friday?

ANSWER:

This prayer, an appeal for Divine forgiveness, takes the place of the Evening Sacrifices which were offered as an atonement for sin. Since no Sacrifices were ever offered in the Temple on Friday evening, this prayer need not be recited at Friday evening services.

(*Beth Yosef, Ch. 237*)

187. QUESTION:

Why is the Biblical verse Veshamru ("And the Children of Israel shall keep the Sabbath ...") (Ex. 31:16-17), inserted between the prayer for redemption and the Evening Tefillah of Friday night?

ANSWER:

To imply that if you will keep Sabbath, you will not be in need of protection.

If Israel were to observe only two Sabbaths in succession they would be redeemed immediately!

(Tur, Ch. 267)

One should be very careful to observe the Sabbath strictly. Storekeepers should close their establishments when the day (Friday) is still high, for temptation is likely to come in the late afternoon just before the Sabbath in the form of crowds of customers.

One should therefore be careful to close his doors early in the afternoon.

188. QUESTION:

At the conclusion of all Festival Benedictions, we make mention of the people of Israel — e.g. "Blessed art Thou, O L-rd, who hallowest Israel and the Festive Seasons" (Mekadesh Yisrael ve-hazmanim). Why by contrast do the Sabbath Benedictions make no mention of Israel, concluding simply with the words, "Who hallowest the Sabbath" (mekadesh ha-Shabbos)?

ANSWER:

The Sabbath already existed before the people of Israel was created, as it is written: "For in six days the L-rd made heaven and earth, and on the seventh day He ceased from work and rested" (Ex. 31:17).

(Abudraham)

189. QUESTION:

> Why is the Friday evening service concluded with Magen Avoth ("Shield of the Fathers") which is an abridged version of the Sabbath Amidah?

ANSWER:

To give late comers additional time to complete their prayers so that they will be able to go home with the rest of the congregation rather than walk unescorted through the fields in the dark.

(*Tur, Ch.* 268)

190. QUESTION:

> Why is Magen Avoth not recited when Friday evening services are held in the house of a bridegroom, or in the house of a mourner.

ANSWER:

Unlike the synagogue, private homes were not usually located in some deserted field. Accordingly, there is no reason to prolong the service.

(*Orakh Hayyim* 268:10)

191. QUESTION:

> The passage from the Mishna beginning with Bameh Madlikin — "With what materials may the Sabbath lights be kindled ...," (Mishna in Sabbath, Chap. 2), is read on Friday evening, but not when the Sabbath coincides with a Festival. Why Not?

ANSWER:

This passage states: "Three things must a man ask his household toward dusk on the Sabbath eve: Have you separated the tithe? Have you prepared the eruv? Have you kindled the Sabbath lamp!"

But part of this passage is not applicable to Festivals, for one does not tithe on those days.

(*Levush, Ch.* 270)

192. QUESTION:

What is the origin of the Sabbath Kiddush?

ANSWER:

It is written: *"Remember (Zachor)* the Sabbath day *to keep it holy" (l'kadsho)* (Ex. 20:8).

This is interpreted to mean that we should "remember" the Sabbath day by "sanctifying" it with a cup of wine and the recital of the Kiddush.

We must remember the Sabbath day with *Kiddush* when it enters and with *Havdalah* when it leaves.

(Maimonides, Laws of Sabbath, Ch. 29)

The Rokeach writes (Ch. 297): *Mikra kodesh yiyeh lachem* — "ye shall have a *holy* convocation (Lev. 22:7). From this verse we deduce that Kiddush is to be recited also on Festivals.

193. QUESTION:

Formerly, the Kiddush would be recited at the synagogue because transients would frequently lodge and eat in the synagogue premises. Today, however, the synagogue premises, as a rule, are no longer put to this use.

Why, then, is Kiddush still recited at the synagogue at the conclusion of the Friday evening service?

ANSWER:

For the benefit of those ignorant of Hebrew. It is felt that if they will hear the Kiddush often enough, they will eventually be able to recite it properly on their own, at home.

(Kol Bo)

Rabbenu Yaakov of Marmirsh was accustomed to ask questions of Heaven, which would be answered without fail. One of his questions was whether it was right to omit reciting the Kiddush and Havdalah in the synagogue on Sabbaths when there were no transients staying there.

Came the answer from above: "Although the Kiddush should

be recited where one is eating (*kiddush bimkom seudah*), it is still proper to recite both Kiddush and Havdalah in the synagogue, because it is written "In the *multitude of people* is the King's glory" (Proverbs 14:28).

194. QUESTION:
Why is it customary to put two cloths on the Sabbath table, one above the challa, and another underneath?

ANSWERS:
1. The *Challa,* which symbolizes the Sabbath meal, is kept covered until the feast has been properly "introduced" by the Kiddush.

2. Because in the Kiddush, the blessing over the wine precedes the blessing made over the bread. Once the wine has been blessed, the bread may be uncovered.

(*Tur, Ch.* 271)

3. To recall the *Mannah* of the wilderness which did not fall on Sabbaths and Festivals, and which would be found encased between two protecting layers of dew, one above and one below.

(*Tosfoth Pesahim* 100b, *sub voce, She-en*)

195. QUESTION:
Why did the Rabbis ordain that the Sabbath should be sanctified with a cup of wine?

ANSWER:
Because the Sabbath is likened to a bride in whose honor wine should be drunk to make her rejoice.

Rabbi Shmuel ben Nachmeni said in the name of Rabbi Jonathan: "From where do we learn that the (*Hymn of Praise*) *shirah* must be recited over wine? It is written: "And the vine said to them: Should I leave my wine which cheers G-d and man..." (Judges 9:13).

Now — if wine cheers man, with what is G-d to be cheered? From this we see that the Hymn of Praise must be recited over wine."

(*Tolaath Yaakov*)

196. QUESTION:

Why do certain Jews make it a practice not to recite Kiddush between the hours of six and seven on Friday night?

ANSWER:

Because these are the hours when Mars (*Maadim*), the planet of war and disaster, is in the ascendecy.

(See Rashi, Sabbath 129b; ibid., Eruvin 56a; Machtzith Ha-Shekel 271:1)

197. QUESTION:

The Kiddush cup must be filled to the brim. Why?

ANSWER:

If the cup were not completely filled, it would seem as if one were making Kiddush over wine left over in the cup from some previous occasion.

(Abudraham)

198. QUESTION:

Why must Kiddush never be recited over water?

ANSWER:

While water symbolizes grace and compassion, wine denotes fire and judgment. We therefore make a *Blessing* over wine to nullify the fire and judgment contained therein.

(Levush, Ch. 182; see No. 132)

199. QUESTION:

Why do we begin the home Kiddush with Va-yehulu — "And the heaven and the earth were finished . . ." (Gen. 2:1-3)?

ANSWER:

So that those members of the family who did not attend the synagogue service might hear this verse, which contains the commandment to rest on the Sabbath.

(*Tosfoth Pesachim* 106a, *sub voce, zakhreihu*)

200. QUESTION:

Why is the blessing over the wine (bore P'ri hagafen) said before the blessing over the Sabbath (mekaddesh haShabbos)?

ANSWER:

The blessing over wine is said whenever one drinks wine which may be several times a week, while the Sabbath Day comes only once a week.

According to tradition, the event which occurs more frequently is given precedence over one which does not occur so often.

(*Abudraham*)

201. QUESTION:

Why do we preface the Kiddush with the words sabri maranan — "By your leave, gentlemen?"

ANSWER:

To call the family and guests to attention while the master of the house recites the blessing over the wine, so that they will not have to recite the blessing for themselves.

(*Abudraham*)

202. QUESTION:

Why does the master of the house say bir'shuth — "With your consent," before he breaks the bread after Kiddush, but not before drinking the Kiddush wine?

ANSWER:

While it is obligatory to recite the Kiddush over wine, it is not mandatory to eat bread as part of the meal. Etiquette therefore requires that the host must ask the consent of all those assembled around his table before partaking of the bread.

(*Shibalei HaLeket, No.* 140)

203. QUESTION:

Why does the Kiddush include the phrase Zecher liyetziath mitzrayim — "In remembrance of the exodus of Egypt?"

ANSWER:

These words should be read in the context of the preceding phrase *Tehilla lemikraei kodesh* — "This day is the first day of the holy convocations," meaning that the Sabbath comes first on the list of the holy days (Lev. 23), meant to recall the exodus of Egypt.

The Sabbath as such, however, was instituted as a memorial to the Creation.

(*Seder Hayom*)

204. QUESTION:

Although women are not obliged to perform those Mitzvos that depend on a fixed time, they are duty-bound to hear the Kiddush recited. Why?

ANSWER:

Men and women were made equally liable to punishment for violations of precepts laid down in Biblical Law in the Rabbinic Codes.

But since women were burdened with numerous household duties, they were exempted from those religious obligations which could only be performed at a set time (*mitzvath asei shehazman gerama*), such as donning the Tefillin (Kiddushin 29a).

This exception does not, apply to negative precepts, and to

precepts which contain both positive and negative aspects such as the observance of the Sabbath.

"Remembering" the Sabbath by hearing the Kiddush recited is an essential component of Sabbath observance (Berakhoth 20b).

205. QUESTION:

Why should the Kiddush be recited at the time and place of the Sabbath meal?

ANSWER:

Because it is written: *Ve-karatha le-Shaabos oneg* — "And ye shall call the Sabbath a delight" (Isaiah 58:13).

Comment the Rabbis: "Where there is delight, i.e., a festive meal, there shall you recite the Kiddush."

(*RaSHBaM, Rabbi Samuel ben Meir, Pesahim* 101a)

206. QUESTION:

Why must we have two loaves of bread at every Sabbath meal?

ANSWER:

Because it is written concerning the Mannah in the wilderness: *Liktu lehem mishna* — "And it came to pass that on the sixth day they gathered twice as much bread" (Ex. 16:21). However, only one of these loaves may be broken at a time, lest one would appear to be a glutton.

(*Abudraham*)

207. QUESTION:

Why is it a Jewish custom to eat fish on the Sabbath?

ANSWER:

To remind us of the mercies of G-d.

Even as fish have no eyelids, so that their eyes are never closed, so the eyes of the L-rd are open at all times to watch over those who fear him.

(Minhath Yaakov)

In his commentary in the Book of Genesis, the Redak, Rabbi David Kimchi, writes in connection with the verse, "And G-d blessed the seventh day and hallowed it" (Gen. 2:3) — that there is a certain fish in the sea which does not swim on the Sabbath but rests close to dry land or in a crevice all that day.

208. QUESTION:
Why do we not don the Tefillin on the Sabbath?

ANSWER:

There are three commandments in which the word *OS* ("token" or "sign") is mentioned: Milah (circumcision), Sabbath observance and the donning of Tefillin.

Concerning circumcision it is written: והיה לאות ברית ביני וביניכם — "And it shall be a *token* of a covenant betwixt Me and you" (Gen. 17:11).

Concerning Sabbath observance it is written: ביני ובין בני ישראל אות היא לעולם — "It (the Shabbos), is a *sign* between Me and the Children of Israel forever" (Ex. 31:17).

Concerning the Tefillin it is written: והיה לאות על ידכה "And it shall be for a *sign* upon thy hand" (Ex.13:16).

These aforementioned three signs or tokens bear witness to the Children of Israel that they are servants of the Holy One, blessed be He.

According to Jewish law, evidence at court is admissible only if it is based on testimony from two witnesses. Cf. "At the mouth of two witnesses...shall a matter be established" (Deut. 19:15).

A Jew, therefore cannot be truly "Jewish" unless he has two witnesses to attest to his Jewishness.

On weekdays the Tefillin act as one of the two witnesses — the other being Milah. On the Sabbath, however, the role of the second witness is taken by the Sabbath itself; hence it is not necessary to don the Tefillin on the Sabbath.

(Abudraham)

209. QUESTION:

Why is the prayer beginning with Ve-Hu Rahum ("And He being merciful...") not said at any time during the Sabbath?

ANSWER:

This prayer was instituted by the Rabbis to offset "the awakening powers of rigor and justice," for this verse is a plea to G-d to turn aside His anger and not to stir up all His wrath...

We omit it on the Sabbath because this is not the day on which to raise the subject of Divine wrath and righteousness.

(*Responsa Yaavetz, Part 2, Ch.* 120)

210. QUESTION:

What are the nine Sabbath Psalms added to the morning service on the Sabbath after Hodu and what is their purpose?

ANSWER:

On Shabbos, worshippers have more leisure time for devotion (Tur, Ch. 281). All these Psalms have reference — direct or indirect — to the Sabbath.

The first Psalm is Psalm 19 which describes the Creation and the Torah, which was given on a Sabbath.

The second, Psalm 34 speaks of King David, who feigned madness for fear of being recognized at the Philistine court where he had taken refuge from the wrath of Saul. This incident also took place on a Sabbath.

The third, Psalm 90, contains the verse, "O satisfy us in the morning with Thy lovingkindness...," which refers to the new Day of the World to Come, when every day will be a Sabbath.

The fourth, Psalm 91, prays for deliverance from demons, evil spells and other calamities. It is proper to recite this Psalm on the Sabbath so that these misfortunes should be banished from our midst on the Day of Rest.

The fifth, Psalm 135, is the preface to Psalm 136, the "Great Psalm." It is only proper that these two Psalms should be recited on the Sabbath because they extol the justice and the lovingkindness of the L-rd as revealed in nature and in the history of the people of Israel.

The seventh, Psalm 33, contains the verse "By the word of the L-rd the heavens were made..."

All these (heaven and earth) were completed on the Sabbath, as it is written: "And the heaven and the earth were finished" (Gen. 2:1).

The eighth, Psalm 92, was composed by Moses in honor of the Sabbath Day. The initial letters of Mizmor, Shir and HaShabbath spell out the Hebrew consonants of "Moshe."

The ninth, Psalm 93, is a hymn appropriate to the Sabbath Eve, for as soon as G-d finished all His work, He enwrapped Himself in His cloak of glory and splendor in honor of the Sabbath, as it is related in this Psalm.

(*Kol Bo*)

211. QUESTION:

Why is Psalm 136, "O give thanks unto the L-rd, for He is good, for His mercy endures for ever," known as Hallel Ha-Gadol, the "Great Hallel?"

ANSWER:

Rabbi Yohanan said: "In verse 25 of this Psalm it is written that the Holy One, blessed be He, is enthroned in the uppermost heights of the universe, from where He gives food to all His creatures (Noten lehem le-chal basar) (Pesahim 118a).

Since this particular verse lends paramount importance to the "Great Hallel," it is recited on the Sabbath, in the Morning Service.

Verse 25 of Psalm 136, declares that "He giveth food to all flesh."

The Zichron Tov, Rabbi Isaac of Neshitz, asked one of his Hassidim:

"From where do you get your bread?"

— "From the board on which the bread is kept," the man replied.

"And who put it there? the Rebbe asked.

"Why, my wife," answered the Hassid.

Thereupon the Rebbe said to him: "You answered like a fool!" "If you had known who it really is that gives you your bread, you would have been assured of wealth and sustenance for the rest of your life!"

212. QUESTION:

Why is the "ordinary Hallel" (Psalms 113-18), rather than the Great Hallel, recited on happy occasions?

ANSWER:

The "ordinary Hallel" is recited on happy occasions because it alludes to the following five events in Israel's history:

1. The Exodus from Egypt. 2. The splitting of the Red Sea. 3. The giving of the Torah to Israel. 4. The resurrection of the dead and 5. The sufferings of the Messiah.

The Exodus from Egypt — as it is written, "When Israel went forth out of Egypt" (Ps. 114:1).

The splitting of the Red Sea — as it is written, "The sea beheld it and fled" (114:3).

The giving of the Torah — as it is written, "The mountains skipped like rams, the hills like young sheep" (114:4).

The resurrection of the Dead — as it is written, "I shall walk before the L-rd in the lands of the living" (116:9).

The sufferings of the Messiah — as it is written, "Not unto us, O L-rd, not unto us, etc." (115:1).

(*Kad Ha-Kemach*)

213. QUESTION:

Why does the Sabbath Tefillah contain only seven blessings instead of eighteen?

ANSWERS:

1. In order not to burden the congregation with an overly-long service.

2. The Sabbath service was meant for joyful communion with

G-d. It is only right, therefore, that all those blessings in the Eighteen Benedictions that refer to guilt, want, tribulation or sorrow should be omitted on the Sabbath, so as not to mar the worshipper's joy and serenity on the Day of Rest.

(Halokhoth Ketanoth)

214. QUESTION:

Why does the text of the Sabbath services refer to the Sabbath first in the feminine gender, then in the masculine and finally in the third person plural? (In the Friday evening service, we say, veyanukhu vah, **"And may Israel rest in her"; in the Sabbath morning service we say,** veyanukhu vo, **"May Israel rest in him"; and in the afternoon service we say,** veyanukhu vam, **"may Israel rest in them")?**

ANSWER:

On Friday night, the Sabbath is compared to a bride who is still at the home of her father where she, the bride, is the cause of all the rejoicing. Therefore, the feminine form (vah) (in *her*).

On Saturday morning, the Sabbath is likened to a bride who has entered the home of her parents-in-law, where the bridegroom is the main source of joy. Therefore the masculine form (vo) (in *him*).

Finally, in the afternoon, the bride and the groom are a source of happiness to one another. Therefore, the third person plural (vam) (*in them*).

(Tosefeth Shabbos 268:4)

215. QUESTION:

Why is the beautiful doxology beginning with Al ha-kol yisgadal ve-yiskaddash, "Magnified and hallowed . . . ," recited only on Sabbaths and Festivals?

ANSWER:

Because the leisure of the Sabbath or holiday enables the worshipper to recite this solemn prayer with the devotion it deserves.

(Levush 134:2)

216. QUESTION:

Why does the Reader (Baal Koreh) say Amen aloud
before beginning to read each portion of the Law?

ANSWER:

The *Amen* is the response of the *Baal Koreh* to the blessings
recited by the person called to the Torah for that particular portion.

It is said aloud to call the worshippers to order so that they
will know the reading is about to begin and will listen to it with
the proper attention.

(*Hagaoth Minhagim*)

217. QUESTION:

Why did the Rabbis rule that the actual reading
from the Law should be done by one reader (Baal
Koreh), instead of by the worshipper who was
called up to the Torah for that portion?

ANSWER:

Originally every person who was called to the Torah read his
own portion. But as ignorance spread, it became increasingly difficult
to find "men of learning"; indeed, there were hardly any laymen left
who were able to read properly from the Scroll at all. Therefore,
in order to avoid embarrassment, the custom was instituted to engage
a *Baal Koreh* who would read each portion, regardless of the educational level of the person called to the Torah.

(*Peri Hadash* 141:2)

The same considerations were taken into account in the procedure set down for the Offering of the First Fruits (*Bikkurim*),
which was made in the Temple in Jerusalem (Deut. 26) and in
which Hebrew prayer (see Verses 5-10) had to be recited by each
person. Those unable to read the prayer repeated it after the
officiating Priest. Eventually, to avoid embarrassment to the less
educated, it was ruled that each person, regardless of his degree of
learning, had to repeat the prayer after the Priest (Mishna, Bikkurim
3:7).

218. QUESTION:
Why are seven men called up to read from the Torah on the Sabbath?

ANSWER:
This is done for the benefit of the persons who were unable to attend services during the rest of the week, so that they did not hear the *Barekhu,* "Bless ye the L-rd who is to be blessed" pronounced all week long.

On the Sabbath, these people are given the opportunity to hear the *Barekhu* pronounced seven times by the seven men called up to the Torah, once for the Sabbath, and six times for the six other days of the week.

(*Beth Yosef, Ch.* 282)

219. QUESTION:
The person called upon to read from the Law should be joined on the Bimah (reading platform) by two other persons — the Baal Koreh and the Gabbai (Warden) of the congregation.
What is the reason for this custom?

ANSWER:
It is written: העידותי בכם היום "I call heaven and earth to witness against you this day..." (Deut. 4:26).

According to Jewish law, a "warning," in order to be valid, must be made in the presence of two witnesses, that is, at any court trial involving capital punishment, testimony was required from two witnesses to the effect that the accused had been forewarned of the consequences of the crime he had been about to commit. Accordingly, the person who reads to the congregation the admonitions contained in the Torah, must have beside him "two witnesses" whose presence makes the admonitions "official."

(*Elijah, Gaon of Vilna; see Magen Avraham* 141:8)

The *Levush* (141:4) writes that the *Gabbai* (Warden) symbolizes the authority of G-d, since he calls to the Law whoever he pleases; the *Baal Koreh* acts as the "agent" in the sense of Moses, who was the "agent" through whom the Torah was given; the one who receives the 'aliya, represents the entire people of Israel to whom the Torah was revealed.

220. QUESTION:

Why may hosafoth **('aliyot beyond the mandatory seven) be given on the Sabbath?**

ANSWER:

According to the Law, "seven men of learning" are to be called to the Torah. If there should be among the "first seven" called to the Torah, an ignoramus, who does not know even one letter of the portion, this requirement would not be met. To obviate this possibility, we call a few additional men to the Torah.

(*Eliyahu Rabbah*)

Although it is customary to call up some unlearned people to these *'aliyot,* it is considered more desirable to accord this honor to "learned men," so that we may be certain that the mandatory seven "men of learning" had indeed been called to the Law.

(*Peri Megaddim* 135:5)

221. QUESTION:

Why should the Tohaha **(Reproof) in Leviticus 26:14-43, be read in its entirety and without any interruptions?**

ANSWER:

It is written: מוסר ד' בני אל תמאס, ואל תקוץ בתוכחתו "My son, despise not the chastening of the L-rd, neither spurn thou His chastisement" (Proverbs 3:11).

Tokotz, the Hebrew for "spurn thou," is derived from *Kutz,* "to cut off."

The latter part of this verse therefore implies that we are not to allow any distraction to "cut off" (interrupt) the reading of the "reproof." Accordingly, only one person should be called to the Torah for this entire portion.

(*Tosfoth, Megilla* 31b, *sub voce, En mafsikin*)

222. QUESTION:

After the completion of the reading of each of the Five Books of Moses, the Reader and Congregation exclaim חזק חזק ונתחזק "Be strong, be strong, and let us strengthen one another." What is the origin of this custom?

ANSWER:

To recall a solemn moment in the life of Joshua, who succeeded Moses as leader of the Children of Israel.

G-d said to Joshua: "This Book of the Law shall not depart out of thy mouth" (Joshua 1:8). The Rabbis comment that Joshua was holding the Scroll of the Law in his hands at the time and reading from it (Gen. Rabbah).

It was when Joshua concluded the Reading that G-d said to him "Be strong and of good courage" (Joshua 1:9).

(*Abudraham*)

223. QUESTION:

What is the origin of the reading of a Lesson from the Prophets (Haftarah) after each Reading from the Law?

ANSWER:

At one time the Syrian overlords of Palestine had forbidden the Reading of the Law. To circumvent this prohibition, appropriate selections from the Prophets were substituted.

(*Abudraham*)

224. QUESTION:

What is the origin of the term Haftarah applied to the Lesson from the Prophets?

ANSWER:

The word Haftarah is derived from *patur*, "free."

At the time when the reading from the Pentateuch was prohibited by the pagan overlords, the reading of the Lesson of the Prophets "freed" or exempted the congregation from the duty to read from the Law.

(*Ibid.*)

225. QUESTION:

Why must the person called to read the Lesson from the Prophets, first read the final section of the portion of the Law assigned for that Sabbath?

ANSWER:

When it was possible, once again, to read from the Law without danger to life or liberty, it was pointed out that if the person called to read the Lesson from the Prophets were not to read at least several verses from the Law, it would appear as if the Books of the Prophets were considered equal to the Law of Moses. This would be wrong, for the teachings of the Prophets are only supplementary to the Torah, which contains the basic doctrines of our religion.

(*See Levush* 282:5; *TaZ* 282:2)

226. QUESTION:

When Rosh Hodesh falls on a Sabbath, why is no mention made of the New Moon in the benediction "Who hallowest the Sabbath," with which the Haftarah is concluded?

ANSWER:

The Haftarah is read only because the day happens to be a Sabbath. If Rosh Hodesh falls on a week day no Haftarah is read.

(*Shulhan Arukh Ha-Rav*)

227. QUESTION:

Why is it considered obligatory for every individual to rehearse for himself the weekly Sedrah twice and the Targum (Aramaic translation) once?

ANSWER:

So that every individual become thoroughly familiar with the words of the Torah.

(*Levush* 285:1)

228. QUESTION:

When reciting the El Malle Rahamim (Memorial Prayer), it is customary to donate money to charity in memory of the departed. Why?

ANSWER:

We give charity in memory of the departed, so that they, who are guiltless and pure, may pray for the families who survive them.

(*Sodei Razi*)

229. QUESTION:

Why is the prayer beginning with Yekum Purkan ("May salvation come . . .") recited in Aramaic?

ANSWER:

Because it was composed in Babylonia, where Aramaic was the vernacular of the Jews.

(*Eliyahu Rabbah* 284:11)

230. QUESTION:

Why is it customary for the Cantor to hold the Scroll of the Law in his arms when reciting Yekum Purkan?

ANSWER:

Because this is a prayer for the health and happiness of the Heads of the Talmudical Academies, the Rabbis and the students who devote their lives to the Law.

(*TaZ* 96:1)

231. QUESTION:

The Prayer for the Martyrs, Av HaRahamim —
"Father of Mercies...," is not recited on the Sabbath preceding Rosh Hodesh except for the Sabbaths preceding the New Moons of Iyaar and Sivan.
What is the reason for this exception?

ANSWER:

Because the months of Iyaar and Sivan of the year 4856 (soon
after the First Crusade in 1096), saw the destruction of many
Jewish communities in Germany either by massacre, or by voluntary
martyrdom to escape baptism. Accordingly, *Av HaRahamim* is recited on these two Sabbaths.

(*Peri Megaddim* 284:8; *ibid, Machtzith HaShekel*)

The *Arvei Nachal* (*Parshat Masse*), writes in the name of the
Responsa of MaHaRaM (Rabbi Meir of Rothenburg), concerning
an oral tradition handed down from Rabbi to Rabbi, that one
who lays down his life in honor of G-d's Name does not suffer, and
feels no pain.

This is so because the martyr who is prepared to sanctify the
Name of G-d by laying down his life for Him goes to his death
with enthusiasm and zeal. All his inmost thoughts and feelings are
centered on his act of supreme sacrifice. This love and yearning for
G-d ennables him to overcome the physical agony of violent death.

We see this clearly in the case of Rabbi Akiba, who longed for
the time when his daily profession of love for G-d would be put to
the test. That long-awaited moment came after his valiant efforts in
the final Jewish revolt against Imperial Rome, when the executioner
was tearing into his flesh with combs of iron.

"All my days," Akiba told his weeping disciples, "I have longed
for this hour. I have loved G-d *with all my heart* and *with all my
might.* Now that I can love Him *with all my soul* (Deut. 6:5),
even when He is about to take my soul from me, my happiness is
complete" (Berakhoth 61b).

It was this conception of the *Shema* (Confession of Faith), that
gave Jewish martyrs the inner strength to lay down their lives for
their beliefs.

A medieval Jewish saint used to pray: "My G-d, Thou hast given

me over to starvation and poverty. Thou hast plunged me into the
depths of darkness. But even if they should burn me with fire, I
will only love Thee and rejoice in Thee all the more."

(Bachyah ibn Pakuda)

232. QUESTION:

**In the prayers for the sick, we pray for "healing
of soul and body." What does the soul have to do
with the sickness of the body?**

ANSWER:

This is in accordance with a passage in the Gemara (Nedarim
41a) which states: "The sick person does not recover from his
sickness until all his sins are forgiven, for it is written, "Who
forgives all thine iniquity; Who heals all thy diseases" (Psalms
103:3).

We therefore pray that the soul should be "healed" through
Divine forgiveness, because only then can we expect healing for
the body as well.

(Imrot Tehorot)

Maimonides (Ethics 2:1) writes: "To the sick in body, the
bitter tastes sweet, and the sweet, bitter... Even so are people
whose souls are sick."

Toldot Yaakov Yosef puts it as follows: A person sick in body,
who has not eaten for several days so that his stomach has shrunk,
will find when he begins to take some nourishment that even sweet
food will leave a bitter taste in his mouth. One might say the same
of one who is sick in his soul.

One who returns to the study of Torah after an absence of
several days will find at first that "the sweet will taste bitter in
his mouth," i.e. he will not gain the proper pleasure and inspiration
from his studies.

233. QUESTION:

**When the Scroll is returned to the Ark after the
Reading of the Law, "Let them praise the Name of**

the L-rd, for His Name alone is exalted" is recited.
Why?

ANSWER:

When we pronounced the Benedictions over the Torah, we bowed in honor of the Torah. Now, when we return the Scroll to the Ark, we say "Let them praise the Name *of the L-rd*" to show that we did not bow to the Scroll but to the *Shekhina*, the Divine Presence, which rests upon the Law, and which alone is to be exalted.

(*Rokeach, Ch.* 319; *see Magen Avraham* 139:6)

234. QUESTION:

On the Sabbath, "Let them praise the Name of the L-rd..." is followed by the chanting of Psalm 29. Why?

ANSWERS:

1. This Psalm describes seven different attributes of the voice of the L-rd ("The voice of the L-rd is over the waters... is mighty... is majestic... breaks the cedars... strikes flames of fire... causes the desert to quake... strips the woods bare"), corresponding to the Seven Benedictions in the *Musaph* service, which immediately follows the return of the Scrolls to the Ark.

(*Peri Megaddim* 284:2)

2. Because the Rabbis are generally agreed that the Torah was revealed on Sabbath, and this Psalm is a hymn extolling the day when the Law was given on Mount Sinai.

(*Eshel Avraham, Ch.* 149)

235. QUESTION:

In the Kedusha of the Sabbath Musaph service we recite the passage עולם מלא כבודו "His Glory fills the Universe, and His Ministering Angels ask one another: Where is the place of His glory?"
Why is this passage not also part of the Kedusha recited on weekdays?

ANSWER:

On weekdays, the Infinite Light of His Countenance reaches the lower world in a reduced degree only, and the Ministering Angels when sanctifying His Name, rise on High, reaching towards the Seraphim and exclaiming, ממקומו 'ד כבוד ברוך "Blessed be the glory of the L-rd from His dwelling place."

On the Sabbath, however, both worlds — above and below — are uplifted and His Infinite Light reaches even the lower worlds, so that the entire universe is filled with His Infinite Light.

On that day, the Ministering Angels ask one another: איה כבודו מקום "Where is the abode of His glory?" i.e. where can His glory *not* be found?

(*T'zvi Hirsh, Rebbe of Zidichov*)

236. QUESTION:

Why do we say Mim'komkha, "From Thy dwelling place..." in the Kedusha of the Sabbath morning service, but Mim'komo, "From His dwelling place," in the Kedusha of the Musaph service?

ANSWER:

The Morning Service is usually read during the first three hours of the morning, when the L-rd is enthroned on the Seat of Mercy, apportioning food to all the inhabitants of the world. It is therefore proper to speak to Him in personal terms, i.e. "From *Thy* dwelling place, shine forth, O our King, and reign over us..."

By the time *Musaph* is recited in the late morning hours, however, he has moved on to the Seat of Judgment from which He judges the world impartially and without regard to person. We therefore pray to Him to move once again from the Seat of Judgment to the Seat of Mercy, i.e. "From *His* dwelling place may *He* turn in mercy..."

For this reason, too, we say *Mim'komo* ("From His dwelling place") in all the Kedushoth of the Yom Kippur liturgy, for on that Day he is enthroned on the Seat of Judgment all day long, and we must beseech Him to return to the Seat of Mercy.

(*Mateh Moshe*)

237. QUESTION:

Why do we recite the first line of the Shema ("Hear O Israel ...”), and also the last line "I am the L-rd your G-d," at the conclusion of the Kedusha?

ANSWER:

In the days of Rav, founder of the Talmudical Academy of Sura, King Yuzdegar of Persia, issued a decree prohibiting the reading of the *Shema* in the synagogues. The sages of that generation therefore decided to insert the first and last line of the *Shema* into the Kedusha, where they would not be conspicuous, but would still keep the *Shema* from being forgotten by the young.

In response to our fervent prayers, the King's law was annulled by a Higher Power, for King Yuzdegar was killed by a snake which had made its way into his regal bedchamber.

The sages then decided that this short form of the *Shema* should be retained in the Kedusha, as an everlasting memorial of the miraculous turn of events which enabled the Jews of Persia to recite the *Shema* once again openly and unafraid.

(*Beth Yosef, Ch.* 423, *in the name of the Gaonim*)

238. QUESTION:

Why is the Kiddush recited on Sabbath morning called Kiddusha Rabba ("the Great Kiddush")?

ANSWER:

By way of euphemism, to keep the morning Kiddush from being disregarded. The Kiddush of Sabbath morning is not so important as the Kiddush recited on Friday night, because the Friday evening Kiddush is a Biblical commandment, while the Kiddush of Sabbath morning was only instituted by the Rabbis. Accordingly, the former calls for a larger cup of wine then the latter.

Even as a blind man is designated in Hebrew by the euphemism *sagi nahar* ("abundant in light"), so, too, the less important morning Kiddush is referred to as "the Great Kiddush."

(*Rabbenu Nissim, Arvei Pesachim* 24a)

239. QUESTION:

What is the origin of the custom (in certain localities) of eating onions and garlic on the Sabbath?

ANSWER:

It is written, "And thou shalt call the Sabbath a delight" (Isaiah
58:13). This means that one should partake of all kinds of choice
or exotic foods and beverages so that the Sabbath will indeed be
a delight in the full sense of the word.

Since it is impossible to have all the foods existing in the world
on one's table..., we must accept the fact that the food cooked and
prepared specifically for the Sabbath has the exquisite taste of
the *manna,* which the Children of Israel ate in the wilderness and
which contained all the flavors found in the world except those of
onion and garlic. These had been excluded because they were considered harmful to pregnant women.

We therefore make it a point on the Sabbath to eat onion
and garlic, so that we may enjoy these flavors, too, to help make
our Sabbath pleasure complete.

(*Ge'ulat Yisrael*)

240. QUESTION:

What is the origin of the custom of eating "food
made of feet," i.e. meat dishes like feet of chicken,
etc. on the Sabbath?

ANSWERS:

1. It is written of Israel in exile: "Its feet go down to death,"
since strangers are dwelling in its land.

In the days of redemption, however, even the feet, the lower
extremities of the body, will be raised on high, as the Rabbis say,
"One should always hope for the feet of the Redeemer."

Since the Sabbath affords us a foretaste of the World to Come,
we eat "food made of feet" on that day to show that we are
awaiting the day when "the feet will be raised on high," and when
the Light of the Almighty, which He has kept hidden from us
since Creation, will shine upon us.

(*Yad Aaron, by Aaron Leib, Rebbe of Nadvorno*)

2. It is a well known adage that "falsehood has no feet," unlike truth, which has feet to stand upon. We therefore eat "feet" on the Sabbath, to show that the Sabbath is based on a profound truth, the Word of G-d.

(In the name of a Holy Man)

241. QUESTION:

What is the origin of the custom of eating some sort of pudding on the Sabbath?

ANSWER:

Since the *manna* did not come down from heaven on Sabbaths, it was considered proper to preface some delicacy to recall the *manna,* which was covered with dew.

(See ReMa, Ch. 242; *see Tosfoth Pesachim* 100b, sub voce, Sh'en)

242. QUESTION:

What is the origin of the custom widespread among the pious to sing zemiroth (Sabbath Table Hymns) or to ask someone else to sing, when the Sabbath food is brought to the table?

ANSWER:

According to the Rabbis, food can be sanctified by holy utterances pronounced at the table, and food thus hallowed becomes "a food of healing."

(Mishkenoth Ha-Ro'im)

243. QUESTION:

What is the symbolic significance of the foods we eat on the Sabbath?

ANSWER:

Since the Sabbath is a foretaste of the "perfect Sabbath" of the World to Come, we eat foods symbolizing the delicacies we will enjoy on that hoped-for day which will be "all Sabbath." The fish represents the Leviathan, and the *shor-ha-bor,* the lengendary ox, whose meat the righteous will enjoy in the World to Come. The wine with which we sanctify the Sabbath represents the *yayin ham'shumar,* the "guarded wine" which the righteous will be permitted to drink.

(The Gaon, Baal Torath Hayim)

244. QUESTION:

> In the Grace after Meals on the Sabbath, we recite the prayer beginning with Retzei ("Be pleased, O L-rd..."). One verse in this paragraph reads... "that there be no trouble, grief or lament on the day of our rest..." Would it not have been more fitting to pray that "there be no trouble, grief or lament in the entire world all week long?"

ANSWER:

As the heart keeps man alive by giving nourishment to his entire body, so the Sabbath gives life and substance to the other days of the week. Therefore, just as our main concern in human health is to guard the health of the heart, so we pray that our Sabbath may be free of grief and trouble, for if our Sabbath is happy, all will be well with us during the rest of the week.

(Tzemach David, by Rabbi David of Dinov)

One should greet the Sabbath with joy and ecstasy, and honor it by making it "a day of delight."

The keynote of the Sabbath should be rejoicing, and all care, grief and sorrow should be banished.

With our own eyes we have seen grief and sorrow visit a family on the Eve of the Sabbath, but because the family accepted the Sabbath with joy and banished sorrow for that day, their sorrow eventually turned to joy and their darkness to light.

(Masok Midvash)

245. QUESTION:

In the Retzei prayer, the Rabbis added the word be-ahavah, לנוח בו באהבה "... that we may rest and repose thereon with love ..." What is the significance of this addition?

ANSWER:

The Law as a whole was not accepted by Israel willingly but only under duress. The Sabbath, however, was given to the Children of Israel in Mara (before the) rest of the Law was imposed on them (Sanhedrin 56b and Sabbath 87b).

Accordingly, we emphasize the devotion with which the Children of Israel, out of their own free will, kept the Sabbath.

(*Rabbi Mordechai Yaffe*, 188:6)

246. QUESTION:

In the Grace after Meals on Sabbath we pray: הרחמן הוא ינחילנו ליום שכלו שבת ומנוחה לחיי העולמים This is usually translated as "May the All-Merciful let us inherit the day which shall be wholly a Sabbath and rest in life everlasting."

What is the interpretation given in Rabbinic literature for this verse?

ANSWER:

It is written in *Shulhan Arukh Ha-Rav* that one who recites this verse as quoted above is perpetrating a textual error, for the last but one word, *le-hayyei* — "in life everlasting," is not the correct version of the original text. Rather, it should read, *le-hay* — meaning, "to the One Who lives forever," i.e. to G-d Himself.

In other words, we pray to Him that this day which will be "all Sabbath" may come as speedily as possible, for then, on that ultimate Sabbath Day — G-d will rest forever.

Rabbi Sholom of Belz (*Parshat Pinhas*), in the name of the Maggid of Mezhirich, interprets the verse quoted above as follows:

הרחמן הוא ינחילנו ליום שכולו שבת — ואז — ומנוחה לחי העולמים "May the All-Merciful let us inherit the day which shall be wholly a Sabbath — *and then* — there will be rest for Him Who lives forever."

At the present time, G-d has no rest, because of the tribulations of His people Israel. It is only on *that day*, when deliverance, consolation, blessing, salvation, life, peace and all things good will come to Israel, that He will enjoy true rest.

247. QUESTION:

Why do we recite the verse "And as for me, may my prayer unto Thee, O L-rd be acceptable..." (Psalms 69:14), during Minha Services on the Sabbath?

ANSWERS:

1. The Children of Israel say to G-d: "See, O L-rd, although we drank wine today, we still remember to pray to Thee, unlike the other nations (whom strong drink tends to remove from them all thoughts of G-d).

(Tur, Ch. 292)

2. Because this time on the Sabbath day is "an acceptable time" before G-d — for it was in the afternoon of the Sabbath that it entered His Mind to create the world with all its goodness and abundance.

How do we know that the world had its beginnings on a Sabbath? Because it is written: "And it was evening and it was morning, the First Day." Accordingly, it must be assumed that the decision to start the work of Creation was made the day before the First Day, i.e. late on the day which preceded man's first Sabbath by one week.

When we read this particular passage, we say to G-d, in effect, "May Thy abundant goodness be upon us now even as it was on that Sabbath, when it just entered Thy mind to create the world in which we live."

(Zerah Kodesh, Parshath Hukkath, in the name of Menahem Mendel, Rebbe of Rimanov)

248. QUESTION:
Why is the Torah read during Minha Services on the Sabbaths?

ANSWER:
Ezra the Scribe instituted this practice for the benefit of those merchants who did not attend the Readings on Mondays and Thursdays (Bava Kama 82a). This is one of the ten famous *takanoth* (ordinances) instituted by Ezra.

249. QUESTION:
Why does the Sabbath Shemone Esrei consist of only seven Benedictions, instead of eighteen?

ANSWER:
The Eighteen Benedictions of the weekday service, include benedictions referring to needs of ours which we ask G-d to fulfill. The Rabbis saw fit to exclude these benedictions from our Sabbath prayers, for they felt that recalling our needs would detract from our enjoyment of the Sabbath. The Sabbath prayers were meant primarily for joyful communion with G-d, with no mention of guilt, want, tribulation or sorrow to mar the worshipper's serenity.

Accordingly, the thirteen intermediate Benedictions, which refer to our needs and wants are replaced on the Sabbath by a prayer containing Seven Benedictions that convey the beauty of the Sabbath spirit.

(Shulhan Arukh Ha-Rav)

250. QUESTION:
Why is the passage "They that keep the Sabbath and call it a delight shall rejoice in Thy Kingdom ..." (Yithmehu), which is recited in the Sabbath Musaph service, not included in the Sabbath Minha service.

ANSWER:
Because tradition has it that a number of saintly men in our

history, including Joseph, Moses and King David, each passed away on Sabbath, at this particular hour. Since our joy, therefore, cannot be complete, a prayer of this sort would not be in order at this time.

(*Yaavetz*)

251. QUESTION:

Why do we recite instead, the passage beginning with Tzidkath'cha "Thy Righteousness . . ." (Psalms 36:7, 71:19 and 119:142)?

ANSWERS:

1. These verses, which we repeat three times, imply our submission to the Divine Judgment (*tzidduk hadin*), as in the case of the death of a loved one.

The introduction of this strange note into our Sabbath service is also linked with the tradition (cited above) that Joseph, Moses and King David, peace be upon them, each passed away on a Sabbath afternoon.

(*Yaavetz*)

2. This passage implies submission to Divine Judgment also on the part of the souls of the wicked in Gehenna which are released from their imprisonment each Sabbath but must return there as soon as the Sabbath is over, as it is written in Genesis Rabba, "The angel who presides over the spirits calls out on the Eve of the Sabbath, 'Go forth, ye wicked, from Gehenna and rest, even as the Israelites are now resting on the Sabbath.' On the conclusion of the Sabbath, the same angel calls out, 'Return, ye wicked, to Gehenna, for the Israelites have finished their Sabbath prayers.' "

Until the hour of Minha, the wicked give no thought to their impending return to Gehenna, for they tell themselves that the sun is still far from setting. But when Minha is recited and night begins to fall, fear and trembling overtake them, for they know that their freedom will soon be at an end. They recite the above-named passage in an effort to resign themselves to the Divine Judgment which doomed their souls to imprisonment in Gehenna.

252. QUESTION:
Why is Psalm 104 ("Bless the L-rd, O my soul")
read on Sabbath afternoons between Shabbat Bereshith and Passover?

ANSWER:
In this most wonderful hymn, King David, enraptured by the
marvels of Creation, loses himself in the adoration of G-d. It is
therefore recited at the Sabbath Minha hour beginning with the
Sabbath on which the story of the Creation is read from the Torah,
so as to bring to mind G-d's Majesty as revealed in Creation, since
the Sabbath itself which is then about to leave us is a "memorial of
the Creation."

253. QUESTION:
Why is the above passage followed by the Fifteen
"Pilgrim Psalms" (Shir Ha-Maaloth, Psalms 120-
134)?

ANSWER:
In accordance with a Rabbinic tradition to the effect that "when
King David was digging the foundation of the Temple, the waters
of the deep which were buried underground at the time of Creation
rose to the surface and threatened to inundate the world. Thereupon,
David recited the fifteen Pilgrim Psalms and the flood receded"
(Sukkah 53a; Makkoth 11a).
(*Orchoth Hayim, Ch. 292, in the name of the Kerem Shlomo*)

254. QUESTION:
Why are the "Ethics of the Fathers" (Pirkei Avoth)
recited on Sabbath afternoons during the summer
season?

ANSWER:
Summer being a season of pleasures and enjoyments, the Rabbis
considered it proper at this time in particular to have us study tractate
Avoth, which deals with rules of proper and dignified conduct.
(*Ibid.*)

255. QUESTION:

Why is each of the Six Chapters of the "Ethics of the Fathers" prefaced by the statement: "All Israel have a portion in the World to Come..."?

ANSWER:

As a tactful gesture to the unlearned, to let them know that even Jews of little Jewish learning are not excluded from the World to Come.

(*Mateh Moshe, in the name of the Kol Bo*)

256. QUESTION:

Why are neither Psalm 104 nor "Ethics of the Fathers" recited on Sabbaths coinciding with one of the Festivals?

ANSWER:

It is generally agreed that "the celebration of the Festivals is one-half G-d's and one-half yours!" (Pesachim 68b; Betza 15b).

In other words, the first half of the day should be spent in prayer and study, but the latter half of the day is meant for one's own enjoyment. Accordingly, both Psalm 104 and the "Ethics of the Fathers," which are meant to be read during the latter half of the day, are omitted when the Sabbath coincides with a Festival.

(*Orchoth Hayim, Ch.* 430)

257. QUESTION:

Why is every Jew duty-bound to eat no less than three meals on the Sabbath; one on Friday night and two in the daytime Saturday?

ANSWERS:

1. One who eats to excess will be forced to put off his next meal. However, when one knows that it is a religious act to fulfill the precept of eating at each meal no less than three meals on the Sabbath, he will eat just enough at each meal to satisfy his hunger,

so that he may be able to eat the three prescribed meals at their appointed times, particularly the third and last meal (*shalosh seudos*).

If he will keep this rule, he will be eating all his meals for the sake of the religious act involved and also to do no more than just satisfy his hunger. He will then be able to find time for the study of Torah, at the same time curbing any tendency to gluttony.

It will then follow that he will not spend too much time on meals even on weekdays, and he will therefore have enough time to perform his daily duties without finding them too burdensome.

(*Abudraham*)

2. *The Levush* (291:1) maintains that the eating of these three meals is not merely a Rabbinical precept but a Scriptural Command, for it is written in the Talmud: "The word *today*, occurs three times in the Biblical verse (Ex. 16:25) regarding the partaking of food on the Sabbath, viz., "And Moses said: Eat this (the *manna*) *today;* for *today* is a Sabbath unto the L-rd; *today* ye shall not find it in the field" (Sabbath 117b). (אכלוהו היום, כי שבת היום לד׳, היום לא תמצאהו בשדה).

This message is taken to imply that at least three meals must be eaten on the Sabbath.

3. Concerning the sentence quoted above, viz., *"Eat this today, for today* is a Sabbath unto the L-rd...,"* the Rebbe of Rimanov commented: "Absorb the sanctity of the Sabbath Day into your inmost parts, even as you consume the Sabbath foods."

258. QUESTION:
Why do many pious people say "Le-Kaved Shabbos" (in honor of Sabbath) when performing certain acts on that day?

ANSWER:
The Rebbe of Rimanov said: "Know ye that with the holiness of the Sabbath, an abundance of good things comes down to the world, and he who wishes to receive them, must give voice to this thought in *speech* by saying aloud, "I do this, or I am eating this, in honor of the Holy Sabbath!"

In this way do the good things come down from Above. This thought is intimated by the saying of the Rabbis: זכור ושמור בדיבור אחד נאמרו "Observe and remember [these two commands] were uttered by the Almighty in one breath" (Shavuoth 20b). This is interpreted to mean that we must observe and remember the Sabbath by the spoken word.

Therefore, too, when visiting a friend on the Sabbath, one should not greet him in the usual weekday manner, i.e. with "Good Morning" or "Good Afternoon," but with "Good Shabbos" or "Shabbat Shalom," in fulfillment of the Scriptural command זכור את יום השבת "Remember the Sabbath day" (Ex. 20:8).

(Ahavath Shalom, Parshat Va-Yera)

259. QUESTION:

What is the significance of the third Shabbos meal, and what is the origin of its Hebrew designation, Sh'alosh S'udoth, which, literally translated, does not mean "The Third Meal" but "Three Meals?"

ANSWER:

By partaking of the third and last meal of the Sabbath, we complete our observance of the command to eat at least three meals on that day.

During the first two meals of the day, we were actually hungry and ate our food with particular enjoyment. By the time of the third meal, we are no longer hungry. Nevertheless, we sit down to partake of this meal with song and rejoicing in order to fulfill the commandment of G-d. It is not the food which draws us to the table but the desire to carry out His precepts.

This act is therefore considered as if we had actually eaten all the three Sabbath meals in this spirit. Accordingly, the last Sabbath meal is called *Sh'alosh S'udoth*, referring to all the three meals.

(Divrei Emeth)

The Rebbe of Rimanov, Rabbi Tzvi Ha-Cohen, amplifies the verse סועדים בו — לברך שלש פעמים "They feast on the Sabbath in order to be able to recite the Grace after Meals three times" (from the Friday night table hymns) — to mean that "they feast on the Sabbath, not because they want to satisfy their hunger and give pleasure to their palate, but only in order to have occasion to recite the Grace after Meals three times during the Sabbath."

260. QUESTION:

Why was it the custom of the Hassidic Rabbis to delay reciting the Grace after the Third Sabbath Meal until the Sabbath was over and they could put on lights?

ANSWER:

They drew out the Third Meal well into the evening, so that by expounding the Law, and by chanting songs and hymns of praise, they might be able to bestow some of the holiness of the Sabbath upon the week that was about to begin.

In this way, too, the souls of sinners which had been set free from Gehenna for the Sabbath, would be able to prolong their stay on earth as much as possible.

(Atereth Tzvi, Bereshith)

The *Derekh Emuna* writes in the name of the *Noam Megaddim* (*Parshath Tzav*), as follows:

Concerning those souls which enter Gehenna but are given rest on the Sabbath, we have a tradition from our masters, that not all of them need to return to Gehenna at the same time after the conclusion of the Sabbath.

Many of these souls have their rest periods prolonged until well after the conclusion of the Sabbath, and they do not return to Gehenna until very late in the evening. This is thanks to the pious Jews, who, by sitting at their tables and prolonging the Third Sabbath Meal, bring some of the holiness of the Sabbath into the new week. As long as these pious Jews are at their tables, the souls need not return to Gehenna, and they proclaim: "Happy are you, O righteous and pious men, in this world and happy shall you be in the World to Come!"

But this privilege is granted only to those, who, though they themselves had sinned, never showed disrespect for the righteous.

Those sinners who scoffed at the righteous, and especially those who jeered at the pious for prolonging the Sabbath well into the night, must return to Gehenna as soon as three stars appear in the sky, heralding the end of the Sabbath.

261. QUESTION:

Why did the Rabbis insert the Havdalah prayer ("Thou hast favored us with a knowledge of Thy Torah... and ... hast made a distinction between the holy and the profane ..."), into the Eighteen Benedictions recited in the Evening Service at the conclusion of the Sabbath?

ANSWER:

When the Jews returned to Palestine from captivity, most of them were too poor to be able to buy wine for Havdalah.

The Rabbis of that time therefore instituted the custom of having the Havdalah recited as part of the Eighteen Benedictions rather than after the Evening Service. When the Jews prospered once again, Havdalah would be recited after the service, over a cup of wine. But whenever they came upon hard days, Havdalah would be shifted back to the Eighteen Benedictions so that it could be recited without wine. Eventually, to keep the Havdalah service from being shifted back and forth, the Rabbis decided that it should be recited both times — in the Eighteen Benedictions *and also* over a cup of wine (or another beverage if wine is not available).

(Shulhan Arukh Ha-Rav)

262. QUESTION:

Why was the Havdalah prayer placed before the passage "O favor us with knowledge ..."?

ANSWER:

Because man should not petition G-d for his personal needs, such as, knowledge, wisdom, etc., before the end of the Sabbath has been proclaimed by the Havdalah prayer.

(Magen Avraham 294:1)

263. QUESTION:

Why are the passages "And let the graciousness..."
(Psalm 90:17), and "He who dwells in the shelter
of the most High..." (ibid. 91), recited after the
Eighteen Benedictions at the conclusion of the
Sabbath?

ANSWER:

These two Psalms assure us of Divine protection from adversity.
On Saturday night, all the evils of the weekday world arise
again and roam through the world, doing their worst wherever they
appear. Accordingly, it is only appropriate that we recite these
Psalms as the Sabbath comes to an end.

(*Yaavetz*)

264. QUESTION:

Why is the prayer "And Thou art holy...," recited
at the conclusion of the Sabbath?

ANSWER:

Because the world survives by virtue of this prayer of sanctification which shields us from harm and misfortune. Since the end of
the Sabbath is the time when the evil impulses resume their work,
it is only appropriate that it should be recited at that hour.

(*Yaavetz*)

265. QUESTION:

What was the origin of the custom in certain localities, not to recite the prayer beginning with "G-d
grant you dew from heaven...," in the synagogue?

ANSWER:

Because many people could not recite this lengthy prayer by
heart and would have to read it by the light of a candle. However,
this passage comes before "the blessing over light," and it is not
considered proper to enjoy the light of a newly-lit candle before
that blessing has been recited. As a result, it was thought best to

wait until after making Havdalah at home to recite "May G-d grant you dew from heaven..."

(*Eshel Avraham, Ch.* 298)

The *Ha-Ari, Rabbi Yitzhak Luria Ashkenazi,* when worshipping with Ashkenazim, would recite the prayer along with them in the synagogue. But when he would worship with Sephardim, whose custom it was not to recite it in the synagogue, he would follow their way and recite it at home after Havdalah.

266. QUESTION:

Why is it customary to recite Psalm 128: "Happy is everyone that fears the L-rd..." after the reading of "G-d grant you dew from Heaven?"

ANSWER:

This Psalm is an exhortation to man to begin the week of work and business, in a spirit of integrity and honesty.

This is the meaning of the second verse of this Psalm: "When thou shalt eat the labor of thine hands, (i.e. not gain from theft or plunder — then —) happy shalt thou be, and it shall be well with thee."

267. QUESTION:

Why are the blessings "Blessed shall be the fruit of thy body..." (Deut. 28:4), and "Blessed shall be thy basket and thy kneading-trough" (ibid. 28:5), in the prayer "G-d grant you dew from heaven...," not quoted as in the Biblical sequence but in reverse order?

ANSWER:

This prayer was composed in the Diaspora. In view of the hardships of exile, it is proper to start our prayer with the blessings dealing with "our basket and kneading-trough," that is, the blessings pertaining to the essentials of our day-to-day existence, rather than with a blessing of less immediate character, such as a blessing on our offspring.

(Sefer Ha-Hayim)

268. QUESTION:
Why should Havdalah be recited over a cup of wine?

ANSWER:
We make Havdalah over a cup of wine to restore our strength after the departure of the *Neshama Yethera*, the "Additional Sabbath Soul," to fortify us for the cares of the coming week, and to restore some of the Sabbath joy and gladness to our hearts.

(Tolaat Yaakov)

269. QUESTION:
Why do we inhale the aroma of spices at the conclusion of the Sabbath?

ANSWER:
During the Sabbath, man is given an "additional soul," the Neshama Yethera, which adds "spice" to his life throughout the Sabbath day. When the Sabbath ends and this "second soul" leaves us, we inhale the aroma of spices to make up for this loss and to add some fragrance to our lives, as it were.

On Saturday nights falling on a festival, the spices are omitted, since the joy of the incoming festival is at least the equivalent of the enjoyment we get from inhaling the aroma of fragrant spices.

(Abudraham; see Tosfoth Pesachim 102b, sub voce, Rav)

270. QUESTION:
Why do we not recite the blessing over spices also at the conclusion of a Festival?

ANSWER:
Because the "additional soul" comes to us only on the Sabbath. We do not receive it on Festivals.

(Tosfoth Betza 33b, sub voce, Kee)

271. QUESTION:

Why do we pronounce the benediction over light after the conclusion of the Sabbath?

ANSWER:

It was at the end of the first Sabbath that man first learned how to kindle a light. The Jerusalem Talmud records the following legend: "When Adam saw the sun go down for the first time, leaving all of creation in ever-deepening darkness, his heart was filled with terror. Thereupon, G-d took pity on him and gave him the intelligence to take two stones — the name of one was Darkness, and the name of the other was Shadow of Death — and to rub them against each other. In this manner did man first discover fire. When he saw the flame he had produced, Adam exclaimed with gratitude: "Blessed be He, the Creator of Light!"

(*Kol Bo*)

272. QUESTION:

Why is the blessing over light phrased in the plural form, i.e. "Who createst the lights of fire?"

ANSWER:

The plural refers to the many different colors contained in a flame, red, white and bluish green (Berakhoth 52b).

This, too, is the reason for the use of the braided Havdalah candle which has several wicks.

(*Kol Bo*)

273. QUESTION:

It is forbidden to derive enjoyment from anything before having recited the appropriate Benediction. Why, then, do we not also pronounce a benediction when we kindle lights on weekdays?

ANSWER:

The *Kol Bo* writes: On Saturday night we recite the blessing over the light because we had not been permitted to strike a match or otherwise kindle a light all that day. As for weekdays, on the other hand, we light fires or kindle lights almost every hour of the day. Accordingly, the one blessing we recite after the Sabbath is sufficient for the entire week.

274. QUESTION:

Why do we hold our hands close to the light and look at our fingernails when the benediction over the lights is recited at the Havdalah service?

ANSWER:

We look at our nails to symbolize our hope that we may grow and multiply like the nails of our fingers.

(*Kol Bo*)

275. QUESTION:

Why do we fill the Havdalah cup to overflowing, allowing some of the wine to spill on the ground?

ANSWER:

To symbolize the hoped-for blessing of abundance, as the Rabbis say: "A home in which wine is not spilled like water, is bare of blessings."

Some of the wine used to douse the Havdalah candle is deliberately spilled on the table, to indicate to all those present that this candle had been lit to comply with the specific mitzvah of Havdalah and for the benediction over light.

It is customary to brush some of this spilled wine over our eyelids, to show our love for the precepts of G-d.

(*Levush* 296:1)

276. QUESTION:

Why is it customary on Saturday night, at the Melave Malka meal, to chant "This is the meal of David our King?" '

ANSWER:

To recall the feast King David would hold at the end of each Sabbath in gratitude for having been preserved in life. According to the Rabbis (Sabbath 30a), G-d had informed David he would die on a Sabbath. Hence he was grateful for every Sabbath he was permitted to live through.

277. QUESTION:

Why are more Z'miros sung at the Melave Malka, when we bid farewell to the Sabbath, than on the Sabbath proper?

ANSWER:

Because the *Melave Malka* meal eaten on Saturday night recalls King David, who was known as the "Sweet singer of Israel" (while the three meals of the Sabbath commemorate the three Patriarchs, Abraham, Isaac and Jacob).

(Tzemah David)

278. QUESTION:

Why is Eliyahu HaNavi, the hymn honoring the Prophet Elijah, sung on Saturday night?

ANSWERS:

1. Elijah the Prophet will not come on Friday, lest he disturb Israel's preparations for the Shabbos. The hour when the Sabbath departs, on the other hand, is considered the proper time for saying a prayer that Elijah should come to us and bring us good tidings.

(Tur, Ch. 295)

2. The Midrash states that every Saturday night, Elijah enters Paradise, sits down beneath the Tree of Life, and records the merits of those Israelites who observed the Sabbath.

(Rabbi Jacob Molin, the MaHaRIL)

279. QUESTION:

Why is the Prophet Elijah also called Elijah Ha-Tishbi (Elijah the Tishbite)?

ANSWER:

The Hebrew word *Tishbi* is derived from *Toshav* ("inhabitant, native, settled"). The name indicates that unlike ordinary mortals who are here today and gone tomorrow, Elijah is a permanent inhabitant of both worlds.

(Seder Hayom)

280. QUESTION:

Why was it customary for women to draw water from the well on Saturday night, immediately after hearing the first "Barchu" of the weekday evening service recited? (see Leviticus Rabbah, Ch. 22).

ANSWER:

The Agadda tells us that "each Saturday night the waters from the Well of Miriam, west of Tiberias, flow through all the springs, fountains and rivers of the whole world, and whoever is sick and would drink of these waters, even if he was a leper, will be cured at once."

One Saturday night, a certain woman whose husband was afflicted with a skin disease went to the well to fetch water. She tarried longer than usual, and by fortunate coincidence some of the water she drew up in her bucket had come from the Well of Miriam.

When she came home, her husband, angered by her late return, pushed the bucket from her shoulders so that it fell to the floor. A few drops of the water landed on the man's body and in each spot where the drops fell, the skin became clean at once.

(Kol Bo)

281. QUESTION:

Before starting each Sabbath meal, we chant the hymn Askinu Seudatha ("We are preparing to partake of the meal"). It is chanted once before each of the three meals eaten on the Sabbath proper.

Why, at the Melave Malka, is it chanted three times?

ANSWER:

To stress the importance of this "Fourth Meal."

This is considered proper because unlike the three meals eaten on the Sabbath day, the *Melava Malka* is not based on a Biblical precept but only on a Rabbinic regulation and might be held in less regard, were it not for this special emphasis.

(Divre Yehezkel)

The Zikhron Tov quotes the Rebbe of Neshitz, as having said: "The Melava Malka meal is very important indeed, because it is based on Talmudic law."

He continues with the following story: One Friday afternoon, when he was still a young man, long before he became famous, the Rebbe of Lublin visited the famed Maggid of Mezhirich. As he entered the Maggid's home, Rebbe Shlomo of Skol, the administrator of the Maggid's household, was just placing twelve Sabbath loaves on the table for the Friday night dinner.

At that time, the young guest from Lublin was very poor and knew that he would have no food for the Melava Malka meal the next night. After everyone had left the room, he broke off a piece from one of the twelve loaves at the table, and took it with him so that he might have at least some bread with which to observe the precept of the "Fourth Meal."

When the Maggid of Mezhirich came to the table for the Friday night dinner, he noticed the broken loaf and asked Rebbe Shlomo what had happened. Rebbe Shlomo replied that it must have been the doing of the young man of Poland, for he had been the last to leave the dining room.

The Maggid immediately summoned the young man from Lublin to take him to task. But when the latter told him that he had taken the bread solely for the purpose of performing the *mitzvah* of the "Fourth Meal," the Maggid placed his hands on the shoulders of the Lubliner and blessed him, saying: "May it be the will of G-d that in the future you may have sufficient means to perform this *mitzvah* in wealth and abundance."

282. QUESTION:
What is the origin of the Yiddish expression Sh'beise Nacht?

ANSWER:
It is a corruption of *"spet zu nacht"* (late at night), a euphemism for "Saturday night," implying the desire to prolong the Sabbath to as "late at night" as possible by such practices as delaying the recital of *Havdalah*.

(Avkath Rocheil 3:11)

The Blessing of the New Moon

283. QUESTION:
What is the origin of the custom followed by some to fast on the Eve of the New Moon (Erev Rosh Hodesh)?

ANSWER:
G-d punished the moon by reducing it in size (see below), so that it is now smaller than the sun. Some people fast on the Eve of the New Moon so that G-d may restore the moon to its original size, making it as large as the sun once more.

(Magen Avraham 417:3)

Rabbi Shimon ben Pazzi pointed out a contradiction between two verses in the Book of Genesis. One verse reads, "And G-d made the two great lights" (Gen. 1:16); but immediately the verse continues, "The greater light...and the lesser light?"

These two seemingly contradictory statements were reconciled by the following legend: It seems that originally the sun and the moon were of the same size. But the moon said to the Holy One, Blessed be He: "Sovereign of the Universe! Is it possible for two kings to wear one crown?"

Thereupon the Holy One, Blessed be He, punished the moon for its arrogance by making it smaller than the sun (Hullin 60b).

284. QUESTION:
What is the origin of the custom to stand while reciting the Blessing over the New Moon?

ANSWER:

In olden times, the New Moon would be announced by the Rabbis on the basis of testimony from two witnesses who had seen the New Moon.

The Rabbis would make the announcement standing up. Hence our present custom.

(*Magen Avraham* 417:1)

285. QUESTION:
Why is the Eve of the New Moon (Erev Rosh Hodesh), called Yom Kippur Kattan (lit. "Lesser Day of Atonement")?

ANSWER:

Because on this day, we are pardoned for all the sins we have committed through the entire month. In the days of the Temple, a goat would be sacrificed at that time as a sin offering. Today, in the Musaph service of the New Moon, we refer to Rosh Hodesh as זמן כפרה לכל תולדותם "A time of forgiveness throughout their generations."

(*Peri Hadash, Ch.* 417,
in the name of Rabbi Moses Cordovero)

286. QUESTION:
Why is it customary for women to refrain from work on Rosh Hodesh?

ANSWER:

G-d gave the women *Rosh Hodesh* as a full festival to recall the merit of Israel's women in the wilderness. When the men asked their wives to give them their golden trinkets for the casting of the Golden Calf, the women refused to do so, for they did not want to have any part in the making of the idol.

(*Pirke d'Rabbi Eliezer, Ch.* 45)

287. QUESTION:
Why is half of the Hallel recited on Rosh Hodesh?

ANSWERS:

1. Because of a difference of opinion amongst the Codifiers as to the origin of the rule that the Hallel is to be recited on Rosh Hodesh.

Maimonides held that the reading of the Hallel on Rosh Hodesh is not an observance based on religious precepts, but merely a custom started by Babylonian Jewry during the second century C.E., so that it does not warrant a "full" Hallel.

(*Abudraham*)

2. Because Rosh Hodesh is "a day of forgiveness," comparable in solemnity to Rosh Hashanah and Yom Kippur, as it is stated in the Musaph service זמן כפרה לכל תולדותם "A time of forgiveness throughout their generations." At such times, hymns of joyous praise are not considered appropriate.

(*Hagahot Minhagim*)

288. QUESTION:
The Rabbis say: "One who reads the Hallel every day is a scorner and a blasphemer" (Sabbath 118b). What do they mean by this statement?

ANSWER:

One of the verses in the Hallel Psalms says of the heathens: "Their idols are silver and gold" (Psalms 115:4).

If one were to recite this verse every day rather then only on special occasions, it would seem as if he were scoffing at G-d, nagging Him, as it were, saying, "The idols are still around and You seem unable to remove them from the world!"

(*Midrash Talpiyoth, Oth Hay, anaf Hallel Hagadol;*
Jerusalem Talmud)

289. QUESTION:
Why should Hallel be recited standing?

ANSWER:

It is written: הללו עבדי ד' העומדים "Praise Him, ye servants of the L-rd; ye that *stand* in the house of the L-rd..." (Psalms 135:1-2).

(*TaZ* 422:4)

Accordingly, it is forbidden to lean against a bench or wall while reciting the Hallel, for "leaning" is not considered "standing."

(*Magen Avraham* 422:11)

290.   QUESTION:

Why are Verses 21-29 of Psalm 118 each repeated twice in the reading of the Hallel?

ANSWER:

To stress that each of these verses was recited by a different outstanding figure in the life of King David. According to the Gemara (Pesachim 119a), these verses were said by Jesse, David, David's brothers and the Prophet Samuel.

Rabbi Shmuel ben Nachmeini said in the name of Rabbi Jonathan:

Verse 21 of Psalm 118 ("I will give thanks unto Thee, for Thou hast answered me, and art become my deliverance") was said by David.

Verse 22 ("The stone which the builders rejected is become the cornerstone") was said by Jesse, the father of David when David, though he was only the youngest son in his family and a mere shepherd, became King of Israel.

Verse 23 ("This was the L-rd's doing; it is marvellous in our eyes") was said by the brothers of David in amazement at David's sudden rise to the most exalted position in the land.

Verse 24 ("This is the day which the L-rd has made; we will be glad and rejoice thereon") was said by Samuel, who had prophesied the victory of the Israelites under the leadership of David.

The first half of Verse 25 ("Save, we beseech Thee, O L-rd") was said by David's brothers. The second half ("We beseech Thee,, O L-rd, make us now to prosper") was said by David, as he prayed that G-d might cause him to continue to prosper in his reign as King of Israel.

The first part of Verse 26 ("Blessed be he who comes in the name of the L-rd") was said by Jesse when David returned from the pastures where he had been keeping his sheep and met Samuel for the first time.

The latter part of the verse ("We bless you of the house of the L-rd") was said by Samuel, when he invited David and his entire family "to come to the sacrifice he was preparing unto the L-rd" (I Samuel, 16:5).

Then David, his family and Samuel all joined in reciting the first part of Verse 27 ("The L-rd is G-d, He has given us light").

The latter part of the verse ("Order the festive procession with boughs, even unto the horns of the altar") was said by Samuel, advising the entire family of David, to offer up peace-offerings on the altar.

Verse 28 ("Thou art my G-d and I will give thanks unto Thee...") was said by David.

Then the entire family and Samuel all said Verse 29 ("O give thanks unto the L-rd; for He is good...").

(*Abudraham*)

291. QUESTION:

What is the origin of the custom in certain communities to recite "the Psalm for the Day" (Shir Shel Yom) after Morning Services on Rosh Hodesh?

ANSWER:

To recall the procedure followed in the Holy Temple.

The Levites would recite the "Psalm for the Day" immediately after the Morning Sacrifice of Rosh Hodesh, and before the Musaph Sacrifice.

(*Yesod Ve-Shoresh Ha-Avodah, Section* 8)

292. QUESTION:

What is the origin of the custom to read Psalm 104 ("Bless the L-rd, O my soul...") on Rosh Hodesh?

ANSWER:

Because it is written therein עשה ירח למועדים "He made the moon for Festivals" (104:19).

(Tur, Ch. 423)

293. QUESTION:

Why is it customary to have a festive dinner on Rosh Hodesh?

ANSWER:

To recall the dinner which was set before the witnesses who saw the New Moon. (Early in the morning of the last day of each month, the Sanhedrin would convene, and take testimony from two reliable witnesses who had seen the New Moon. After satisfying themselves that the New Moon had indeed appeared, they would proclaim aloud: "The New Moon is hereby consecrated".)

(Kol Bo)

The author of the Shulhan Arukh, Rabbi Yosef Caro, devoted a *separate* paragraph to the religious duty of eating a festive dinner on Rosh Hodesh (Ch. 419), and to the *mitzvah* of partaking in a *Melaveh Malka* meal on Saturday night (Ch. 300).

The Rebbe of Lublin commented: "This was done by the author on purpose, to impress upon us the importance of partaking of these two meals mentioned above."

294. QUESTION:

Why does the consecration of the New Moon always take place on a Saturday night?

ANSWERS:

1. In order to proclaim a message of hope at a time that recalls tragedy.

It was on a Saturday night that the Temple was destroyed and the *Shekhina*, the Divine Presence, went into exile. When the New Moon appears, we say: "For in days to come, they (Israel), are also to be renewed like her (the moon)."

Thus, at the same time of day that the Temple was destroyed, we proclaim the good tidings that Israel and G-d will be renewed and revived as in the days of yore.

(Peri Etz Hayim, Sec. Rosh Hodesh, Ch. 13, *in the name of Rabbi Hayim Vital)*

2. Because we are still in a happy Sabbath mood at that hour and still dressed in our Sabbath attire.

(See Magen Avraham 426:3)

295. QUESTION:

Why should the New Moon be consecrated not under a roof but out in the open street?

ANSWER:

The ceremony should not be performed "under one roof" with defiled or impure objects.

(MaHaRIL, Rabbi Jacob Molin)

According to the *BaH, Rabbi Joel Sirkes,* we go out in the street to consecrate the moon because this is how one welcomes an important personage, like a King.

If one cannot perform the ceremony in the open air, one may do so from inside one's home, standing at one of the windows.

296. QUESTION:

What is the origin of the custom to recite "David, King of Israel, lives and endures" when blessing the New Moon?

ANSWER:

This sentence alludes to Psalm 89:38 when we are told that the throne of David will be "established forever like the moon."

Just as the moon shines brightly at some times and is hidden at others, so it is with the children of David. When they walk in the way of the L-rd, they shine brightly as the light throughout the world.

Just as the moon is eclipsed in the latter part of the month, but then renews itself with the advent of the new month to spread its light over the world, so will it be with Israel, who will be redeemed in the near future. The kingdom of David will be restored and will endure forever.

(Eshel Avraham, Ch. 426)

297. QUESTION:

Why do we say, Shalom Alechem — ("Peace be unto you," after making the Blessing over the New Moon?

ANSWER:

After just having pronounced a curse upon our foes ("May fear and dread fall upon them..."), it is only proper that we should say to our neighbors who recited the blessing with us, that the "fear and dread" is not meant for them and that we wish them happiness and peace.

(Mate Moshe)

298. QUESTION:

What is the origin of the custom to shake the corners of one's tzitzith (ritual fringes), at the conclusion of the Blessing over the New Moon?

ANSWERS:

1. This is done in order to shake off impure thoughts like those which occasioned the complaint of the moon [when it envied the sun for its size].

(Emek Beracha)

2. The *Siddur Ha-Ari* writes: One should shake the corners of his ritual fringes, to remind one of the Kingship of G-d, which they represent.

3. We shake our *tzitzith* (ritual fringes) after the consecration of the moon and not after the performance of any other Mitzvah, because in this particular case we feel the need to stress that when

we bless the New Moon we do so not to worship the moon, but simply to observe G-d's commandment to consecrate the New Moon, just as we keep the Divine precept of wearing *tzitzith*.

(*Rabbi Eliezer of Kamarn*)

299. QUESTION:

Why do we conclude the consecration of the New Moon with the Alenu (Adoration) prayer, which proclaims the Unity of G-d?

ANSWER:

This prayer concludes with the words: "For we bend the knee and offer worship and thanks before the Supreme King of Kings, the Holy One, blessed be He!"

Thus we declare that when we bless the New Moon, we are not worshipping the moon but solely "the Holy One, blessed be He."

Passover Customs

300. QUESTION:

The Rabbis say that one should ask one's questions concerning the laws of Passover thirty days before the Festival arrives (Pesahim 6a; Megilla 29b; Sanhedrin 12b; Avoda Zarah 5b). Why?

ANSWER:

This is in keeping with the statement of *Ha-rav Hessed Le-Avraham*, that "every year, thirty days before Passover, G-d shows lovingkindness to Israel, and in His Divine mercy He sets out to free the souls of the Israelites, little by little, from the clutches of their impurity, (as represented by the leaven). This cleansing of souls takes place each night during those Thirty days, one-thirtieth of the impurity being removed each day."

The Rabbis say: בניסן נגאלו, ובניסן עתידין ליגאל "In the month of Nissan the Jews were redeemed in the past, and in this very same month they will be redeemed also in the future" (Rosh Hashanah 11a). For in the month of Nissan they are ready for redemption, their souls having left the domain of the Evil Power during the thirty days that went before. On the night of Passover, the process is completed and they become free from all impurities, and they are then worthy of redemption.

(Lev David, by Rabbi Hayim Yosef David Azulai)

301. QUESTION:

Why is the month of Nissan known in Hebrew as the month of aviv (אביב)?

ANSWERS:

1. To denote the time of year in which Passover comes. *Aviv* being the Hebrew for "spring."

2. The Hebrew letters in the word *aviv* may be divided into two words — אב, meaning father, and י"ב, the numerical symbol for "twelve."

In other words, Passover is the "father" of the twelve months of the year.

(Binath Moshe, by Menahem Mendel, Rebbe of Koznitz)

Just as a son is fed and nourished by his father, so do all the other months of the year receive their spiritual sustenance from the month of Nissan.

Nissan is therefore considered the "first to all the months of the year" (Ex. 12:2), for all the physical and spiritual abundance of the world renews itself during the month of Nissan. In this spirit, too, all the religious acts and good deeds one intends to perform should be performed at the beginning of the month of Nissan.

(Daath Moshe)

302. QUESTION:

Why are the Special Daily Supplications (Tahanun) not recited throughout the month of Nissan?

ANSWER:
Because most of the month bears a festive character. When Israel was in the wilderness, the twelve tribal Chieftains, offered special sacrifices on each day of the month of Nissan (Numbers, Ch. 7).

Each of these days was considered as a festive occasion for the chieftan who was scheduled to offer this sacrifice on that day.

The twelve days of offerings were followed by the Eve of Passover, and then by the Passover festival itself, ending in *Isru Hag,* the day after Passover. Thus, a total of twenty-three days. In other words, most of the month of Nissan, bore the stamp of festivity and holiness.

(Beth Yosef, Ch. 429)

Agra de-Kalla (Parshath Pekude), quotes Rabbi Meir of Rothenburg, the *MaHaRaM,* as follows: "The first twelve days of the month of Nissan were the days when identical offerings were presented by the twelve tribal Chieftains at the dedication of the Altar (Ex. Ch. 7). These days are considered propitious days auguring sustenance, strength and vigor (hashpa-ah), for the eleven remaining months of the year.

303. QUESTION:
Why is the Sabbath before Passover called Shabbat HaGadol, **"The Great Shabbos?"**

ANSWERS:
1. Because of the miracle which took place on the Sabbath before the first Passover. G-d commanded the Israelites to offer up lambs for the Paschal sacrifice. This was a dangerous thing to do since lambs were regarded as idols by the Egyptians, who worshipped rams and might have done violence to anyone attempting to harm their idols. Still, the Israelites did as they were told. Then a miracle came to pass. The Egyptians were paralyzed with sudden terror so that they could do nothing to protect their sacred lambs. This miracle took place on the tenth day of the month of Nissan, which fell on a Sabbath that year (see Tosfoth, Shabbat 87b, sub voce, *ve-asa*).

The Midrash Rabbah (Bo) tells us: When the Israelites took their Paschal lambs that Sabbath, the Egyptian firstborn asked the Israelites for an explanation. Replied the Israelites: "This is our Passover sacrifice to our G-d, Who will slay all the firstborn of Egypt."

Alarmed, the firstborn rushed to their fathers and then to Pharaoh, pleading with him to let the Israelites go. When the King refused to send the Children of Israel away, the firstborn rose up in armed revolt and killed many of their own countrymen, as it is written, "[G-d] slew the Egyptians through their firstborn" (Psalms 136:10).

Seeing that so many miracles occurred during the four days preceding the first Passover, one might ask whether *these four days* should not all be designated as "great" days?

This question must be answered in the light of the facts that, primarily, the great miracle took place on the first of the four days, that is, on the tenth of Nissan, when fear made the Egyptians incapable of taking action against the Children of Israel, and the Israelites, for the first time, felt that freedom was really near. After the first day, however, they became accustomed to the prospect of freedom and began to take it for granted.

(Beth Yosef, Ch. 430)

2. Because it was the first Sabbath on which the Israelites began to observe the commandments of G-d.

(P'ri Hadash, Ch. 430)

304. QUESTION:
What is the Haftarah reading chosen for Shabbat HaGadol and why was it selected?

ANSWER:
The third chapter of the Book of Malachi. The Haftorah concludes with the promise that Elijah the Prophet will come. Passover, as the Festival of Redemption, was always associated with that future Passover, when all mankind would be delivered from oppression of both body and spirit.

Elijah was traditionally regarded as the herald who would appear on Passover to announce the dawn of the Messianic era.

(Levush, Ch. 430)

305. QUESTION:

Why is it customary for rabbis to deliver discourses on Shabbat HaGadol?

ANSWERS:

1. The Midrash relates that on the Sabbath before he led the Israelites out of Egypt, Moses delivered a discourse to them on the laws of Passover.

2. The rabbis usually deliver discourses on Shabbat HaGadol, for the Jews who are scattered all over the small villages and hamlets may be expected to travel to the larger towns where there is a rabbi, in order to learn how to observe Passover properly. The rabbi has an opportunity, then, to address these people and to explain to them the laws such as those of Passover.

(*Makhtzith HaShekel* 429:1)

306. QUESTION:

Why is it customary, prior to the "search for leaven," to place pieces of bread in every room of the house where the person making the search may find them?

ANSWERS:

1. Since it is expected that the entire house will be cleared of leaven by that time, the deliberate placing of leaven where the searcher will find it, will enable the searcher to perform the precept to burn and to "declare null and void" all the leaven in his household in the morning of Passover Eve.

2. Crumbs are placed in every room, for if the searcher were to begin the search and fail to turn up any leaven, he might stop his search or else just perform it only cursorily in the belief that the entire house was clean of leaven. He would not then have fulfilled the precept of searching every nook and cranny of his home for leaven.

(*Hok Yaakov* 432:14)

3. To remind every Jew of his obligation to free himself from the "leaven" in his own soul, namely, his Evil Impulse.

Just as he removes the leaven by the light of a candle, searching every nook and cranny in his house, so, too, he should eliminate the evil that dwells within his person, searching his heart by the light of his soul which is the "candle of G-d."

The pieces of bread (leaven) put into each room of the house symbolizing the "leaven" of Evil, reminds us of the imperfections that are yet to be removed from our hearts.

(Avodath Yisrael)

307.   QUESTION:

> The benediction recited prior to the search of leaven is "...and commanded us to remove the leaven." Why is it not ... "and commanded us to search for leaven?"

ANSWER:

Because the ultimate purpose of the commandment is not the "search" but the "removal" of the leaven.

(Levush, Ch. 432)

308.   QUESTION:

> Why is the declaration: "All manner of leaven which is in my possession that I have not seen or removed, is hereby to be considered null and void and as the dust of the earth," recited in Aramaic and not in Hebrew?

ANSWER:

For the benefit of the unlearned who did not understand Hebrew and knew only the vernacular. [Aramaic was the vernacular used by Jews at the time this declaration was just composed.]

(Darke Moshe)

309. QUESTION:

Why is the Sheheheyanu (the benediction usually recited when carrying out a given religious precept for the first time in a year), not recited before the search for leaven?

ANSWERS:

1. Since the search for leaven is made in honor of the approaching festival of Passover, the *Sheheheyanu* recited on Passover itself is taken as referring to this precept also.

(*Tur, Ch.* 432)

2. Because one is apt to be sorry for having to get rid of so much leaven (and *Sheheheyanu* is meant to be recited on happy occasions only).

(*Abudraham*)

310. QUESTION:

Why is the "Psalm of Thanksgiving" (Psalm 100) not recited on the Eve of Passover?

ANSWER:

Because this Psalm is associated with the sacrifice of Thanksgiving, which, was not offered on Passover Eve.

(*Magen Avraham* 429:7)

311. QUESTION:

Why is it customary for the firstborn to fast on the Eve of Passover?

ANSWER:

To recall the fact that when the firstborn of Egypt were slain, the firstborn of the Children of Israel were spared.

(*Levush, Ch.* 470)

312. QUESTION:

What has been the attitude of the Rabbis toward the work of baking matzoth for Passover?

ANSWER:

It is proper and fitting that a G-d-fearing man should personally supervise the kneading and baking of the matzoth; let him not feel that it is below his dignity to go to the well, to carry pitchers and pails of water, and so forth, for their task.

All these "menial" tasks should be performed for the L-rd with joy and happiness, as King David said: "I have rejoiced in the way of Thy testimonies as much as in all riches" (Psalm 119:14) and, as Maimonides said, "One who is haughty and proud and honors himself, is sinful and a fool" (Laws concerning the *Lulav*).

Concerning such a man, Solomon said: "Glorify not thyself in the Presence of the King" (Proverbs 25:6). Furthermore, whoever humbles himself when performing a religious precept, with all the menial tasks it may entail, is the one to be honored, for honor and glory are to be given to G-d alone, and to Him we should pay homage, with joy and humility.

313. QUESTION:

Why is it forbidden to eat Matzoth the entire fourteenth day of Nissan (before the Seder)?

ANSWER:

One who eats matza during the day on Passover Eve, is comparable to one who seduces his betrothed while she is still in her father's house, an offense punishable by lashes, because it shows that the offender is unwilling to control his animal instincts; he cannot restrain his desire until after the wedding and after the recital of the "seven benedictions."

The same applies to one who cannot wait to enjoy his *matzoth* until night time, after the "seven blessings" which precede the eating of *matzoth* at the Seder have been read.

(*Levush* 471:2)

314. QUESTION:

Why should we refrain from work beginning with noontime on the Eve of Passover?

ANSWER:

Lest preoccupation with daily pursuits may cause one to forget
to burn his leaven, to slaughter his Paschal offering, or to prepare
his matzoth for the Seder. It is an important religious duty to
prepare all the aforementioned during the day, in order to be
ready for the Seder when the time arrives.

(*Rashi, Pesahim* 50a)

315. QUESTION:

**The Torah calls Passover, Hag HaMatzoth (the
Feast of Unleavened Bread), but in general Jewish
parlance it is called Pesach (the Feast of Passover).
What is the significance of this difference in
nomenclature?**

ANSWER:

It is written: "I am my beloved's, and my beloved is mine"
(Song of Songs 6:3). Likewise, we extol the greatness and holiness
of G-d, while He, in turn, praises the worthiness of Israel.

By referring to Passover as the "Feast of Unleavened Bread,"
G-d means to praise us for our meticulous observance of the commandment to eat unleavened bread on this Festival.

We, in turn, call the Festival, "Feast of Passover," to extol G-d
and to thank Him for "passing over" our homes, as it is written,
פסח הוא לד' "And ye shall say: It is the Pass-Over sacrifice to the
Eternal because He passed over the houses of the Children of
Israel in Egypt when He smote the Egyptians" (Ex. 12:27).

(*Kedushath Levi, Parshath Bo*)

316. QUESTION:

**Why is the Friday night "Summary of the Sabbath
Amidah" beginning with "He was a Shield to our
forefathers with His word ...," not recited when
that night is a Seder night?**

ANSWER:

This prayer was instituted by the Rabbis "to shield us from evil spirits." According to this tradition, Passover night being a *Lel Shimurim*, a "night of watching unto the L-rd" (Ex. 12:42) makes the prayer for protection unnecessary.

(*Tur, Ch.* 487)

317. QUESTION:

Why is the home celebration of the first two nights of Passover known as the Seder?

ANSWER:

Seder is the Hebrew term for "Order," implying the "Order" of the Passover celebration as set down in the Haggadah.

318. QUESTION:

Why is the book from which we read the Seder service known as the Haggadah?

ANSWER:

Haggadah connotes a "telling" or "narration," as in *ve-higad'ta levinha*, "You shall *tell* your son on that day" (Ex. 13:8).

(*Abudraham*)

319. QUESTION:

Why is it customary in some localities for the man conducting the Seder to wear his kittel during the Seder?

ANSWER:

The wearing of this burial shroud is meant to prevent excessive, unseemly merriment at the Seder table.

(*TaZ* 472:3)

NOTE: The *Kittel* (lit. "gown"), is a white garment owned by every Jewish married male which is meant to serve as his burial shroud.

320. QUESTION:

We are commanded to recline at the Seder table to recall the position of free men at banquets in olden times. What is the correct posture for carrying out this precept?

ANSWER:

One should always recline on the left side. One should not recline on one's back or face, because this is not a posture appropriate to a sense of freedom. One should not recline on the right side because of the danger that the epiglottis might open before the esophagus, and that the cartilaginous lid covering the entrance to the upper part of the windpipe might open of itself, permitting food to enter and cause choking.

(Levush 472:3)

Even if one is left-handed, he should recline on the left side.

(Ibid., Tur)

The actual reading of the Haggadah should not be performed in a reclining position, but sitting up straight, with awe and reverence for the Almighty!

(P'ri Megaddim 473:29)

321. QUESTION:

What is the significance of the Four Cups of wine every participant is required to drink at the Seder?

ANSWERS:

1. The Rabbis tell us (Shemoth Rabbah, Ch. 8) that the Four Cups of wine drunk at the Seder, symbolize the four Divine promises of Redemption found in the Scripture in connection with Israel's liberation from Egypt: "I will bring you out; I will deliver you; I will redeem you; I will take you to Me" (Ex. 6:6-7).

The Frst Cup of wine is drunk at the Kiddush, when we thank G-d for having "chosen us from among all peoples." It stands for the fourth promise — "I will take you to Me." Because of its importance, it is the first of the four cups.

The Second Cup of wine is drunk while the story of Israel and its tribulations in Egypt is related. It symbolizes the promise, "And I will bring you out" (i.e. from bondage).

The Third Cup following the Grace is drunk after the festive dinner, when we declare G-d's bounty and His goodness to us, and praise the beauty of the Land of Israel. This cup recalls the second promise, "I will deliver you" (i.e. from all types of slavery).

The Fourth Cup of wine marks the reading of the Hallel, wherein we sing praises to G-d for having redeemed us with an "outstretched arm." This cup represents the third promise, "I will redeem you" (i.e., we say to Him: Even as You have made us a great name amongst the nations of the world, so do we praise, exalt and glorify Your Name, for ever and ever).

(Hessed le-Avraham)

2. These Four Cups may also be taken to represent the four virtues which the Israelites displayed while they were in Egypt and for which they were considered deserving of liberation from slavery:

1. They refused to change their Hebrew names.
2. They refused to speak any other language but Hebrew.
3. They did not indulge in vicious gossip about each other.
4. They led pure lives, free of adultery and other immorality.

(Leviticus Rabbah, Ch. 32)

322. QUESTION:

Why are women also obligated to drink the Four Cups of wine?

ANSWER:

Because the Passover miracles occurred primarily thanks to the merits of the pious women of that generation of Israelites. Accordingly, it is only appropriate that the women of every generation should participate fully in the Seder service and drink the Four Cups of wine.

(Magen Avraham 472:16)

323. QUESTION:

What is the significance of the roasted shankbone with bits of meat left upon it (z'roa), and the roasted egg (betza), on the Seder dish?

ANSWER:

The shankbone commemorates the Paschal sacrifice called *z'roa* in Hebrew; it symbolizes also the *z'roa netuyah,* the "outstretched hand" with which the L-rd brought us forth from Egypt.

The egg recalls the Festival Offering eaten on Passover Eve.

324. QUESTION:

What is the significance of the haroseth, (the brownish mixture of wine, nuts, cinnamon and apples) on the Seder dish?

ANSWER:

The *haroseth* symbolizes the *clay* with which our forefathers were forced to make bricks in Egypt.

The *two fruits* allude to two verses in the Song of Songs which is closely linked with the spring season, i.e., "Under the *apple-tree* I awakened thee" (8:5) and "I went into the garden of *nuts*" (ibid. 6:11).

(*Tur, Ch.* 473; *see Abudraham*)

325. QUESTION:

What is the origin of the term haroseth?

ANSWER:

The term in Hebrew designates *clay* such as may be used also by a potter (*maa'se harassin*).

(*Mordekhai, quoting the Jerusalem Talmud, in Arvei Pesahim*)

326. QUESTION:

Why do we not pronounce a special benediction over the haroseth?

ANSWER:

Because the eating of *haroseth* on the Seder night is not based on precept but on custom only.

(Yaavetz)

327. QUESTION:

Why do we eat karpas (parsley or celery)?

ANSWER:

In the word *karpas* there lies a special clue — for if the numerical value of the letters is read in the reverse order, we discover the "sixty myriads" of Israelites who were oppressed with heavy and arduous work.

(Magen Avraham 473:4)

328. QUESTION:

What is the significance of the "bitter herbs" (maror)?

ANSWER:

We eat bitter herbs at the Seder to recall the bitterness of the lot of our forefathers in Egypt.

The best choice for *maror* is a piece of horseradish, because horseradish has a particularly sharp and bitter taste.

(See Levush 473:5)

The author of *Ho-il Moshe* writes in chapter 9:

"Over a period of many years, the holy *Rabbi Hayim of Tzanz* rigidly adhered to his custom of eating the horseradish in its raw form. In his later years, however, when his health began to fail, his physicians forbade him to do so lest he impair his health still further by eating this sharp and bitter vegetable.

When the time came for eating the bitter herbs, he would take the horseradish in his hand, begin the blessing ... "Who hast sanctified us by His commandments ...," but, in place of the words, "and hast commanded us concerning the eating of the bitter herbs" — he concluded with Verse 15 from the Fourth Chapter of Deuteronomy — "Take ye therefore good heed unto yourself" (showing that G-d desires us to do whatever is required to preserve our health). Then he would put the horseradish back on the table without having eaten any of it."

329. QUESTION:
What is the origin of the custom to place Three Matzoth, rather than two, on the Seder plate?

ANSWER:

The Three Matzos recall the "three measures of fine meal" which Abraham bade his wife Sarah prepare for the three angels who visited him (Gen. 18:6). According to tradition, this visit took place on the night of Passover.

(Tosafists: Daath Z'kenim)

There are some who give names to the three matzoth — the top one is called Priest; the middle one, the Levite; and the bottom matzah, the Israelite.

330. QUESTION:
Why is the middle matzah on the Seder dish broken?

ANSWER:

To recall the splitting of the Red Sea, "down the middle," as it were, which took place on the night of Passover.

(Ibid.)

331. QUESTION:
What is the reason for the dipping of the greens (karpas) into salt water at the start of the Seder, long before the meal is due to begin?

ANSWER:

To emphasize that the Seder is indeed "different" from all other nights of the year, for it is not customary to dip vegetables into salt-water before the meal. It is hoped that this unusual procedure will prompt the children at the Seder table to ask questions, which will lead into an explanation of the meaning of the Seder.

(See Rashi, Commentary on Pesahim 114a)

332. QUESTION:

Why do we wash our hands at the Seder even before the first dipping (of the greens into the salt water?

ANSWER:

This, too, is an unusual procedure, aimed to elicit a question from the children at the Seder.

(Hok Yaakov 473:28)

333. QUESTION:

Why do we dip the greens into salt water not merely once, but twice?

ANSWERS:

1. Again, to elicit a question from the children, since this is not the usual way.

2. One dipping commemorates the redemption from Egypt, as it is written: "And ye shall take a bunch of hyssop, and *dip it* (in the blood of the Paschal lamb) that is in the basin" (Ex. 12:22).

The second dipping symbolizes the dispersion of Israel which came about as the result of the wicked deed of Joseph's brothers, in that they sold Joseph into slavery, as it is written: "And they *dipped* the coat of Joseph into blood" (Gen. 37:31) (in order to make their aged father believe that Joseph had been killed by wild beasts).

(Maasei HaShem)

334. QUESTION:

Why is it customary to break the middle one of the three matzoth on the Seder plate before beginning the reading of the Hagaddah?

ANSWER:

So that the passage "This is the bread of affliction..." may be recited over a broken piece of matzah, as it is taught in the Gemara: "This bread (matzah) is called the 'bread of poverty' and, just as it is the custom of the poor to save broken pieces of bread, so do we now break the bread of poverty in two" (Pesahim 115b).

(*Abudraham*)

335. QUESTION:

Why do we hide the afikoman?

ANSWER:

This, too, has an educational purpose, namely, that the children should ask why we are hiding the Afikoman even before having eaten our meal. This will give the parent the opportunity to tell the children the story of the Exodus from Egypt.

(*Levush*)

It is customary to wrap the Afikoman into a napkin and to hide it between the cushions.

(*Mate Moshe, No.* 627)

Says the Talmud: "We snatch away the matzah from the children on the Seder night, in order that they should not stuff themselves with it and become drowsy and then, no questions will be forthcoming from them" (Pesahim 109a).

(*Hok Yaakov* 472:2)

336. QUESTION:

What is the origin of the custom to have the children "steal" the Afikoman on the Seder night?

ANSWER:

This is a game to keep the children awake, so that they will not miss any part of the Seder.

(*Ibid.*)

337. QUESTION:
Why do we lift up the Seder plate when we recite "This is the bread of affliction ..."?

ANSWER:
A number of commentators hold that this is done to elicit questions from the children. However, there must be a more profound reason than this.

It is written in the Midrash: "He raises up the needy from the dunghill" (Psalms 113:7). This refers to the "Children of Israel, who were sunk in the mire in Egypt, and G-d raised them on high!"

When we eat the bread of affliction, the symbol of abject misery, we raise the Seder plate, to imply that throughout the ages, He has always raised us up from the dunghill of affliction.

(*Mateh Aaron, author of Bigdei Aaron, on Scriptures*)

338. QUESTION:
Why is "This is the bread of affliction ..." recited in Aramaic?

ANSWER:
The custom of inviting all those who were hungry to join in the Passover celebration originated in Babylonia. Hence, the invitation was extended in Aramaic, the everyday language of the Jews of Babylonia at that time, so that all might understand it.

(*Abudraham*)

339 QUESTION:
Why are the final words of "This is the bread of affliction" — "Next year may we be free men" — recited in Hebrew?

ANSWER:
This change from the all-Aramaic text was instituted in the Jewish communities of Persia, so that the Persians, who spoke Aramaic, should not suspect the Jews of wanting to flee the country.

(*Gevurath HaShem*)

340. QUESTION:

Why is it customary to dash a little wine from one's cup with one's finger when enumerating the Ten Plagues and when mentioning the mnemonic signs of the initials of the Ten Plagues (Detzach, Adash, Beachav)?

ANSWERS:

1. To imply that our cup of joy cannot be full to overflowing when human beings lose their lives, not even when they are our enemies, as the Egyptians were.

2. The finger is used to recall the cry of the magicians of Egypt, "This is the *finger* of G-d" (Ex. 8:15).

(*Hok Yosef* 473:34)

341. QUESTION:

Why do we not pronounce the Benediction over the Hallel before reciting the Hallel at the Seder table?

ANSWER:

In the synagogue the Hallel is chanted as a part of the order of worship. At home, at the Seder table, on the other hand, it is recited in a less formal mood, interrupted by blessings, by talk about the Exodus, and so forth. Accordingly, the reading of the Hallel at home is not preceded by the formal benediction.

(*Abudraham*)

342. QUESTION:

In the synagogue the Hallel is recited standing. Why, then, do we remain seated when we read it at the Seder at home?

ANSWER:

In the synagogue Hallel is recited standing because it is written, "Praise Him, ye servants of the L-rd; ye that *stand* in the *House of the L-rd* . . ." (Psalms 135:1-2).

The Seder at home, on the other hand, is a less formal occasion. The Hallel is interrupted several times and we are permitted to spend most of the evening in a reclining position.

(*TaZ* 422:4)

343. QUESTION:

Why is the recital of the Hallel at the Seder divided into two parts?

ANSWER:

The first half of the Hallel, recited prior to the festive dinner, consists of Psalms referring to the Exodus from Egypt. It is therefore an appropriate part of the narrative of the Exodus which is read before the meal.

The latter part of the Hallel, recited after the meal, parallels the second half of the Haggadah in that both refer to Israel's future redemption.

(*Levush, Ch.* 480)

344. QUESTION:

Why do we open the door of our homes before reciting the curse on our enemies, "Pour out Thy wrath . . ."?

ANSWER:

To show our implicit faith in G-d. On this "Night of Watching unto the L-rd," we are not afraid to open our doors and shout it out for all the world to hear that we are awaiting the true Messiah!

(*Ibid.*)

345. QUESTION:

Why do we raise our cup before reciting "Therefore it is our duty to praise . . ."?

ANSWER:

We lift up our wine cup even as we are about to lift our voices in song and praise: to laud, glorify, exalt, honor, bless and extol, and adore Him Who performed these wonders for our fore-fathers and for all of us. The Rabbis tell us that "song and praises should be recited only over wine" (Berakhot 35a).

(Pardes HaGadol, Ch. 132)

346. QUESTION:

Why do we pronounce the benediction over each of the four cups separately?

ANSWER:

Because the drinking of each of the four cups represents a religious act in its own right.

(Magen Avraham, Ch. 474)

347. QUESTION:

In the days of the Temple, the bitter herbs (maror) were eaten at the end of the Seder meal.
Why, today, do we eat them at the beginning of the meal?

ANSWER:

The bitter herbs symbolize the bitterness of oppression and exile. In the days of the Temple, the Israelites ate the bitter herbs at the end of the meal because they knew that "in the end" they would have to go into exile.

Today, however, we are actually in exile, and await redemption "in the end." Accordingly, we eat the bitter herbs first, and then spend the rest of the evening giving expression to our hope for future deliverance.

(Menahem Tziyon, by the Rebbe of Rimanov)

348. QUESTION:

Why are eggs eaten prior to the Seder?

ANSWER:

The eggs symbolize mourning. On the very day when we are eating *matzoth,* the symbol of freedom, we will taste the bitterness of exile, as symbolized by the *maror*. For the first day of Passover always falls on the same day of the week as Tisha B'Av, the anniversary of the destruction of the Temple. Thus, even at our time of joy, we are reminded of our lost Temple in Jerusalem.

(*Levush* 476:2)

349. QUESTION:
What is the origin and significance of the "Cup of the Prophet Elijah" that is placed on the Seder table?

ANSWER:

In the Talmud there is some debate as to whether, in fact, a fifth cup of wine should not be drunk, for Scripture contains one more "promise of redemption," namely, "And I will bring you in into the Land" (Ex. 6:8). The sages deferred the decision pending the arrival of the Prophet Elijah, who will pass the final decision on this and all other moot questions.

We therefore have at the Seder table a fifth cup, from which, however, we do not drink. We call it the "Cup of Elijah," for this is the cup concerning which the Prophet alone can decide.

(*The Gaon of Vilna*)

It is written in *Toldoth Esther*: "The practice of pouring a fifth cup of wine, known as the "Cup of the Prophet Elijah," is based on the Jerusalem Talmud, where it is written: "On what do we base the drinking of the Four Cups of wine?" — On the four promises of redemption found in Scripture, whereby the Holy One, Blessed be He, promised to deliver Israel out of Egypt, as it is written, "Therefore say to the Children of Israel: I am the Eternal, and I will bring you out from under the burdens of the Egyptians, and I will deliver you from their bondage, and I will redeem you with an outstretched arm, and with great judgments; and I will take you to Me for a people, and I will be to you a G-d" (Ex. 6:6-7).

Upon further scrutiny, we find in the following verse (6:8), one more promise of redemption, namely, "and I will bring you into the Land."

Seeing that we have, in fact, five promises of redemption, should there not have been a fifth cup to represent the final promise, i.e., that the L-rd will bring us into the Land? On the other hand, our stay in the Land of Israel after our deliverance from Egypt, was a temporary one. Only with the advent of the Messiah, heralded by the coming of Elijah, will we be brought to the Land to remain there forever.

For this reason, we pour a fifth cup of wine, which we call the Cup of Elijah and from which we do not drink, waiting, instead, for Elijah and the time when we will truly be able to drink from the cup of complete redemption."

350. QUESTION:

Why must we not drink any thing but water after drinking the Four Cups of wine at the Seder?

ANSWERS:

1. In the olden days, the poor would be given enough wine from the public soup kitchen to last them for the two Sedarim; that is, enough for about eight cups of wine — four for each night. To make sure that they would not drink up all the wine on the first night and not have enough left for the second Seder, the rule was laid down that no more wine may be taken that night after the Four Cups had been drunk.

2. We are not permitted to drink additional wine after the Seder, in order that we do not become drunk. We are supposed to devote the remainder of the evening with the study of the laws of Passover and to the history of the Exodus of Egypt, until we get sleepy, at which time we are supposed to retire for the night.

(*Hok Yaakov* 481:1)

It is proper NOT TO SMOKE after the Seder, in order that the taste of the AFIKOMAN (matza), linger in one's mouth.

(*Shaarei Teshuvah* 511:5)

351. QUESTION:

Why is the complete Hallel recited only on the First Two Days of Passover and just half the Hallel on the remaining days?

ANSWER:

On the Seventh Day of Passover, the Egyptians were drowned in the Red Sea. When the angels wanted to offer praises to G-d for the miraculous escape of the Children of Israel, G-d said to them: "My creatures are perishing, and ye would sing!" (Megilla 10b).

For this reason, only half the Hallel ("Half-Hallel") is recited on the Seventh and Eighth day of Passover. Lest the Intermediary Days of Passover should receive more honor than the last two full Festival Days, Half-Hallel is recited on the Intermediate Days also.

(TaZ 490:3)

352. QUESTION:

Why is it customary in some communities for those whose parents are still living to leave the synagogue when Yizkor is begun, and stay outside until after the memorial service is over?

ANSWER:

It is awkward to stand quietly and not join the rest of the congregation in its prayers. Also, one should not put himself in a position where he may be the object of envy for still having his parents (see Yevamoth 106a). It is therefore best that one who has parents should wait outside the synagogue during the *Yizkor* service.

(Shaarei Ephraim)

353. QUESTION:

On Shemini Atzereth (last day of Sukkot), before the Musaf service — the Sexton calls out aloud the words "Maashiv haruach umorid hagashem" — "Thou causest the wind to blow and the rain to fall," to remind us that from this day on, and until Passover, this passage must be incorporated into the Amidah. But on the First Day of Passover, the Sexton does not explicitly announce that this passage is not to be recited again until the fall. Why?

ANSWER:

If the Sexton were to announce aloud on the First Day of Passover, that the congregation should cease reciting the prayer "Thou causest the wind to blow and the rain to fall" — it would seem as if we are no longer in need of rain at all. The Sexton therefore simply says aloud, before the start of the Amidah, *Morid HaTal* — "Thou causest dew to descend," to imply that the congregation should begin the paragraph with these words, omitting the prayer for rain that went directly before.

(*Levush* 114:3)

354. QUESTION:

Why is it customary for the Cantor to wear a Kittel (see No. 319 above) when reciting the Prayer for Dew on the First Day of Passover?

ANSWER:

To remind the Cantor to pray with devotion and with a contrite heart for life, healthy offspring, and for sustenance.

355. QUESTION:

What is the significance of Sefirah, the Counting of the Omer?

ANSWER:

We count the forty-nine days from the second night of Passover until the Feast of Weeks (Shavuoth), the anniversary of the Giving of our Torah.

"Just as one who expects a close friend on a certain day counts the days and even the hours until his coming, so do we count the forty-nine days from the anniversary of our departure from Egypt, to the anniversary of the Giving of the Torah, for this last event was the sole purpose of our deliverance from Egypt" (Maimonides).

In later centuries, this period came to have sad connotations for Jews the world over. Tradition tells of an epidemic that swept away tens of thousands of Rabbi Akiba's disciples during the *Sefirah* weeks.

Accordingly, the *Sefirah* has evolved into a period of half-mourning. Throughout the month of Iyar, Jews do not arrange weddings and other festivities except on the 18th of Iyar, which is the thirty-third day of the Omer (*Lag Beomer*), the day on which the epidemic suddenly stopped. Only on *Lag Beomer* proper was festivity permitted, and it came to be known as Scholars' Day.

Another tradition links this day (*Lag Beomer*) with the great teacher Simeon Bar Yohai. Because he had refused to obey the Roman decree against the study of Torah, and continued to teach his pupils, his life was steadily in danger. He succeeded in escaping to a cave in the mountains of Galilee. For thirteen years he lived with his son in this hideout, feeding on the fruit of the carob tree and drinking from a nearby spring.

Each year, his students paid him a visit on *Lag Beomer*. Lest the Roman soldiers suspect their destination, Bar Yohai's students disguised themselves as hunters and carried bows and arrows. Bar Yohai died on *Lag Beomer* and his last request to his disciples was that the day of his death be observed by celebration rather than by mourning.

Nowhere in the world is *Lag Beomer* celebrated with so much joy as at Meron, a village near Safed in Israel, which is said to be Bar Yohai's burial place. Hundreds of pious Hassidim from all parts of Israel and from neighboring countries come to Meron to honor the great teacher and the ideals for which he stood. While waiting for the celebration, they chant Psalms, sing hassidic songs, and study the *Zohar*, the holy book ascribed to Bar Yohai.

The real festivities begin when a huge bonfire is lit at midnight. The women throw silken scarfs and other clothing into the flames. The men, young and old, sing and dance around the fire until early morning. The three-year-old boys receive their first haircuts, and the hair is thrown into the flames, accompanied by ecstatic singing and dancing.

356. QUESTION:

Why were we originally commanded by the Torah to "Count the Omer?"

ANSWERS:

1. In connection with the daily offerings of an *Omer* of grain made between Passover and Shavuoth (Lev. Ch. 23).

2. The Jews of olden times in Israel were told to count the Omer lest, busy as they were at that season with their fields, they would forget to make the mandatory Shavuoth pilgrimage to Jerusalem.

(*Abudraham*)

357. QUESTION:

Why do we not pronounce the Sheheheyanu **benediction before counting the Omer?**

ANSWERS:

1. Because this religious act does not now carry a connotation of rejoicing.

(*Hok Yaakov* 498:7; *Kol Bo*)

2. Because we look forward not to each day we count but to Shavuoth, the anniversary of the Giving of the Torah when our counting will be done. When that day arrives, we will pronounce the Sheheheyanu blessing in which we give thanks to G-d for permitting us to reach this season.

(*B'nei Yisaschar, quoting Rebbe Pinchas of Koretz*)

358. QUESTION:

What is the significance of the prayer "May it be Thy will . . . that the Temple be speedily rebuilt . . . ," which we recite after counting Sefirah?

ANSWER:

The counting of Sefirah today is based on Rabbinical ordinance only, because in the absence of a Temple in Jerusalem and of the *Omer* offerings, the original purpose of counting the *Omer* no longer applies.

We hope that the day will soon come when this act will be restored to its original purpose.

(*Mate Moshe, Ch. 667*)

359. QUESTION:

Why is it customary on each night of the Sefirah weeks to refrain from work from sundown until after the counting of Sefirah?

ANSWER:

To commemorate the deaths among the disciples of Rabbi Akiba, which, according to tradition occurred around sundown.

(*TaZ* 493:3)

360. QUESTION:

When writing a letter during the seven weeks of Sefirah — some people add to the date and super-scription the words: Le-mishpar b'ne Yisrael ("Ac-cording to the counting of the Children of Israel"). What is the reason for this custom?

ANSWER:

Since the forty-nine days of Sefirah must be "complete," we must never lose sight even for a moment that these are the days of the Omer, as it is written in the *Zohar*: "We must not forget the number of days we have been counting, not even for one minute."

(*Menahem Tziyon*)

Shavuoth Customs

361. QUESTION:

What is the origin of Shavuoth, the Hebrew name for the Feast of Pentecost?

ANSWERS:

1. The root of the word is *sheva,* meaning "seven."

The *Ahavat Shalom* writes: The number seven always has the connotation of holiness. The seventh day of the week is a holy day (the Sabbath); the day after the counting of the "Seven Weeks" is the festival of Shavuoth. The seventh year is the Sabbatical year, and the fiftieth year which follows the seventh Sabbatical year is the year of Jubilee.

2. The literal meaning of *Shavuoth* is "weeks," recalling the seven weeks we counted from Passover until This Festival, which commemorates the Giving of the Law.

3. It is related also to *Shevua,* the Hebrew for "taking a vow." This implies that G-d vowed He would not exchange us for any other nation, and we, the Jewish people, vowed in return that we would not exchange Him for any other god.

(*Or HaHayim*)

362. QUESTION:
What is the origin of the custom in many communities to decorate synagogues and homes with flowers and greenery in honor of Shavuoth?

ANSWERS:
1. To stress that the fruits of the trees are being judged on Shavuoth and that we should pray for them.

(*Magen Avraham* 494:5)

2. To recall the "grass which grew around about Mount Sinai" at the time of the Giving of the Law. How do we know that there was grass in that spot? Because it is written: "Neither let the flocks nor the herds feed before that mount" (Ex. 34:3). Obviously, grass must have been growing there.

(*Levush, Ch.* 494)

363. QUESTION:
What special observances mark the first night of Shavuoth?

ANSWER:
The entire first night of Shavuoth is spent in preparing oneself to receive the spiritual message of the festival. Men stay up most of

the night in the synagogue. Selections from Scripture, from Rabbinic literature and from the writings of the mystics are read from a work entitled *Tikkun Lel Shavuoth.*

(*Magen Avraham, Ch.* 494)

364. QUESTION:
Why is the Book of Ruth read on Shavuoth?

ANSWER:
The Book of Ruth was written by the prophet Samuel, to trace the descent of King David from Ruth, the Moabitess, who voluntarily forsook idolatry and entered the Covenant of Sinai.

Shavuoth marks the anniversary of the birth, and of the death of King David (Tosfoth, Hagiga 17a, sub voce, AF, quoting the Jerusalem Talmud).

(*Binyan Ariel*)

365. QUESTION:
Why is it customary to eat dairy food on the first day of Shavuoth before partaking of the regular meat meal?

ANSWERS:
1. It is customary to eat milk and honey on Shavuoth because the Law is likened to them. (Cf. Song of Songs 4:11: "Honey and milk is under thy tongue").

(*Kol Bo*)

2. The white color of milk symbolizes Divine lovingkindness, and thus recalls the grace and compassion with which G-d gave us His Law in order to allow His creatures to fathom His mysteries.

(*B'nei Yisashar*)

3. According to the Midrash, Mount Sinai was called by six names: the "Mount of G-d," "Mount of Bashan," "Har Gavnunim," "Mount Moriah," "Mount Horeb" and "Mount Sinai" (Bamidbar Rabbah, Ch. 1).

The name *Gavnunim* is derived from *g'vinah*, the Hebrew term for cheese, so that one of the names of Mount Sinai was literally "Cheese Mountain." Hence, cheese is eaten on Shavuoth.

(Rabbi Shamshon Ostropoler)

However, meat must be eaten after the dairy foods, because meat meals are needed to make our enjoyment of the festival complete.

(Hagaoth Minhagim)

4. Dairy products signify smallness and humility, symbolistic virtues of modesty, humility and meekness which the Torah loves. In the olden days, people would sit on the floor when studying the law as a sign of their obedience to G-d.

(Pinhas, Rebbe of Karetz)

366. QUESTION:

Why, in some communities, are long Hallot with four corners baked for Shavuoth?

ANSWERS:

1. To recall the two loaves of bread which were offered in the Temple on Shavuoth, and to symbolize Gemini, the sign of the zodiac into which the sun enters in the month of Sivan, the month of Shavuoth.

(Kol Bo)

2. The Torah is likened to bread, and it is written: "The measure thereof is longer than the earth" (Job 11:9). The long Shavuoth loaf therefore symbolizes the "length and breadth of the Law."

The four ends on the Hallah, symbolizes the four methods of interpreting the Scriptural text: the simple meaning; the esoteric meaning and the homiletical and allegorical interpretations.

(Lev David)

Tisha B'Av —
Mourning for the Temple

367. QUESTION:
Why is the month of Av referred to as Menachem Av in the blessing of the New Moon?

ANSWER:
Menachem is the Hebrew word for "comforter," implying the hope that the day will soon come when the L-rd will comfort His people, so that the month of Av will be one of consolation instead of mourning.

(Devir Hamutzna)

368. QUESTION:
It is customary not to eat meat on the first nine days of the month of Av, including Rosh Hodesh, when it is usually considered a religious act to eat meat. Why?

ANSWER:
We abstain from meat on Rosh Hodesh Av, not because of the mourning for the Temple but because the first day of Av is the anniversary of the death of Aaron, the brother of Moses.

(Orakh Hayyim, Ch. 551)

369. QUESTION:
Why is the last meal taken before the fast of Tisha B'Av eaten sitting on the floor?

ANSWER:
Because this is supposed to be a meal of mourning. However, one need not remove one's leather footgear until later.

(Beth Yosef, Ch. 552)

370. QUESTION:
Why is it forbidden to eat two different foods from separate dishes at the final meal before the fast?

ANSWER:

Eating a variety of foods at this time would make the meal appear too festive for the occasion (Levush 552:2).

It is customary to eat lentils and eggs, since they symbolize mourning. Lentils and eggs are round, even as mourning surrounds everyone in the world at some time in his life. Moreover, they have no openings, just as mourners are enclosed within themselves at the hour of grief.

(*Ibid.*, 552:5)

It is written in *Pirkei deRabbi Eliezer* (Ch. 35):

Rabbi Eliezer says: Lentils are a food of misfortune and mourning. When Abel was slain by his brother Cain, his parents, Adam and Eve, mourned over him and ate lentils, as a sign of grief and sorrow. When Haran, brother of Abraham, was burned to death in the fire of Kasdim, his parents ate lentils as a sign of mourning. The lentils for which Esau sold his birthright had been prepared by Jacob as a meal of mourning, for their grandfather Abraham had just died that day.

The Jewish people eat lentils on the Eve of Tisha B'Av in commemoration of the destruction of the First and Second Temples' to symbolize the grief and distress that have accompanied us ever since.

371. QUESTION:
Why is the synagogue not brightly lit on Tisha B'Av?

ANSWER:

As a sign of mourning. When the Temple was destroyed, G-d asked the angels, "What does a king of flesh and blood do when he goes into mourning?" "He puts out all his lanterns," the angels replied. Thereupon G-d said to them: "I will do likewise," as it is written: "The sun and the moon are become black" (Joel 4:15; Echa Rabthi).

(Abudraham)

372. QUESTION:

The Book of Lamentations is one of the "Five Scrolls." Why is it not customary to read the Book of Lamentations from a parchment Scroll as we do the Book of Esther, another one of the Five Scrolls?

ANSWER:

Because the holiday of Purim will never cease from Israel, and the Book of Esther, which contains its story, will be retold year after year. As for the Book of Lamentations, on the other hand, the Rabbis were not desirous to have it written down on parchment in permanent form, for we hope the time will come when Tisha B'Av will be turned into a day of rejoicing and happiness. As a result, we read the Book of Lamentations from books of ordinary paper.

(Levush 559:1)

Imrei Tzaddikim quotes Rabbi Levi Yitzchak of Berdichev as follows:

The Scroll (of Lamentations) is one of the Five Holy Scrolls. In the days of the Messiah, its reading will be prefaced with the Sheheheyanu blessing, for then Tisha B'Av will be turned into a day of rejoicing.

When asked how the Book of Lamentations will be read "in a joyous manner" on Tisha B'Av once the Temple will be rebuilt, the Berdichever replied: It will be read as follows:

(Up to now) "doth the city sit solitary" (but now) "she *is* great among the nations; she *is* a princess among the provinces — to whom she once *was* tributary."

(Up to now) "She wept sore in the night" (but now) "she needs none to comfort her" (Lam. 1:1-2).

In this vein, will Lamentations be read; with the good tidings which have now come to pass inserted into the text.

373. QUESTION:
Why is Psalm 91 (which is ordinarily recited at the conclusion of the Sabbath and which ends, "Establish Thou also upon us the work of our hands, yea, the work of our hands do Thou establish") not recited when Tisha B'Av falls on a Saturday night?

ANSWER:
Since this Psalm was composed to commemorate the completion of the Tabernacle in the wilderness, the forerunner of the Temple, it should not be recited on the anniversary of the destruction of the Holy Temple.

(Mateh Moshe, Ch. 729)

374. QUESTION:
As a rule, mourners are not supposed to go to the synagogue during the Shivah (the first seven days of mourning). Why are they permitted to do so on Tisha B'Av?

ANSWER:
Because the entire congregation is in mourning on that day and all sit on the floor or on low benches like the mourner during Shivah.

(Levush, 559:6)

The mourners may even be called up to the Torah and for Maftir on Tisha B'Av.

(Shaarei Teshuvah, 554:1)

375. QUESTION:
Why are the phylacteries not put on in the morning of Tisha B'Av?

ANSWER:
Since the phylacteries are considered an "adornment," we do not put them on when in deep mourning, as on Tisha B'Av.

Because of deep mourning, we also do not enwrap ourselves with the Tallith.

(Magen Avraham, Ch. 555)

376. QUESTION:

Why is the Priestly Benediction not read in the Morning Service of Tisha B'Av?

ANSWER:

On Tisha B'Av, we are not permitted even to greet one another with the words, "Peace be unto you." How, then, could we recite the Priestly Benediction which concludes with the words..., "and grant thee peace?"

(Dagul Mervavah)

377. QUESTION:

Circumcisions taking place in the morning of Tisha B'Av, are performed only after the Kinoth have been recited. Why?

ANSWER:

Because circumcisions must be performed amidst rejoicing, as it is written: "I rejoice at Thy Word" (Psalm 119:162).

Therefore it is only after the Lamentations, with their concluding verses of comfort, have been read, that the circumcision may properly take place!

(Levush 559:7)

When a Circumcision takes place on Tisha B'Av, it is customary to name the infant Menachem (Comforter).

(Responsa TaSHBeTZ)

378. QUESTION:

Why is the passage "Comfort O L-rd our G-d ..." (Nachem), omitted in the evening and morning services, but included in the afternoon service?

ANSWER:

Until Mincha time on this day of mourning, it is as if one's dead were still lying before him, and it is a rule that one should not attempt to accept consolation until after the burial.

Hence, we do not recite "Comfort us...," until late in the afternoon of Tisha B'Av when the mourning has abated somewhat, "after the burial," as it were.

(HaManhig)

379. QUESTION:

Why is it forbidden to study the Torah on Tisha B'Av?

ANSWER:

Because it is written: "The precepts of the Torah are right, *rejoicing the heart*" (Psalm 19:9), and all rejoicing is forbidden on Tisha B'Av (Taanith 30a).

On the other hand, we are permitted to study literature that saddens the heart, such as the prophecies of calamity found in the Book of Jeremiah, the Book of Job, Midrash Echa and all other subjects considered permissible for a mourner to study.

(*Orakh Hayyim* 554:1-2)

380. QUESTION:

Why is the consecration of The New Moon (Kiddush Halvanah) for the month of Av deferred until the conclusion of Tisha B'Av?

ANSWER:

Tradition has it that the Messiah will be born at the conclusion of Tisha B'Av. This is therefore the proper time to perform the consecration of the New Moon, in which we proclaim the good tidings that Israel and the Moon will renew themselves as of yore.

(*Ari; see Baer Hetev*, 551:25)

381. QUESTION:

Why may the consecration of the New Moon of Av not take place on the night of Shabbath Hazon (the Saturday preceding Tisha B'Av)?

ANSWER:

When we perform the consecration of the New Moon, it is as if we were welcoming the Divine Presence, which is always greeted with joy and happiness. This cannot be done on Shabbath Hazon, since we are explicitly forbidden to rejoice on that day.

(MaHaRIL — Rabbi Jacob Molin)

382. QUESTION:

The Rabbis tell us: "Jerusalem was destroyed because the Rabbis at that time insisted on fulfilling the letter of the law found in the Torah (Baba Metzia 30b).
What did the Rabbis mean by that statement?

ANSWER:

This statement is based on the following Midrash:

The Torah was asked, "How can a person who has sinned obtain forgiveness?" Answered the Torah: "Let him offer a sacrifice!"

They next put the same question to G-d, Who replied: "Let him repent first and then offer a sacrifice!"

The L-rd desires that man repent before offering his sacrifice. A sacrifice without repentance will be of no avail because it will not bring the sinner forgiveness.

This is the meaning of the words of the Rabbis, who said: "Jerusalem was destroyed because they fulfilled the letter of the law of the Torah." They followed the strict letter of the Torah which states that we must offer a sacrifice when we transgress the law. But, they did not follow the spirit of the law as expressed in G-d's own reply "that the sacrifice must be preceded by repentance."

Had the Jews followed the spirit of the law and repented first, Jerusalem would not have been destroyed.

(Hasde Avoth)

383. QUESTION:

According to the Rabbis, "The Fifteenth day of Av was the most festive day in Israel — more festive than all the other holidays" (Mishna, Taanith 26b). What is the significance of that day?

ANSWER:

Said the *RAVeD*, Rabbi Abraham ibn Daud: "On that day, the 15th Day of Av, the last of the generation destined to die in the wilderness perished," as it is written in the Jerusalem Talmud, "Each year, on the day preceding the Ninth of Av, a voice would go out to the entire camp of Israel in the wilderness, saying, 'Go out and dig, go out and dig.' All the Israelites would then go out, dig their own graves and lie down in them. By the next morning, 15,000 of them would be dead.

This happened each year, until they awoke one morning to find everyone still alive in the graves, with no one dead. Thinking that they might have mistakenly consecrated the New Moon of Av too soon, they returned to their graves on the nights of the tenth of Av, and again on the eleventh, the twelfth, the thirteenth, the fourteenth... When finally the fifteenth day of Av came, they looked up and saw the full moon. They then realized that the ninth day of Av had definitely come and gone, and yet they found that none had died in their midst. They then understood that the death sentence had been annulled, and they made that day, The Fifteenth of Av, a festival."

(Kol Bo)

Fast Days — Communal and Private

It is a positive precept laid down by the Prophets to fast on the anniversaries of sad events in the lives of our ancestors.

The purpose of such fasting is to stir our hearts and to open our eyes to the ways of repentance, and to remind us of the evil deeds of our ancestors, which brought on our tragedy, and of our own sins which cause trouble and sorrow to this very day.

If we commemorate these events, we will mend our ways, as it is said, "And they shall confess their own sins and the sins of their ancestors."

Therefore, it is incumbent on every man to take this to heart in these days, and so search out his evil deeds and to repent of them, for the main thing is not the fast as such, as it is written concerning the people of Nineveh, "And G-d saw their works," (Jonah 3:10), and our Rabbis of blessed memory said, "And He saw their sackcloth and their fast," but, "And G-d saw their *works that they had turned from their evil way.*"

The main thing is not the fasting, but the preparation for repentance. Therefore, those people who fast but spend the day taking walks and engaging in idle pursuits, may have preserved the secondary concern but have cast away the main principle.

(Kitzur Shulhan Arukh, 121:1)

384. QUESTION:

What is the significance of the four principal fast days in the Jewish Calendar?

ANSWER:

"Thus saith the L-rd of hosts: [In the end of days] the fast of the fourth month, and the fast of the fifth, and the fast of the seventh, and the fast of the tenth, shall be to the house of Judah, joy and gladness, and cheerful seasons..." (Zechariah 8:19).

The "fast of the fourth month" refers to the Seventeenth Day of Tamuz (the fourth month of the year). It marks the anniversary of five sad events: 1. On that day Moses descended from the mountain and broke the Tablets of the Law when he saw the Golden Calf. 2. The regular sacrifice was abolished on that day. 3. The city was breached in both Temples on this day. 4. Apostomos the wicked burned the Torah and 5. placed an idol in the Temple.

The "fast of the fifth month" refers to the Ninth of Av (the fifth month of the year). On that day it was decreed that our ancestors in the wilderness would not live to enter the land of Israel, for the spies had spoken ill of the land, and the Children of Israel had wept in vain all that night. Therefore this day was singled out as a day of weeping for many generations to come.

The First Temple, and the Second Temple were destroyed on that day. On that day, too, the city of Bethar was captured and thousands of Jews were massacred. Also on that day, Tineius Rufus, the Roman Governor of Judea, plowed up the site on which the Temple had stood, fulfilling the prediction that "Zion shall be plowed into a field" (Micah 3:12).

The "fast of the seventh month" refers to the fast of Gedaliah, which occurs in the month of Tishri. It marks the anniversary of the murder of Gedaliah, son of Ahikam.

After the conquest of the Land of Israel by Nebuchadnezer, King of Babylonia, Gedaliah had been appointed Governor of Palestine. It was only after his assassination that the Jews lost the last vestiges of their independence.

The "fast of the tenth month" refers to the Tenth day of Teveth (the tenth month of the year), when Nebuchadnezer, King of Babylonia, first laid siege to the walls of Jerusalem.

(*Kol Bo*)

385. QUESTION:
In the reading from the Law on communal fast days (Ex. 32:11-34:1-10), Verse 12 of Exodus 32 ("Turn from Thy fierce wrath...") is recited aloud by the congregation and then repeated by the Reader. What is the reason for the emphasis on this verse?

ANSWER:
This verse is a plea to G-d to turn away His wrath and erase the consequences of the tragedy which the fast commemorates.

(*Magen Avraham* 566:2)

386. QUESTION:
On what did the Rabbis base their ruling that girls must begin to observe fast days in full when they

have reached the age of twelve years and one day,
when boys need not do so until they have attained
the age of thirteen years and one day?

ANSWER:

Certain signs of physical maturity, including the growth of body
hair, sets in earlier in girls than in boys. The ages given above were
considered the normal ages for this adolescent development (see
Nidah 45b).

Rosh Hashanah Customs

387. QUESTION:
What was the origin of the practice to begin sounding the Shofar on Rosh Hodesh Elul and sounding
it throughout that month?

ANSWER:

It was on Rosh Hodesh Elul that Moses ascended Mount Sinai
to receive the second set of Tablets of the Law. During that time,
the sound of the Shofar was heard throughout the camp of the
Children of Israel calling upon them to repent of the sin they had
committed in erecting the Golden Calf. The Rabbis therefore ordained
that the Shofar should be sounded on Rosh Hodesh Elul and throughout the month, to bestir the people to repentance.

(*Tur, Ch.* 581, *quoting Pirkei deRabbi Eliezer*)

388. QUESTION:
Why is it customary to rise early in the morning
to recite the Propitiatory Prayers (Selichoth)?

ANSWER:

The Talmud (Abodah Zarah 3b) states that the spirit of G-d
hovers over the earth as the night comes to an end. It is a time of

"favor and compassion" (*eth ratzon*) and the proper time to approach G-d through prayer and supplication.

389. QUESTION:
Why is it considered proper that the person who leads the congregation in the Selichoth prayers should also act as Reader for the Morning and Mincha services that day?

ANSWER:
Because one who begins a religious act should also be the one to complete it.

(*Levush, Ch.* 581)

390. QUESTION:
What are the Thirteen Attributes of G-d which we enumerate during Selichoth?

ANSWER:
They are enumerated in Exodus 34:6-7.
The Abudraham enumerates them as follows:

1 and 2: *The L-rd, the L-rd*:
The designation "The L-rd" (*Adonai*) denotes G-d in His attribute of mercy; and the repetition is explained in the Talmud to mean, "I am the G-d of Mercy before a man sins, and also after he has sinned. Whatever change has to be wrought must be in the heart of the sinner and not in the nature of G-d.

3. *G-d* (*Elohim*):
The almighty L-rd of the Universe, Ruler over nature and mankind.

4. *Merciful*:
Full of loving sympathy for human frailty.

5. *And Gracious*:
Assisting and helping, consoling the afflicted and raising up the oppressed.

6. *Long-Suffering*:
Affording the sinner ample opportunity to reconsider his evil ways.

7. *Abundant in Loving-Kindness*:
Granting His gifts and blessings in excess of what man would deserve.

8. *And Truth*:
He is eternally true to Himself, steadfastly pursuing His plans for the salvation of mankind and rewarding those who do His will.

Note that the quality of loving-kindness, precedes the virtue of truth, both here and throughout Scripture in general, as if to say, "Tell the truth by all means; but be quite sure that you do it with kindness and mercy."

9. *Keeping Mercy Unto the Thousandth Generation*:
Remembering the good deeds of the ancestors to the thousandth generation, and reserving the reward for their remotest descendants.

10. *Forgiving Iniquity*:
Viewing men's failings with indulgence and, by His forgiveness, restoring their souls to their original state of purity.

Avon, translated as "iniquity," refers to sins committed from evil disposition.

11. *Transgression*:
Evil deeds springing from malicious intent and rebellion against G-d.

12. *Sin*:
Shortcomings due to error and thoughtlessness.

13. *Acquitting*:
Acquitting the penitent; He is merciful, gracious and forgiving.

It is customary for the Cantor to intone the words, "And the L-rd passed by before him and proclaimed" (Ex. 34:6), and for the congregation to continue "The L-rd, the L-rd, merciful and gracious..."

(Abudraham)

It is written in the Kitzur SHeLaH: It would be proper to stand throughout the reading of the Selichoth. But we should definitely stand when reciting the Thirteen Attributes of G-d and when reciting "G-d, The King Who sits upon the Throne of Mercy."

391. QUESTION:
Why does the Reader don a Tallith for the recital of Selichoth despite the fact that, according to the Law, Tzitzith are not ordinarily put on at this early hour?

Note: Since the "Tzitzith" are meant to be "visual" reminders (Cf. "And you shall see them" — Numbers 15:37-41), they should not be put on when it is still too dark outside to see them clearly.

ANSWER:
Because it is written: "G-d wrapped Himself into the Tallith and taught Moses the Thirteen Attributes" (Rosh Hashanah 17b).
(*TaZ* 581:2)

392. QUESTION:
Why is the Confession of Sins (Ashamnu) recited in the Selichoth and on the High Holy Days, phrased in the plural form, (i.e. "We have sinned, etc.") and not in the singular, ("I have sinned, etc.")?

ANSWER:
Rabbi Isaac Luria, the renowned mystic, asked: "Why was the Confession phrased in the plural, so that we say 'we are guilt-laden,' instead of 'I am guilt-laden,' and so forth?"

"Because Israel is one body, of which each and every Israelite is an integral part. Hence it follows, that all the members of that body are responsible for the whole, even as I am responsible for my brother. If my fellow-Jew sins, it is as if I myself had sinned.

Even when we recite the Confession alone, at home, *Ashamnu*

should be phrased in the plural, for we are all guarantors for one
another . . .

(Yesod HaTeshuvah, Ch. 6)

We associate ourselves in the burden of guilt of all those who
sin, because we know that society as a whole is responsible for
much of the wrong done by our fellowmen.

This may be compared to the case of one who drills a hole in
a boat, and who replies to the protests of his fellow-passengers:
"What business is that of yours? The hole is only under my own
seat!"

"Fool!" the others say to him. "Do you not understand that
once the water comes through that hole under your seat it will
eventually flood the whole boat and we will all be drowned?"

393.   QUESTION:

What is the meaning of the sentence in the Confession: "Forgive us for the sin which we have committed before Thee with the word of the mouth?"

ANSWER:

This means the Sin we have committed by repenting only with
the word of our mouths, without true repentance in our hearts.

Said the SHeLaH HaKodosh: "He who confesses, but does so
without a contrite heart, will be severely punished," for this would
make it appear as if the one confessing were haughty and arrogant,
saying, "Who is master over me?"

394.   QUESTION:

Why do we not perform the Blessing of the New
Moon for the month of Tishrei?

ANSWER:

So that the Adversary not become aware of the exact date of
the Day of Judgment and be not ready with his "case" against
the people of Israel. This is alluded to in the sentence "Blow the
Shofar on the New Moon, at the appointed time, on the day of
our feast" (Psalms 81:4).

The Talmud (Rosh Hashanah 8b) explains that the term בכסה also means "concealed" or "hidden," implying that on Rosh Hashanah the moon is "hidden" to mislead the Adversary.

(*Levush, Ch.* 581)

395. QUESTION:

The Shofar is sounded throughout the month of Elul, except on the Eve of Rosh Hashanah. Why is it not sounded on that day?

ANSWER:

To stress the distinction between the blowing of the Shofar during the month of Elul which is "voluntary" and based on Rabbinical ruling, and that of Rosh Hashanah, which is "mandatory," having been specifically commanded in the Bible.

(*TaZ* 581:4)

396. QUESTION:

Why is the word le'ela (far above) repeated twice in the Kaddish recited during the Ten Days of Penitence?

ANSWER:

To stress His exalted place far above and beyond all the hymns and blessings uttered in the world, for during these Days of Awe, He is seated on His Judgment Seat, and all must praise Him and plead with Him for mercy.

(*Levush* 582:8)

397. QUESTION:

Why is the prayer "Remember us to life, O King who delightest in life...," inserted in the Shemonah Esrei for the Ten Days of Penitence immediately before the benediction lauding G-d as the "Shield of Abraham"?

ANSWER:

Because life wakens memories, and it is written of Abraham — "he *remembered* Thy Holy Word" (Psalms 105:42).

(Tur, Ch. 582)

398. QUESTION:

Why do we not refer to Rosh Hashanah and Yom Kippur as ..." appointed times for gladness, festivals and seasons for joy .." in the appropriate prayers, as we do to Passover, Shavuoth and Sukkoth?

ANSWER:

Rosh Hashanah and Yom Kippur are not termed festivals in the sense of the Hebrew term *Mo'ed,* which literally implies an "assembly."

On Passover, Shavuoth and Sukkoth, the entire people would come from all parts of the world to gather in Jerusalem, worship in the Temple and bring their offerings amidst great rejoicing. These assemblies were required only "three times a year," as it is written: "Three times in the year shall all thy males appear before the L-rd..." (Deut. 16:16-17).

Since these assemblies were not held on Rosh Hashanah and Yom Kippur, we do not use the sentence "Appointed times for gladness, etc." in our prayers on those days.

(Levush 582:8)

399. QUESTION:

Why is Rosh Hashanah called Yom HaZikkaron (Day of Remembrance)?

ANSWER:

All our prayers and supplications on this Day of Judgment, are fervent prayers that the L-rd, in remembering our merits and the merits of our fathers, may show us mercy in the year to come.

(Nachlath Yaakov)

Rosh Hashanah is called *Yom HaZikkaron* (Day of Remembrance) because it is the first day of the Ten Days of Penitence, and the only way to show penitence is by "remembering" that there is a G-d above.

(*MaHaRaN*)

400. QUESTION:

Why is it considered particularly meritorious to weep during Rosh Hashanah and Yom Kippur prayers?

ANSWER:

The *Vavei Ha-Amudim* writes: It is good to shed tears during prayers. One whose heart is obdurate and cannot shed a tear should at least pretend to be weeping, "for the L-rd hath heard the *voice of my weeping*" (Psalms 6:9).

The *Shulhan Arukh Ha-Ari* of blessed memory writes:

"The soul of him who does not weep on the Holy Days, is incomplete and imperfect."

401. QUESTION:

Why, during the Ten Days of Penitence, do we change the concluding words of the Eleventh Benediction of the Shemonah Esrei from "the King Who loves righteousness and judgment" to "the King of judgment"?

ANSWER:

Throughout the year, we conclude the Eleventh Benediction with the words, "the King who loves righteousness and judgment," to show that in His great loving-kindness, He transforms justice into mercy.

During the High Holy Days, however, we conclude this benediction with the words, "the King of judgment," for at this season He does not replace judgment with loving-kindness. Still, in His mercy, He gives man additional time in which to repent of his sins.

(Binyan Ariel)

402. QUESTION:

What special foods are eaten on the evenings of Rosh Hashanah and what is their significance?

ANSWERS:

1. *A slice of apple dipped in honey.*
To symbolize our hope for a "sweet year." The apple has Kabbalistic connotations.

(TaZ, Ch. 583)

2. *The head of a sheep.*
This symbolizes the *ram* which Abraham sacrificed in place of Isaac. It also symbolizes our hope for success and prosperity in the year to come, and we recite the words, "May it be Thy will that our position be that of the head and not that of the tail."

3. *Pomegranates.* To symbolize our resolve that our merits may become as numerous as the seeds of the pomegranate.

4. *Chick Peas.*
It was thought that the moonlight caused these to grow, and the moon is associated with the flow of water and hence with "merit and favor."

The Hebrew word for chick peas, *Kara,* implies that they are "cold" *(Kar)* on the inside. Accordingly, these vegetables are taken to symbolize the "cooling down" of G-d's stern judgment.

(Pinchas, Rebbe of Karetz)

5. It is customary not to eat nuts and almonds on Rosh Hashanah because the total numerical value of the letters in *egoz,* the Hebrew for "nut" corresponds to that of the letters in *het,* the Hebrew for "sin."

Besides, nuts and almonds stimulate an increased flow of saliva, which interferes with the recital of the prayers.

(Orakh Hayyim and TaZ, Ch. 583)

403. QUESTION:
Why do some people refrain from sleeping in the afternoon of Rosh Hashanah?

ANSWER:
Because of the statement in the Jerusalem Talmud that "one who sleeps at the beginning of the year dims his luck."

(*TaZ* 583:3)

404. QUESTION:
Why is Hallel not recited on Rosh Hashanah and Yom Kippur?

ANSWERS:
1. It is written in the Talmud: Rabbi Abahu said: The ministering angels said unto the Holy One, praised be He: "Sovereign of the Universe! Why does Israel not recite Hallel before Thee on the New Year and on the Day of Atonement?"

Thereupon G-d replied: "When the King is seated on the Throne of Divine Judgment and the books wherein life and death are inscribed lie open before Him — can Israel burst into song?"

(*Tur, Ch.* 584; *Rosh Hashanah* 32b; *Archin* 10b)

Says the Talmud: Rabbi Kruspedai quotes Rabbi Yohanan as follows:

"Three books are opened on New Year's Day: One for the perfectly righteous, one for the grossly wicked, and one for those who are neither all righteous nor all wicked.

The perfectly righteous are promptly inscribed and sealed for life. The wicked are promptly inscribed and sealed for death. As for the others, their verdict is left over from the New Year until the Day of Atonement. If they prove themselves worthy of it, they will be inscribed for life. If they prove unworthy, they will be inscribed for death."

(*Rosh Hashanah* 16b)

2. Hallel is a hymn of praise and joy, and it is not proper to be joyful before knowing what sentence has been passed.

(*Levush* 584:1)

405. QUESTION:

What is the origin of the Avinu Malkenu ("Our Father, our King...," which is recited during the Ten Days of Penitence?

ANSWER:

The Talmud relates that Rabbi Eliezer recited twenty-four benedictions so that the L-rd might cause rain to fall, but they were to no avail. Next, Rabbi Akiba stepped up to the reading desk and said: "*Avinu Malkeinu*, Our Father, our King! Thou art our Father. Our Father, our King! We have no King but Thee; Our Father, our King! We have sinned before Thee; Our Father, our King! Have mercy upon us; Our Father, our King! Deal kindly with us for the sake of Thy Name." And behold, his prayers were answered immediately.

(*Taanith* 25b)

These stirring pleas were eventually incorporated into the order of worship during the Ten Days of Penitence. In the course of the centuries that followed, other verses, all starting with "Our Father, our King" and beseeching G-d to grant us life and forgiveness, were added.

(*Kol Bo*)

406. QUESTION:

Why is Avinu Malkenu not recited on the Sabbath?

ANSWER:

Because it is forbidden to pray for the fulfillment of one's personal needs on the Holy Sabbath.

(*RaN* — *Rabbi Nissim Gerandi; last Chapter of Baba Bathra*)

407. QUESTION:

If a circumcision is to take place at the synagogue on Rosh Hashanah, it should be performed after the Reading of the Law, but before the Sounding of the Shofar, and not at the conclusion of the service, as is usually done on a Sabbath or other festival. Why?

ROSH HASHANAH CUSTOMS 227

ANSWER:

Because the circumcision should be performed before noon, and on Rosh Hashanah the services are quite long, often continuing until the early afternoon.

The circumcision should be performed before the Sounding of the Shofar, as it is appropriate to bring to mind the Covenant of Abraham before recalling the sacrifice of Isaac, symbolized by the Shofar (the horns of a ram, the animal which Abraham sacrificed instead of Isaac).

(*Levush* 584:4)

408. QUESTION:

Why is the Shofar not blown until just before the Musaph Service?

ANSWER:

By right, the Shofar should be Sounded during the Morning Service, because religious acts should be performed as early as possible. However, it happened one time in a certain place that the Shofar was Sounded early in the Morning Service, and the enemy heard it. Mistaking the blasts of the Shofar for a call to battle, the enemy's men rushed to the synagogue, fell upon the defenseless Jews at prayer there and massacred them.

Since that tragic incident, the Sounding of the Shofar was deferred until the Additional Service (Musaph). By that late hour, everyone might be expected to understand that the Jews have been praying all morning long, Reading from the Law, and praying again, and that the Sounding of the Shofar is just another part of the worship that has gone on all morning, and not a call to battle.

(*Levush* 585:3; see *Abudraham*; see *Rashi, Rosh Hashanah* 32b; *Ibid., Tosfoth, sub voce, Beshaath*)

409. QUESTION:

What is the origin of the custom to recite Psalm 47 seven times before the Sounding of the Shofar?

ANSWER:

The name of G-d is mentioned seven times in this Psalm and we repeat it seven times to bring to mind that He is about to judge us on this solemn day. The Shofar is then Sounded to proclaim His sovereignty and to evoke His mercy upon us on This Day of Judgment.

410. QUESTION:

In the case of all the other offerings listed in Numbers 28-29, it is written "Ye shall present an offering ..." Why, then, is it written concerning the Rosh Hashanah sacrifice, "And ye shall make a burnt-offering ..." (Ibid., 29:2)?

ANSWER:

When one truly repents on Rosh Hashanah, G-d considers it as if that person had just been created, quite literally, "newly-made" in the world. He is like a new-born infant without a blemish, and G-d gives him a new name.

One who truly repents of his past sins on Rosh Hashanah, literally makes of himself a burnt-offering, and receives complete forgiveness from G-d.

(Abudraham, quoting the Midrash)

411. QUESTION:

Why is the final blast of the Shofar called Tekiah Gedolah ("the Long Blast")?

ANSWER:

The final blast is a sustained note to impress the congregation with the fact that the *Tekioth* have ended and that they may now proceed to the rest of the service, as it is written, "When the ram's horn sounds long, they shall come up to the mount" (Ex. 19:13), i.e., the long sustained note is the *signal* that the revelation is at an end, and that the mountain has reverted to its ordinary character.

(MaHaRIL — Rabbi Jacob Molin)

412. QUESTION:
What do the Rabbis mean when they tell us that "since the days of the destruction of the Temple, all the gates of Heaven have been locked except the gate of tears?" (Berakhoth 32b; Baba Metzia 59a).

ANSWER:
All the gates of Heaven are guarded by angels, except the Gate of Tears, which has no one guarding it except G-d Himself, and He accepts the tears of men at all times?

(*Ahavath Jonathan*)

413. QUESTION:
What is the origin and significance of the practice on the first afternoon of Rosh Hashanah to go to a stream of water containing fish (Tashlich Ceremony)?

ANSWER:
To recall the sacrifice of Isaac. It is told in the Midrash that "when our father Abraham was on his way to sacrifice his son Isaac, the Adversary turned himself into a large brook of water in the road. Abraham and Isaac attempted to wade through the brook, but the further they went, the deeper the brook became, so that the water soon reached up to their necks. Realizing that the Adversary had done this to keep him from carrying out the command of G-d, Abraham cried out: "The L-rd rebuke thee, O Adversary. Terrified at the voice of Abraham, the Adversary fled and the place became dry land again as it was at first (so that Abraham and Isaac could proceed on their way to Mount Moriah)."

We should choose a body of water that contains fish, to remind us that we are like so many fish caught unawares in the net of judgment and justice. This awareness should impel us to sincere repentance.

(*Levush*)

Fish have no eyelids and so recall the ever-open-eye of the One Above, Who neither slumbers nor sleeps but keeps His eye at all times on His people Israel.

(*Machzeh Avraham*)

414. QUESTION:

What is the significance of the custom to shake the corners of our clothes after completing the Tashlich ceremony?

ANSWER:

By shaking the dust from our clothes we remind ourselves that we should also search our souls and shake from them every lingering trace of evil so they may become pure and free from sins.

415. QUESTION:

Why is it customary on the Second Night of Rosh Hashanah, to place a new fruit on the table or to put on a new garment before reciting that night's Kiddush?

ANSWER:

In order to have at least one valid reason for reciting the *Shehehe-yanu* benediction. While both days of Rosh Hashanah are considered as having the same degree of holiness, the authorities differ on whether *Sheheheyanu* should be recited again in the Kiddush on the Second Night, as it has already been recited in the Kiddush on the first night, and the two days are regarded as "one long day."

It is therefore best to place a new fruit on the table, or don a new garment on the second night prior to reciting the kiddush because new fruits or garments rate this benediction even if, in some opinions, the second night of Rosh Hashanah does not. But even if such articles should not be available, the *Sheheheyanu* must still be recited.

(*Rosh Hashanah* 30b; *TaZ* 600:2)

416. QUESTION:

Why was the month of Tishrei chosen as the Season of Divine Judgment?

ANSWER:

Because this is a month which gives us the occasion to perform a variety of religious acts, e.g. the Sounding of the Shofar, the observance of Yom Kippur, dwelling in the Sukkah and taking up the Four Plant Species.

(*Abudraham*)

417. QUESTION:

What do our Rabbis have to say concerning the true spirit of penitance?

ANSWERS:

1. The Rachmei Ha-Av quotes the famous Tzaddik, Rabbi Yehudah Tzevi of Razdil, who related the following story: One Sabbath, Rabbi Feibish of Dobritch visited Rabbi Menachem Mendel of Rimanov. When he bade his host farewell the next morning, he broke into loud sobs and said: "Behold, I am already seventy-four years old and I have not yet repented!" In reply, Rabbi Menachem Mendel, too, began to weep bitterly and whispered, "I am even as you are." And the two men blessed one another.

2. When a person wishes to repent, the first thing he must do is to part from his former wicked ways, and in future to keep away from all those things which bring man to sin.

He should then labor very diligently in the service of the L-rd, and try to make amends for his past transgressions. Just as in war a man cannot adequately attend to his wounds under a hail of bullets, but must remove himself from the battlefield to get a chance to bind up his wounds, so, too, it is with one who wishes to repent sincerely of his sins before he can atone for the sins he committed, he must remove himself from those paths which led him to sin in the first place.

Yom Kippur Customs

418. QUESTION:

Why is it customary Erev Yom Kippur to bake rounded Hallot shaped like wings?

ANSWER:

On Yom Kippur Day, the Israelites resemble the angels, of whom it is written that "each one had six wings" (Isaiah 6:2).

419. QUESTION:

Why are Psalm 20 and 100 not recited on the Eve of Yom Kippur?

ANSWER:

Psalm 20 is built around the verse "the L-rd answer thee in the day of trouble...," and Erev Yom Kippur is not a day of trouble.

According to tradition, Psalm 100, the Psalm of Thanksgiving, was sung whilst the thanksgiving offering was being sacrificed in the Temple. On the Eve of Yom Kippur, however, this offering was not brought (see below) and, accordingly, Psalm 100 was not recited. For this reason we today, also do not recite Psalm 100 on the Eve of the Day of Atonement.

The *Levush* explains: "When the Temple was in existence, the offering of Thanksgiving could not be sacrificed on the Eve of Yom Kippur because it would not be possible to perform the religious act in its entirety. The offering had to be eaten during the whole of that day *and* evening until midnight. The night being Yom Kippur, this part of the Commandment could not have been fulfilled."

(*Ch.* 604:2)

420. QUESTION:

Why is it a religious duty to eat a proper meal on the Eve of Yom Kippur before starting the fast?

ANSWER:

In order to feel the pain of fasting more intensely on Yom Kippur Day, for one finds it more difficult to fast *after* having been accustomed to eating.

(MaHaRIT — Rabbi Joseph Trani)

421. QUESTION:

Why is it customary Erev Yom Kippur to eat Kreplach (pancakes filled with meat) on the Eve of Yom Kippur?

ANSWER:

Meat symbolizes stern judgment, while the dough in which it is wrapped symbolizes the mercy with which we hope G-d's justice will be "coated."

(Zerah Kodesh)

422. QUESTION:

Why did the Rabbis rule that the Confession of Sins had to be recited during the Mincha services of the Eve of Yom Kippur?

ANSWER:

The Rabbis feared that people might become intoxicated at the final meal, which is eaten at home after the Mincha service, and that they would then be incapable of concentrating properly on the Confession.

They therefore ruled that, for good measure, the Confession should be recited in the Afternoon Service, before the final meal is eaten.

(See Yoma 87b; see Matte Ephraim 619:8)

423. QUESTION:

How should one recite his own private Confession of sins?

ANSWER:

The Midrash Rabbah (Vayikra Ch. 3), quotes the Jerusalem Talmud (end of Yoma) as follows:

Said Rabbi Bibi, the son of Abaye: "How should one confess on the Eve of Yom Kippur?" He should say: "I confess to Thee, O L-rd, that all the wicked deeds that I have committed before Thee, were committed when I was in an evil state of mind; all that which I have done, I shall never do again! May it be Thy Will, O L-rd, my G-d, to forgive me for all my transgressions; to pardon me for all my iniquities, and to grant me remission for all my sins, as it is written, "Let the wicked forsake his way, and the man of iniquity his thoughts; and let him return unto the L-rd, and He will have mercy upon him; and to our G-d for He will abundantly pardon" (Isaiah 55:6).

It is written in the Sefer Mussar: "Happy is the man who forsakes his wicked ways while he is still in the prime of life, and says, "Woe unto me, what have I done! I have rebelled against the King of Kings, the Holy One, Blessed be He! How came it that the fear of the L-rd was not before my eyes? I forgot that it was He who created me; He has lavished kindness and favors upon me to this very day; He endowed me with knowledge to understand, to learn, to teach, to heed, to fulfill the Words of His Laws in order that I might be found deserving of Life in the World To Come. But I have reversed all this, and have sinned with all the limbs of my body; every member of my body has become blemished and I have become defective because of my sinfulness; Where O where, will I hide my shame on the day when my father and mother, my relatives and friends will see me in my shame and will back away from me, and what will I do when my day of judgment will arrive!"

If man will speak thusly in the prime of his life, he will become truly contrite, and G-d will hear his lamentations and forgive him, for he will be sure to be careful not to sin again!

424. QUESTION:

Why is it forbidden to wear shoes made of leather on Yom Kippur?

ANSWERS:

1. As a sign of mourning. Mourners, too, are forbidden to wear leather shoes or leather slippers.

2. The author of *Agra DePirka* writes that shoes are put on in order that one's fllesh touch not the naked earth, for the earth was cursed because of the sin of man (Adam and Eve). Thus our shoes serve to separate our flesh from the accursed earth.

But when we tread on holy ground, we are bidden to remove our shoes, for that soil is not accursed and our feet should touch it. We learn this from Holy Writ, "as Moses was bidden to remove his shoes from off his feet, for the place whereon he was standing was holy ground" (Ex. 3:5).

On Yom Kippur, all the ground in the entire world is sanctified by the holiness of the day. Therefore, every place on earth being holy ground, we should not wear shoes at all on Yom Kippur.

425. QUESTION:

Why is it customary to wear white garments on Yom Kippur?

ANSWERS:

1. The white garments are to remind us that on Yom Kippur man resembles the angels.

2. The *Kittel* or shroud worn by the men is part of the garb in which they will be buried. This thought should make the heart contrite and lead man to repentance.

(*Levush* 610:4)

3. To recall "Though your sins be as scarlet, they shall be as white as snow" (Isaiah 1:18).

(*P'ri Hadash, Ch.* 581, *in the name of the MaHaRSHaL*)

The *Yismach Moshe,* Rabbi Moses Teitelbaum, writes that he would address his congregation before *Kol Nidrei* as follows:

"My brethren, Children of Israel! Take to heart the white clothes you are now wearing and mark them well. In these very same white clothes we will go to the world above one day to give an accounting before the Supreme King of Kings, the Holy One, Blessed be He! Let us imagine that we are standing before His Throne this minute, wearing our white shrouds... Let us therefore repent fully now — for once life is at an end, repentance will be of no avail. Let us resolve not to return to our sinful ways, and let us beg the forgiveness of Him Who pardons and forgives iniquities!"

426. QUESTION:
Why is it customary to spread grass or paper on the floor of the synagogue on Yom Kippur?

ANSWER:
On Yom Kippur Day, it is customary to prostrate oneself when reading the *Avodah,* the order of the Service in the Temple, and when one falls down on one's knees, there should be a separation between oneself and the bare earth.

(*Megillah* 22b)

427. QUESTION:
Why was the Tenth Day of Tishrei chosen by the Torah as the Day of Atonement for all generations?

ANSWER:
After the incident of the Golden Calf, Moses descended with the second set of Tablets of the Law. This was the tenth day of Tishrei. Moses found the people fasting and repenting of their great sin. G-d accepted their sincere penitence and proclaimed that day as a day of forgiveness and pardon for all generations to come.

428. QUESTION:
Why is the chanting of Kol Nidrei begun on the Eve of Yom Kippur while it is still day?

ANSWER:
Vows and oaths may not be annulled on Sabbaths or Festivals

unless their cancellation is begun before the Sabbath or holiday has
actually begun.

(Magen Avraham 619:5)

429. QUESTION:

What is the meaning of the formal declaration All
Dass HaMakom, "By the knowledge of the Almighty ..., we give permission to pray with those
who have transgressed ..." which is made before
the chanting of Kol Nidrei?

ANSWER:

It is written in the Talmud: "Any congregational fast in which
sinners do not take part, is not considered a fast" (Kerithuth 6b).

The mixture of perfumes which made up the incense used in
the Temple contained eleven different spices, balm, onycho, galbanum, frankincense, etc.... Among these eleven aromatic spices,
was galbanum, which was included in the mixture despite its un-
pleasant odor because without it, the mixture cannot be considered
incense.

So it was with the sinners in Israel. At first, the Jewish community, shocked by their behavior, ostracized them. But when Yom
Kippur, the Day of Forgiveness, came, the sinners felt a longing
to join their brethren in public worship. The religious authorities
were loth to repel them, and by this solemn declaration prior to
Kol Nidrei, permitted the transgressors to join the congregation in
prayer, for, as the Rabbis say, "A congregational fast which does
not include sinners is not considered a fast."

(Mateh Ephraim 619:10)

430. QUESTION:

According to the Talmud (Nedarim 23b), the nulli-
fication of vows should actually be performed on
Rosh Hashanah. Why, then, is Kol Nidrei not
chanted until Yom Kippur?

ANSWER:

Because Yom Kippur is the one day when all activity not directly linked with worship ceases, and nearly everyone is in the synagogue. Besides, Yom Kippur comes close on the heels of Rosh Hashanah and is, at times, designated by the term Rosh Hashanah (Lev. 23:27).

(Shulhan Arukh Ha-Rav)

431. QUESTION:

Why did the Rabbis rule that Kol Nidrei must be recited in Aramaic?

ANSWER:

When the Kol Nidrei was first introduced, the vernacular of the great Jewish communities was Aramaic. In view of the importance of the Kol Nidrei, the Rabbis ruled that it had to be recited in the language all Jews understood at the time.

(Levush 619:1)

432. QUESTION:

Why does the Cantor chant the Kol Nidrei in a particularly loud voice?

ANSWER:

To remind the congregation of the vows they have made during the year just past. With each repetition of the Kol Nidrei, the chanting grows louder, to give added emphasis to the solemn implications of vows and their cancellation.

(Ibid., Levush)

433. QUESTION:

Why does the Congregation recite the Kol Nidrei in an undertone together with the Cantor?

ANSWER:

In order to absolve the Cantor of his own vows and oaths, for he cannot nullify his own personal vows.

(Hagaoth Minhagim)

434. QUESTION:

Why is Kol Nidrei repeated three times?

ANSWER:

It is the form of Rabbinical language to repeat certain "key words" three times, e.g. *Magal zu, magal zu, magal zu* — "This sickle, this sickle, this sickle; this basket, this basket, this basket" (Menahot 65a).

In the Levirate (Halitzah) ceremony, too, the command to the woman "Remove the shoe" (from the foot of the brother-in-law) is repeated thrice, as is *Mutar lakh,* the declaration that the childless widow concerned is now free to remarry.

(*Maateh Moshe, Ch.* 864)

435. QUESTION:

What do the Rabbis have to say concerning the custom of some people to raise their voices when praying?

ANSWER:

The *Tur,* Rabbi Jacob ben Asher and the *Beth Yosef,* Rabbi Yosef Caro, the Codifiers of the Law, were concerned about the custom of farmers and those living in remote villages who would gather in the city on the Holy Days to pray with a large congregation and, unmindful of the other worshippers, raise their voices, giving free rein to their pent-up emotions...

The fact is that it is forbidden to raise one's voice when praying, because that may be distracting to the other worshippers.

The Kabbala and the Zohar (works of Jewish mysticism) were very stringent about this issue.

The Codifiers wrote: "It is permissible to raise one's voice a little on these Holy Days. However, it is best not to do so, but to pray quietly and with great devotion.

(*See Menachem Tzyion, by Rebbe Menachem Mendel of Rimanov*)

436. QUESTION:

Why do we not recite "...Accept our rest..." when Yom Kippur falls on a Sabbath?

ANSWER:

Since Yom Kippur is a day of fasting, on which we are bidden to "afflict ourselves," it can hardly be called a "day of rest."

(*Levush, Ch.* 619)

437. QUESTION:

Why are six people called up to the Reading of the Law on Yom Kippur when it falls on a weekday?

ANSWER:

On Yom Kippur Day we are forgiven the sins which we commit in our day-to-day life during the six days of the week.

If Yom Kippur falls on a Sabbath, seven people are called to the Reading of the Law, but never more then seven!

(*Mateh Ephrayim,* 619:3;
Magen Avraham 282:2)

438. QUESTION:

What portion of the Law is read on Yom Kippur and why?

ANSWER:

The Sixteenth Chapter of the Book of Leviticus, to remind us not to take lightly even those commandments which may seem trivial to us, for the sons of Aaron were severly punished for introducing strange fires into the Sanctuary, an act which certainly does not seem a great sin at first glance.

(שהרי אלו נענשו במצוה שאין בו כרת ולא מיתת ב"ד).

(*Kol Bo*)

Concerning the sons of Aaron, we read that "That day promised to be the happiest in Aaron's life, as he, the High Priest, was moving about in his magnificent robes, performing the solemn duties of his exalted office. Yet, within minutes, his two sons lay dead at his feet, for on the very day that the Sanctuary was being consecrated, they ventured to make changes in the essentials of the service according to a momentary whim.

Seeking to help the bereaved father understand why this had happened, Moses said to Aaron: "Through them that are nigh unto Me will I be sanctified" (Lev. 10:3).

In sharp contrast to the common view that highly-placed or gifted men are free to disregard the laws of morality, Judaism teaches that the greater a man's position or knowledge, the stricter is the standard by which he is to be judged, and the greater his consequent guilt and punishment if he should deviate from that standard, for, as the Rabbis put it, "With the righteous, G-d is exacting even to a hair's breadth," and it is G-d's wish that "before all the people may I be glorified" (Ibid). For when He is sanctified by those who are near to Him, the result will be that He will be glorified also by the people who look to the priests and scholars for inspiration and guidance."

(*Mateh Moshe, Ch.* 874)

439. QUESTION:

In the Avodah (the description of the Yom Kippur service in the Holy of Holies), we substitute HaShem or BaShem for the Tetragrammaton, the Ineffable Name which only the High Priest was permitted to pronounce. Why do we not read Adonai as we usually do for the Tetragrammaton when it occurs in the Prayer Book?

ANSWER:

On Yom Kippur, the High Priest, did not call out the Name of G-d as we do, viz. Adonai; but used the Ineffable Name of Four Letters, i.e. יהוה the Shem Ham'forash which we are forbidden to pronounce.

When the High Priest pronounced this Name of G-d during the Avodah on Yom Kippur, all those present would fall upon their faces and exclaim, "Blessed be His Name whose glorious kingdom is for ever and ever."

If we were to read *Adonai* in place of the Tetragrammaton, it would appear as if that was the designation by which the High Priest addressed the L-rd in the Temple on Yom Kippur. Hence we read *HaShem,* indicating that at this point in the Service, the High Priest used the *Shem Ham'forash* — the Ineffable Name which not even he was permitted to pronounce during the rest of the year.

(*Levush* 621:6)

440. QUESTION:

At Mincha services on Yom Kippur afternoon, three people are called to the Reading of the Law, and the portion read deals with forbidden marriages (Lev. Ch. 18). Why?

ANSWERS:

1) Just as the Holy One, Blessed be He, warned us not to "uncover the nakedness" of our next of kin, so do we intimate to G-d our hope that He will not expose our transgressions to their full extent.

(*Tosfoth, Megillah* 31a, *sub voce, BeMincha*)

2) Because a man's lust and desire for his blood relatives are strong... and these incestuous unions are strictly forbidden.

(*Ibid, Rashi; see TaZ* 622:4)

441. QUESTION:

Why is the concluding prayer of Yom Kippur called Neilah?

ANSWER:

The Hebrew word *Neilah* connotes closing. At this time, when Yom Kippur draws to a close, the gates of heaven, which were open all day to our prayers, are about to be closed also.

442. QUESTION:

"Hear O Israel, the L-rd our G-d, the L-rd is One," is recited at the conclusion of the Neilah service. Why is it recited only once?

ANSWER:

We recite the *Shema* to reaffirm our abiding faith in G-d. To recite it again might appear as if we were acknowledging belief in more than one Deity.

(See Berakhoth 33a)

443. QUESTION:

Why is the verse "Blessed be the Name of His Glorious Kingdom for ever and ever" (Baruch Shem) recited three times at the close of the Neilah service?

ANSWER:

To recall the three-fold declaration "The L-rd is King" (in the present), "the L-rd was King" (in the past) and "the L-rd shall be King" (in the future).

(Levush)

444. QUESTION:

Why is ד' הוא האלהים "The L-rd, He is G-d," repeated seven times?

ANSWER:

This declaration, "The L-rd, He is G-d," is to accompany the Divine Presence, the Shekhinah, as it returns from earth to the High Places above the Seven Heavens.

(Ba'er Hetev, 623:5)

445. QUESTION:

Why is the Shofar sounded after the conclusion of Neilah?

ANSWER:

1) It symbolizes the departure of the Divine Presence, as it is written, עלה אלהים בתרועה "G-d ascended with the sound of the Shofar" (Psalms 47:6).

(TaZ 623:2)

2)   To announce that it is now night, so that the children who have fasted may be given food and drink at once. Also, it is the signal to prepare for the conclusion of the Day of Atonement, which is considered a festival in its own right.

(*Tosfoth, Shabbath* 114b, *sub voce, Va-amai*)

It is for this same reason, too, that we greet each other with *Gut Yom Tov* at the end of Yom Kippur.

(*see P'ri Megaddim* 622:2)

3)   The Sounding of the Shofar after Neilah, commemorates the Sounding of the Shofar in the days of the Temple on the Day of Atonement in the Jubilee Year.

(*Kol Bo*)

4)   The Shofar symbolically acts as the advocate for the defense of Israel on Rosh Hashanah, when the L-rd moves from the Seat of Judgment to the Seat of Mercy. It defends Israel against their accusers, as it is written, "G-d is gone up with a shout; the L-rd, with the sound of a Shofar" (Psalm 47:6).

Now that Israel has been proven guiltless before the Tribunal on High, and their innocence has been attested to and sealed for the good, the Shofar, their defender, leaves the tribune with great rejoicing at having won the case, and he lets his voice be heard loud and clear with joy and happiness.

(*Shulhan Arukh Ha-Rav*)

446. QUESTION:

Why is the Sanctification of the New Moon (Kiddush HaL'vanah) performed on Yom Kippur night?

ANSWER:

Because Israel is in a particularly festive and joyous mood at the time, and hence in the most appropriate frame of mind for this ceremony.

(*ReMA*, 426:2)

447. QUESTION:
Why are spices (besamim) not used at the Havdalah service at the close of Yom Kippur?

ANSWER:

It was held that the Sabbath endowed man with an "additional soul" (neshama yethera), and that when this "additional soul" leaves us at the close of the Sabbath, the aroma of fragrant spices will tide us over this loss.

On Yom Kippur, however, we are not given an "additional soul," not even when Yom Kippur falls on a Sabbath, because this is a fast day. As a result, we do not need the spices for Havdalah.

(*Kol Bo*)

448. QUESTION:
Why is the day following Yom Kippur called in Yiddish tzu Gott's Nomen (in the Name of G-d)?

ANSWER:

To denote a change in the wording of a blessing in the Shemonah Esrei. During the Ten Days of Penitence, this blessing, which, throughout the year concludes with "the Holy *G-d*," ends with "the Holy *King*" instead, in keeping with the solemnity of that season. After Yom Kippur, we revert to the regular ending — "the Holy *G-d*." As a result, the day following Yom Kippur, has become known in Yiddish as *tzu Gott's Nomen*.

(*Geulath Yisrael*)

449. QUESTION:
Why are the Propitiatory Prayers (Tahanun) not recited on the days between Yom Kippur and Sukkoth?

ANSWERS:

1) These days are days of rejoicing, for it was then that King Solomon dedicated the Temple in Jerusalem.

(*Shulhan Arukh Ha-Rav*)

2) According to the *Seder Hayom,* Tahanun should not be said from Yom Kippur until the month of Heshvan. The reason is that the month of Tishrei contains most of our joyous holidays; namely, Rosh Hashanah, Yom Kippur, Sukkoth and Shemini Atzereth.

Sukkoth Customs

450. QUESTION:

Why do we not recite the Sheheheyanu blessing when we begin to build a Sukkah?

ANSWER:

Since in many cases, the Sukkah is not built by the person who will use it, the Sheheheyanu is recited only when he enters the Sukkah for the first time, on the first night of the festival when reciting the Kiddush.

(*Levush Ch.* 641)

451. QUESTION:

Why is it forbidden to cover the Sukkah with branches or reeds not detached from the soil or from their source?

ANSWER:

It is stated (Deut. 16:13):

חג הסוכות תעשה לך שבעת ימים באספך מגרנך ומיקבך

"Thou shalt keep the feast of Tabernacles seven days, after thou hast gathered in from thy theshing-floor and from thy winepress." The Gemara comments that the words, "from what thou hast gathered in from thy threshing-floor and from thy winepress" refers to "the spoils thereof." From this it is inferred that only those reeds or branches which have been "reaped" or severed from their soil or source may be used as covering (*S'chach*) for the Sukkah.

(*Levush, Ch.* 626)

452. QUESTION:

Why is it forbidden to use the Sukkah or any of its ornaments for any purpose unrelated to the holiday during the seven days of Sukkoth?

ANSWER:

The materials were set apart for use in the observance of a specific religious precept. It is therefore forbidden to take even a splinter of them to pick one's teeth, for it is written: ,חג הסוכות שבעת ימים לד' "the Feast of Tabernacles for seven days *unto the L-rd*" (Lev. 23:34).

(*Tractate Sukkah* 9a)

453. QUESTION:

Why do we refer to Sukkoth as Z'man Simhatenu — the Season of our Rejoicing?

ANSWER:

Since this festival marked the reaping of the fruits of the years toil, it was an occasion of great rejoicing. Forms of the Hebrew *simha* occur twice in the Bible in connection with Sukkoth, *Vesamakhta behagecha — vehayita akh sameakh* ("Thou shalt rejoice in thy festivals, and thou shalt be altogether joyful" — Deut. 16:14-15).

(*Levush, Ch.* 642)

454. QUESTION:

Why must the blessing over the Sukkah (leishev baSukkah), be pronounced not just when one enters the Sukkah for the first time, but every time one eats a meal there during the holiday, when the blessing over the Matza (al akhilath matza) on Passover is recited only on the Sedarim?

ANSWER:

While we are explicitly commanded to eat Matza only on the Seder, we are duty bound to eat in the Sukkah on each of the seven days of Sukkoth, so that each meal eaten in the Sukkah represents a separate religious act in its own right, to be properly prefaced by a blessing.

(Magen Avraham 639:17; *see Abudraham)*

455. QUESTION:

Why are women exempt from dwelling in the Sukkah during Sukkoth?

ANSWER:

Women have pressing duties in connection with the care of household and family with which the observance of such time-bound precepts might conflict. In order to have peace and happiness prevail in the home at all times, the Torah exempted women from observing positive commandments which must be observed at a definite time.

(Abudraham)

The "Four Species"

456. QUESTION:

What are the "Four Species" used on Sukkoth and what is their significance?

ANSWER:

The *Ethrog* (citron). Shaped like a heart, it symbolizes the hope of Divine forgiveness for the murmurings and desires of our hearts.

The *Hadas* (myrtle). Shaped like an eye, it symbolizes the hope of Divine forgiveness for greed and envy.

The *Arava* (willow). Shaped like a mouth, it symbolizes the hope of Divine forgiveness for idle talk and falsehoods.

The *Lulav* (palm branch). Having only one "heart," this plant symbolizes Israel's single hearted loyalty to G-d.

(Sefer HaManhig)

457. QUESTION:

In the case of the Ethrog, the Torah specifies that it must be beautiful (Cf. P'ri etz hadar — "And ye shall take the fruit of "goodly tree" — (Lev. 23:40). Why does the text not stress beauty also in connection with the other three plant species?

ANSWER:

The Rabbis tell us that because of its shape, the *Ethrog* is likened to the human heart. Since the heart is the most important organ of the body, prompting all of man's actions, G-d "desires" the heart of man.

For this reason the Torah explicitly stated that the *Ethrog* should be "goodly," i.e. beautiful and unblemished.

The other species are likened merely to the eyes and lips, which are subject to the control of the heart.

(*Zerah Kodesh, by the Rebbe of Ropshitz*)

458. QUESTION:

Why is the Lulav taken in the right hand and the Ethrog in the left?

ANSWER:

Because the Lulav consists of three plant species, while the Ethrog represents one.

(*Sukkah* 31b)

459. QUESTION:

Why may no other material than palm leaves be used as clasps and "pockets" to hold the Lulav together?

ANSWER:

Rabbi Judah maintains that the Lulav must be held together with palm leaves, for if another species were used for this purpose, the Lulav would consist not of three, but of four species. Added to the *Ethrog*, this would make five species instead of the required four.

(*Sukkah* 36b)

460. QUESTION:

Why does the blessing we pronounce over the Four Species refer only to the Lulav, (al netilat lulav) with no mention made of the Ethrog at all?

ANSWER:

Because the Lulav is the largest of all the species, so that all four species are considered part of the Lulav.

(*Sukkah* 37b)

461. QUESTION:

Why is the Lulav waved several times in the service?

ANSWER:

It is a gesture of triumph. Just as kings hoist their flags over territory they have won from their enemies, we wave our own standard to proclaim that we have been victorious over our accusers.

(*Abudraham*)

462. QUESTION:

Why is the Lulav waved during the recital of "Give thanks to the L-rd, for He is good, for His mercy endures forever: let Israel declare it that His mercy endures forever," and again at the refrain "O L-rd, help, we beseech Thee?"

ANSWERS:

1) This custom is based on Scriptural text: "Then shall the trees of the wood sing for joy..., O give thanks unto the L-rd, for He is good... And say ye: Save us, O G-d of our Salvation" (1 Chronicles, 16:33-35).

משום שנאמר : אז ירננו עצי היער ... וכתיב בתריה, הודו לד' כי טוב ...
ואמרו הושיענו — כלומר, ירננו בעצי היער כאשר יצאו מלפני ד' זכאין —
כשבא לשפוט את הארץ, ובמה ירננו — בהודו ובהושיעה נא.

(*Abudraham; see Tosfoth, Sukkah* 37b, *sub voce, Be-Hodu*)

2) To indicate that we must take some action on our own if we are to expect help from above.

(*Eshel Avraham, by the Gaon of Buczacz*)

463. QUESTION:
**Why do we not wave the Lulav when reciting "O
L-rd, cause us to prosper?"**

ANSWERS:
1) The symbolic purpose of the waving of the Four Species is
to drive away bad storms and fend off adversity. Accordingly, we
wave the Lulav only when reciting the passage "O L-rd save us"
from harm.

(*Abudraham*)

2) The two phrases are to be found in one Biblical passage
(Psalms 118:25) and we do not wave the Lulav twice during the
recital of one passage.

(*Ibid*)

464. QUESTION:
**What are the motions of shaking the Lulav and
what is their symbolic meaning?**

ANSWER:
The Lulav is shaken thrice each time to recall the "three roots
of intelligence," on which our three Patriarchs drew.

When the Lulav is moved up and down, care should be taken
to keep the Lulav in an upright position, pointing to the sky, just
as "the ladder was set up on the earth, and the top of it reached to
heaven" (Gen. 28:12).

(*Zerah Kodesh*)

465. QUESTION:
**What is the origin and symbolic significance of the
procession in which all the men in the congregation
who own a Lulav and Ethrog march around the
reading desk on each day of Sukkoth?**

ANSWERS:
1) This ceremony symbolizes our joy and happiness on the
festival of Sukkoth. On the first six days, only one circuit is made

around the reader's desk, but on the Seventh Day, Hoshanah Rabbah, seven circuits are made to recall the seven circuits made around the Altar in the Temple on that day.

(*Levush*, 660:2)

2) The seven circuits around the reading desk commemorates the seven circuits made by the Children of Israel around the walls of Jericho (Joshua, Ch. 6).

(*Mateh Moshe, Ch.* 962)

466. QUESTION:

Why is someone holding a Scroll of the Law stationed on the reader's desk during the circuits with the Lulav?

ANSWER:

The Scroll of the Law symbolizes the Altar in the Temple, which atoned for the sins of the congregation.

(*P'ri Megaddim*, 660:1)

467. QUESTION:

Why is it customary to remain awake the entire night of Hoshanah Rabbah **and to recite the Book of Psalms?**

ANSWER:

This is the night when King David is "the guest of honor" in our Sukkah. Since King David was accustomed to remain awake all night singing praises to G-d, we bestir ourselves and recall the virtue of David, with song and praises, by chanting the entire Book of Psalms.

(*Machzeh Avraham*)

468. QUESTION:

On Hoshanah Rabbah and Simhat Torah, all the Scrolls of the Law are removed from the Ark. What is the origin of the custom to place a lighted candle into the empty Ark?

ANSWER:

It alludes to the Scriptural Verse (Proverbs 6:23): "Light is a precept, and the Torah is light."

469. QUESTION:
Why are the "pockets and clasps" removed from the Lulav before it is shaken on Hoshanah Rabbah?

ANSWER:

The removal of the restraining clasps allows the Lulav to be shaken more freely, symbolizing unrestrained rejoicing.

(*Levush* 664:1)

470. QUESTION:
Why do we not pronounce a benediction over the 'arava, as we do over the Lulav?

ANSWER:

Because the *'aravot* ceremony is not based on Biblical law but is a custom handed down to us by the Prophets, and we do not pronounce a benediction when observing a custom.

(*Shulhan Arukh Ha-Rav*)

471. QUESTION:
Why are the aravot taken up on Hoshana Rabbah referred to as Hoshanoth?

ANSWER:

Because they are used and waved in the chanting of the Hoshanoth prayers.

(*Atereth Z'kenim, Ch.* 21)

472. QUESTION:
What is the significance of the ritual performed with the 'aravot (willows) on Hoshanah Rabbah?

ANSWER:

The willows, which grow near bodies of water, remind us to pray for the waters, which are subjected to Divine judgment on Hoshanah Rabbah.

(*Mateh Moshe, Ch. 962*)

473. QUESTION:

Why are the 'aravot (willows) beaten on the ground five times on Hoshanah Rabbah?

ANSWER:

To symbolize our hope that all evil will be ground into the dust so that it will exist no more.

(*Tolaath Yaakov*)

Shemini Atzereth Customs

474. QUESTION:

What is the meaning of Atzereth in the designation Shemini Atzereth?

ANSWER:

The literal meaning of *Atzereth* is "withholding." The Divine Spirit, the Shekhina, "withholds" Israel unto Himself for one more day in order that they may offer another sacrifice unto Him.

Our Rabbis also refer to the day the Law was given as *Atzereth*. We learn from this that the Eighth Day of this Festival of Sukkot is no less important than the Day on which we received the Torah.

(*Kad Ha-Kemach*)

475. QUESTION:

Why is the Sheheheyanu blessing recited on Shemini Atzereth when it is not recited on the last two days of Passover?

ANSWER:

The last day of Sukkoth, Shemini Atzereth, is a Festival in its own right. (Eating in the Sukkah is not obligatory, although commonly observed — Sukkah 47:1).

476. QUESTION:
Why is the Lulav not used on Shemini Atzereth?

ANSWER:

The use of the Lulav during the entire seven days of Sukkoth is in commemoration of the practice which prevailed in Jerusalem in the days of the Temple (Cf. "And ye shall rejoice *before the Lord* (i.e. in the Temple) seven days" (Lev. 23:40).

Those living outside the Temple area were commanded to take the Lulav on the first day only (Cf. "And ye shall take for yourselves *on the first day..."* Ibid).

Since we therefore are not duty-bound to use the Lulav for the entire seven days, we are also not required to use it on the eighth day.

(*Abudraham*)

477. QUESTION:
During the winter season, certain prayers for dew and rain are inserted into the Eighteen Benedictions. What is the basis of the Rabbinical ruling that the phrase "Who causest the winds to blow and the rains to fall" is recited from the last day of Sukkoth on, while the words "dew and rain" are not added until the seventh day of Marheshvan in Israel and even later in the Diaspora?

ANSWER:

Because the "rainy season" begins in Israel immediately after Sukkoth, but the heavy rains do not come until sometime in December, and we want these changes to come no sooner than in their proper season.

(*Kol Bo*)

Simhath Torah Customs

478. QUESTION:

Why is this Festival called Simhath Torah (Rejoicing of the Law)?

ANSWER:

Because of the festivities and rejoicing which attend the completion of the Pentateuchal cycle.

(*Levush Ch. 669*)

479. QUESTION:

Why do we immediately resume the Pentateuchal cycle with the reading of the first chapter of Genesis as soon as we have completed the last part of Deuteronomy?

ANSWER:

To give the lie to the claims of our accusers that once we have completed the Torah we have no intention of reading it again.

(*Ibid*)

480. QUESTION:

What is the origin of the custom of having the congregation join aloud in the recital of the refrain for each day of Creation ("And it was evening and it was morning...") when the first chapter of Genesis is read on Simhat Torah?

ANSWER:

It is the congregation's way of bearing witness to the fundamental truth that G-d created the Universe.

Thus the mood of gladness which prevailed throughout the

Sukkoth, culminates in triumphant rejoicing over the Torah, Israel's inalienable heritage.

(*Bikoreth Ha-Talmud*)

481. QUESTION:

It is customary for the Hatan Torah (the person called upon to read the final paragraphs of Deuteronomy) and the Hatan B'reshith (the person called upon to read the first verses of the Book of Genesis), to hold a reception on the occasion of Simhat Torah. What it the origin of this custom?

ANSWER:

It is written in the Midrash: "And he (Solomon) came to Jerusalem and stood before the Ark of the Covenant and offered up burnt-offerings and peace-offerings, and made a feast for all his servants" (1 Kings, 3:15). To this Rabbi Eliezer comments: "We refer from this that a feast should be given in honor of the completion of the Pentateuchal cycle."

(*Midrash Shir HaShirim, Ch. 1*)

482. QUESTION:

When the Scroll of the Law is lifted up on Simhat Torah, it is customary for the Baal Hagba (the person called upon to perform this act) to "criscross" the Scroll. Why?

ANSWER:

To symbolize the adage: "Turn the Torah, and turn it over again, for everything may be found in it" (Ethics of the Fathers, 5:25).

(*Eshel Avraham, by the Gaon of Buczacz, Ch. 665*)

483. QUESTIONS

Why is the month of Heshvan also referred to as Mar-Heshvan, particularly in the Blessing of the New Moon for that month?

ANSWER:

Ever since the days of the flood, the decree has gone forth from Above, that rains and water should fall during these forty days (beginning with the month of Heshvan).

This month is therefore called MAR-Heshvan, for the Hebrew word *mar* denotes "drops" (as in *mar m-d'li* — "drops from a bucket").

(*Midrash Tanhuma*)

Hanukkah Customs

484. QUESTION:

Why do we celebrate Hanukkah?

ANSWER:

When the Hasmoneans overcame the Syrians and repaired the Temple, they found there only one flask of oil bearing the seal of the High Priest. It contained oil for only one day but a miracle happened and the oil burned for eight days. Next year an eight-day festival was declared by the Rabbis, to be celebrated with songs of praise and thanksgiving, for all times.

(*Sabbath* 21b)

485. QUESTION:

Why is the story of Hanukkah not mentioned at all in the Mishnah?

ANSWER:

Rabbi Judah the Prince, the compiler of the Mishnah, was a descendant of King David. The miracle of Hanukkah, on the other hand, came about through the heroism of the Hasmonean dynasty which was not of Davidic lineage.

Judah, displeased with what seemed like an usurpation of the throne of David, appears to have ignored the achievement of the "rival" dynasty.

(*Hatham Sofer*)

486. QUESTION:
Although the kindling of the Hanukkah lights is a positive commandment depending on a fixed time from which women ordinarily are exempt, it is incumbent on women to see the Hanukkah lights kindled. Why?

ANSWER:
Because of the brave Judith, daughter of the High Priest Johanan, whose courage delivered her community from death. Judith lived in Bethulia. The city was besieged by a large army commanded by Holofernes. When the food began to give out, the people lost all hope of saving their lives. Judith was a beautiful woman, and she decided to risk her own life in a bold attempt to rescue her people. Stealing out of the city, she somehow managed to obtain an interview with Holofernes. He was so charmed with her beauty that he suspected nothing. She entertained him, gave him *cheese* cakes to eat and plenty of wine. When he became drunk, she decapitated him, and brought the head back in a sack. Their commander dead, the enemy lost courage and fled before the Jews. Thus Judith delivered the city.

(*Kol Bo*)

487. QUESTION:
Why is it customary for women not to do any work while the Hanukkah lights are burning?

ANSWER:
To make sure that the Hanukkah lights will not be used for a purpose other than the commemoration of the miracle of Hanukkah. It could happen, for instance, that the lights in the house go out, and if work happens to be going on at the time, the Hanukkah lights

will be put to unlawful use. Women should be more scrupulous about this than their menfolk, as the deliverance of the Jews came about in part through the valor of a woman.

(Mateh Moshe, Ch. 994)

488. QUESTION:

Why are we forbidden to make use of the Hanukkah lights?

ANSWER:

In order that all should know that this light is part of a religious observance. In this way, added emphasis is placed on the miracle which Hanukkah commemorates.

(Levush, 673:2)

489. QUESTION:

On Saturday nights, the Hanukkah lights are kindled in the synagogue prior to Havdalah, but at home the Havdalah ceremony is first and the Hanukkah lights are kindled only thereafter. Why?

ANSWER:

At home, Havdalah is recited first, because, worshipping without a congregation, we are worried lest we might have forgotten to recite the Havdalah blessing of *(Ata honantanu)* in the Shemonah Esrei. In that case, we would actually be kindling the Hanukkah lights on the Sabbath, an act of forbidden work, unless we had first performed the Havdalah ceremony with candle and spices.

(see Ba'er Hetev, Ch. 681)

490. QUESTION:

Why is the full Hallel recited on the eight days of Hanukkah and not just on the first day or the first few days, as is done on, say, Passover?

ANSWER:

Each day of Hanukkah is considered a new festival in its own right, since each day we kindle one more light than we kindled on the previous night. Also the Sacrifices in the Temple varied each day.

(*Abudraham; see Archin* 10ab)

491. QUESTION:

What Biblical portion is read during Hanukkah and why?

ANSWER:

Chapter Seven of the Book of Numbers. The account of the offerings made by the tribal chieftains of the Children of Israel, when the Tabernacle was set up in the wilderness. According to tradition, the Tabernacle was completed on the 25th day of Kislev, the day on which, many centuries later, the Maccabeas rededicated th Temple in Jerusalem.

(*Levush*, 684.1)

492. QUESTION:

Why did the Rabbis institute the custom of kindling the Hanukkah lights not only in the home but also in the synagogue?

ANSWERS:

1) For the same reason that the Friday night Kiddush is recited in the synagogue; namely, for the benefit of transients who ate and slept in the synagogue.

(*Levush*, 671:8)

The reason the custom is still followed today is the same as in the case of the Friday night Kiddush — to enable the ignorant to hear the blessings recited correctly and so to learn to recite the prayers properly themselves.

(*Kol Bo*)

2) Because the original miracle of the cruse of oil occurred in

the Temple and the synagogue today is considered a "Temple in miniature."

(*Atzereth Z'Kenim, Ch. 673*)

493. QUESTION:

Why is the time for kindling the Hanukkah lights in the synagogue set between Mincha and Maariv?

ANSWER:

Because that is the time when the new day enters in, as the Maariv service is already part of the new day.

(*Levush*, 671:8)

One saying his prayers at home should also kindle the Menorah before reciting Maariv.

(*Magen Avraham*, 672:5)

494. QUESTION:

Why do we not observe Hanukkah for nine days, as we do the eight-day of Sukkoth — Simhath Torah Season?

ANSWER:

Because Hanukkah, unlike Sukkoth, is not a Biblical holiday but one instituted by the Rabbis, who fixed the calendar so that we are no longer dependent on determining the dates of festivals by eyewitness reports of the New Moon.

(*Abudraham*)

SOME SCRIPTURAL READINGS 263

Four Important Scriptural Readings

495. QUESTION:

What are the "Four Scriptural Portions" and what is their significance?

ANSWER:

Three of these Four Scriptural Portions — Parshath Shekalim, Parshath Parah Aduma and Parshath Ha-Hodesh commemorate the Temple.

Parshath Shekalim (Exodus 30:11-16) deals with the half-shekel contribution to the Sanctuary. The Haftarah read on Shabbath Shekalim is 2 Kings XI, 17-XII, 17, an account of the gifts made for the repairs of the Temple during the reign of King Josiah.

Every Israelite was to send in his contribution before the first day of Nissan, the beginning of the Jewish year. On the first of Adar, the last month of the year, proclamations would be made throughout the country that the half-shekel was due. Hence, the Biblical passages relating to the Shekel contribution are read on the Sabbath before the First of Adar.

Parshath *Parah Aduma* (Numbers 19:1-22) deals with the laws concerning the sacrifice of the Red heifer, whose ashes were used to purify the Children of Israel. The Haftarah read on Shabbath Para Aduma (Ezekiel 36:16-38) describes the future purification of the Jewish people.

No one who was unclean could offer the Passover sacrifice; hence, an unclean person had to undergo the purification rite sometime before Passover. Accordingly, the pertinent Scriptural portions are read on the Sabbath following Purim, to remind us to take stock of ourselves and to celebrate Passover in the proper spirit.

Parshath HaHodesh (Exodus 12:1-20) is read on the Sabbath preceding the first of Nissan. According to tradition, Exodus 12:2 not only states the designation of Nissan as the first month of the year, but also implies the rules for determining the New Moon, or the First of the Month. This verse was therefore considered the basis of the Jewish Calendar.

The Haftarah read on Shabbath HaHodesh (Ezekiel 45,16-46,18) describes the sacrifices to be offered on the first of Nissan, Passover and other Festivals in the Temple of the future.

The above three Scriptural portions all serve to remind us of the time-honored customs observed in the Temple.

Parshath Zachor (Deut. 25,17-19) commemorates an event from Israel's journey through the wilderness — the attack perpetrated on the Children of Israel by the Amalekites. The Haftarah read on Shabbath Zachor (1 Samuel 15,1-34) tells of the defeat of the Kingdom of Amalek by King Saul several centuries later. These Scriptural portions are read on the Sabbath preceding Purim, because Haman is believed to have been descended from Amalekites.

(*see Abudraham*)

Purim Customs

496.　QUESTION:

Why did Queen Esther set the duration of her fast at three days?

ANSWER:

G-d does not permit the pious to be in distress for more than three days. Cf. the story of Rahab: "And hide yourselves there three days" (Joshua 2:16), and the story of Jonah, "And Jonah was in the belly of the fish three days" (Jonah 2:1).

It is also written concerning the future Day of Redemption, "After two days will He revive us, on the third day, He will raise us up" (Hosea 6:2).

(*Kad HaKemach*)

497. QUESTION:
Why do we observe only one day as the Fast of Esther?

ANSWER:
Because a three-day fast is considered an undue hardship nowadays.

(*Levush* 686:3)

498. QUESTION:
When is the Fast of Esther observed if Purim falls on a Sunday?

ANSWER:
Obviously, the fast cannot be observed on the Sabbath. If it were to be observed on Friday, we would be unable to prepare the Sabbath-food properly since we would not be able to taste from it during its preparation. The fast is therefore observed on the Thursday preceding Purim.

(*Levush* 686:2)

499. QUESTION:
What is the origin and significance of donating three half-dollars for charity before Purim?

ANSWER:
To commemorate the half-shekel the Jews donated in the month of Adar for the purchase of the Public Offerings in the days of the Temple.

We donate three half-shekels today because the word *T'rumah* (Offering) is mentioned three times in the pertinent Biblical portion (Ex. 30:11-16).

(*ReMa* 694:1)

The author of Ahavath Shalom writes: The moral lesson taught by the half-shekel tax is that one Jew by himself is only half a Jew. It is only when he joins with his brother that he becomes a complete individual.

Another reason for the Half-Shekel contribution made on Purim is that it is supposed to atone for the crime committed by the ten sons of Jacob, who sold their brother Joseph into slavery for a profit of one half-shekel each.

By donating this amount to the poor, we are symbolically atoning for their crime by re-purchasing our poor brothers from the slavery of poverty and hunger.

(*Maasei Rokeach; see ReMa* 694:1)

500. QUESTION:

Why is it customary today to make these donations not on Rosh Hodesh Adar but only just before the reading of the Megillah?

ANSWER:

This is considered the most suitable time for making the collection because the entire congregation is then assembled in the synagogue.

Some authorities hold that the donation should be made earlier, that is, before the Mincha service.

(*ReMa* 694:1)

501. QUESTION:

Men and women alike are obligated to hear the Book of Esther read. Why must this reading be performed by a man?

ANSWER:

Because the public reading of the Book of Esther is a religious act like the Reading of the Law which may only be performed by a man.

(*Baer Hetev* 675:3)

502. QUESTION:

What is the origin of the custom to have the entire congregation join with the reader in reading aloud Chapter 2 Verse 5 ("There was a certain Jew in

Shushan the castle, whose name was Mordecai..."); Chapter 8 Verse 15 ("And Mordecai went forth from the presence of the king in royal apparel..."); Chapter 8 Verse 16 ("...the Jews had gladness and joy...") and Chapter 10 Verse 3 ("For Mordecai the Jew was next unto king Ahasuerus...")?

ANSWER:

These high points in the narrative are read aloud by the entire congregation to keep the attention of the audience, and to increase the element of excitement. particularly among the children in the congregation.

The verses chosen for this purpose all relate to Mordecai, whose steadfastness helped bring the miracle of Purim to pass.

(*Abudraham*)

503. QUESTION:

Why is it customary to pound on the benches, to stamp on the floor, or to use noisemakers each time the name of Haman is mentioned in the reading of the Megillah?

ANSWER:

To "drown out" the name of Haman to show that his name should be wiped out for ever, as it is written, "thou shalt blot out the remembrance of Amalek from under heaven, thou shalt not forget" (Deut. 25:19). (Haman was descended from Amalekites).

(*ReMa* 690:17)

504. QUESTION:

Why is the Name of G-d not mentioned one single time in the entire Book of Esther?

ANSWER:

Because the story was originally set down in the chronicles of the Persians and the Medes in their vernacular which did not mention the name of the G-d of the Jews. As a consequence, the name of G-d was omitted also in the later, (Hebrew) version as recorded in the Book of Esther.

(*TdZ*, 334:11)

When the MaHaRIL, Rabbi Jacob Molin, was asked why the name of G-d is not mentioned in the Megillah, the MaHaRIL replied that this omission was made deliberately by way of precaution. Had the Hebrew text mentioned the name of G-d, the (later) version in the Chronicles of Persia and Media would have translated it with the name of their own supreme being.

505. QUESTION:

Why is Hallel not chanted on Purim?

ANSWERS:

1) Because the reading of the Megillah itself is a form of praise for the miracle of Purim.

(*Archin* 10b)

2) Hallel is never chanted on occasions commemorating a miracle that took place outside the Land of Israel.

(*Ibid*)

506. QUESTION:

Why are circumcision ceremonies held on Purim morning performed prior to the reading of the Megillah?

ANSWER:

The Reading of the Megillah contains the verse "The Jews had light and gladness and joy..." (8:16). Accordingly. we want the infant initiated into the ranks of the Jewish people by the time this verse is read so that he, too, may be eligible to have a portion in that joy.

(*Darke Moshe*, 693:4)

507. QUESTION:

Why do we make a point of partaking of strong drink on Purim?

ANSWER:

Although the Torah warns us to be exceedingly careful not to indulge excessively in strong drink (as in the stories of Noah and Lot), the Rabbis permit slight intoxication on Purim because wine recalls the miracle that happened at the time.

Vashti, the first wife of King Ahasuerus, was dethroned on account of the banquet which was given by the king. Cf. "On the seventh day, when the heart of the king was merry with wine, he commanded... to bring Vashti the queen before the king... but she refused to come... and the king was very wroth, and his anger burned in him" (1:10-12). Thus, a decision made by the King in a state of intoxication paved the way for the elevation of Esther, the Jewish maiden, to the throne where, in her position of power, she was able to avert the disaster that threatened her people.

The downfall of Haman also came about as the result of strong drink, as it is written, "And the king said to Esther at the banquet of wine" (5:6). This banquet led to another one, at which, finally, Haman's evil intentions were exposed.

(*Abudraham*)

508. QUESTION:

What is the origin of the custom to don masks and costumes on Purim?

ANSWER:

The following story is told in the Talmud: "The disciples of Rabbi Shimon ben Yohai asked their master: 'By what sins had the Israelites incurred the decree of Haman [to kill all the Jews]?'

"How would you explain it?" the master asked in reply.

"Because the Israelites also participated in the feast arranged by Ahasuerus, the pagan king," the disciples suggested.

"If this were so," the master countered, "only those who lived in Shushan, the capital, and partook of this feast should have suffered.

Why, then, did the Jews in the provinces have to suffer as well? It must be because they knelt before the idol that stood in the king's banquet hall."

"In that case they were actually guilty of a grave sin. Why, then, were they saved from destruction?" the students queried.

"They bowed to the image not because they wanted to sin, but only for appearances' sake," their master explained. "As a result, the Holy One, blessed be He, also decreed their destruction only for appearances' sake, to frighten them into repentance. He actually had no intention of destroying them" (see Megillah 12a).

It is to commemorate the 'pretend' character of G-d's evil decree that we today change our outward appearance on Purim by putting on masks and disguises."

(B'nei Yisashar)

509. QUESTION:

What is the connotation of the name Esther?

ANSWER:

In Hebrew, Esther (אסתר) connotes 'concealing' (סתר). Queen Esther concealed her identity, nationality and faith from Ahasuerus and his court until the time was ripe for Haman's exposure.

(Megillah 13a; *Midrash Rabba Esther)*

510. QUESTION:

In leap years, why is the observance of Purim deferred to the month of Adar 2?

ANSWER:

In order to have the celebration of our deliverance from the hands of Haman fall as close as possible to Passover, the season when we commemorate our deliverance from Egyptian slavery.

(MaHaRIL, Rabbi Jacob Molin)

Circumcision

511. QUESTION:
A feast is held on the first Friday night after the birth of a male child. It is called in Hebrew Shalom Zakhor "Peace to the Male [Infant]." Why?

ANSWERS:

1) It is written in the Talmud: "Rav, Shmuel and Rav Assi passed by a house where a baby had been born, and because the baby had come through the birth safe and unharmed, a feast was made" (Tosfoth, Baba Kamma 80a, sub voce, Lebei).

2) The reason the feast is held on the first Friday night is that everyone is at home that night. It is known as *Shalom Zakhor* "Peace to the Male [Infant]" because the Sabbath is called "Shalom" — "Peace."

512. QUESTION:
Why are a great number of candles lit on the day of a Circumcision?

ANSWERS:

1) It is written: "The Jews had *light,* gladness and joy" (Esther 8:16). "Joy" refers to circumcision, as it is written, "I rejoice at Thy pronouncements" (Psalms 119:162). [This would include the commandment pertaining to circumcision]. Therefore, many lights should be lit when a circumcision takes place.

(*Yaavetz*)

2) At various times, decrees were issued prohibiting the circumcision of Jewish children. In order to obtain the necessary quorum of witnesses without making a public announcement, candles would be lit and placed on the window-sills so that passers-by would know that circumcision was about to take place, and come in to witness the ceremony.

(*Shibalei Ha-Lekett*)

513. QUESTION:

Why is it established custom that the knife used by the Mohel must be sharpened on both sides?

ANSWER:

To eliminate the chance that the Mohel may erroneously use the dull side and thereby endanger the life of the child.

(Derekh Pikudekha)

 514. QUESTION:

Why is it customary to set aside a chair for the Prophet Elijah at every circumcision?

ANSWER:

Elijah is the personification of absolute faith. The prophet of redemption symbolizes implicit trust in the ultimate triumph of truth over falsehood. His zeal for G-d, his devotion to His precepts, and his insistence on the spiritual and ethical values of monotheism have raised him up as the embodiment of the true Torah spirit.

When the King of Israel, under the influence of Jezebel, abolished circumcision in the Northern Kingdom, Elijah, grieved and angered, retired to a cave, and complained to G-d that Israel had forsaken the Covenant of the L-rd (1 Kings 19:10:14).

As a consequence, G-d ordered him to be present at each circumcision, so that he might witness Israel's loyalty.

A throne reserved especially for Elijah is prepared at every circumcision so that he may have a seat befitting his position while witnessing the ceremony.

(Abudraham)

The Agra D'Pirka quotes Rabbi Shlomo Karlin, who cited the Midrash as follows: When the Holy One, blessed be He, told Elijah that he would have to be present at each and every circumcision, Elijah said: "Behold, O G-d, Thou art well aware that I am filled with zeal for Thy Name. Now if the father of the infant should happen to be a sinner, I may not be able to tolerate him and remain in his presence."

The L-rd thereupon promised Elijah that, in such cases, He would cancel the fathers' guilt on his account.

Next, Elijah asked: "But what if the Mohel should happen to be a sinner?" G-d thereupon promised to cancel the Mohel's guilt also, if need be.

Finally, Elijah asked: "But what if the assembled guests should be sinners?" "Then," G-d reassured him, "I will cancel the guilt of the entire assembly."

The Rabbi of Karlin commented: There is an allusion to this in the Torah. The Rabbis say: "Phineas is [identified with] Elijah" (Baba Metzia 114b). Phineas was filled with zeal for His G-d and made atonement for all the Children of Israel (Num. 25:13). Like Phineas, Elijah is a prophet of storm, fire and righteous zeal. Since Elijah would now be present at every circumcision and, being no less zealous than Phineas, would be unable to tolerate sinners present at the rite, G-d will be compelled to cancel the guilt of all those attending the circumcision, just as He forgave Israel in the days of Phineas!

It is customary for everyone present at the circumcision to rise when the infant is brought into the room to be circumcised, and remain standing during the circumcision to honor Elijah the Prophet, who is symbolically present.

(*Or Tzaddikim*)

515. QUESTION:

Why is the Sheheheyanu **blessing not recited at a circumcision?**

ANSWER:

This is not entirely a pleasant occasion calling for *Sheheheyanu*, because it entails considerable pain and distress for the infant.

(*Shibalei HaLekett*)

516. QUESTION:

Why does the father pronounce the blessing, ... "Who hast hallowed us by Thy commandments

and hast commanded us to enter him into the covenant of Abraham our father" only after the circumcision has taken place?

The usual procedure is to recite the blessing before the religious act is performed.

ANSWER:

This blessing is different from blessings recited in connection with the performance of a religious act. It is intended as the father's prayer of praise and thanksgiving to G-d for having given him a son and for having found him worthy to enter the infant into the Covenant of Abraham.

(*Abudraham*)

517. QUESTION:

Why is the infant's foreskin placed into ashes or dust after its removal?

ANSWER:

To commemorate an act performed by Joshua when the Israelites first entered Canaan. G-d said to Joshua: "Do you not know that the Children of Israel are not circumcised properly?" Thereupon Joshua had them circumcised again. Cf. "And Joshua made for himself knives of flint, and circumcised the [male] Children of Israel at Gibeath ha-araloth" (Joshua 5:3).

The name Gibeath ha-araloth means "Hill of Foreskins." It seems that Joshua gathered together all the foreskins of the Israelites to form a mound or hill, which he then covered with earth.

(*Pirke Rabbi Eliezer*)

518. QUESTION:

Why is the verse "O give thanks unto the L-rd, for He is good, for His lovingkindness endures forever" (Psalm 107:1) recited at the circumcision ceremony?

ANSWER:

This Psalm enumerates the four principal reasons for offering thanks to the L-rd; namely, recovery from illness, release from prison, the safe completion of a sea voyage and a safe completion of a journey through the wilderness.

At the circumcision ceremony we give thanks for the recovery of the mother, and for the "release" of the infant from the "prison" in which he lay for nine months.

(*MaHaRIL, Rabbi Jacob Molin*)

519. QUESTION:

Why is it customary to send gifts to a newly-circumcised infant?

ANSWER:

Because Abraham, the first Jew to be circumcised, also received a gift in honor of the occasion. G-d gave him and his descendants title to the Land of Israel (Gen. 17:7-8).

(*Yaavetz*)

520. QUESTION:

Why is it customary to have a feast (s'udah) on the day of circumcision?

ANSWER:

It is written (Ex. 18:12): "...And Aaron came, and all the elders of Israel, to eat bread with Moses' father-in-law (Jethro) *before G-d.*" The phrase "before G-d" is taken to indicate that Jethro became a proselyte. He circumcised himself and made a great feast in honor of the occasion.

(*Midrash Talpiyoth*)

521. QUESTION:

What is the origin of the custom to have the K'vater (the person who brings the infant to the circumcision room) send to the circumcision feast (s'udah) **one Challah** (K'vater koilitch **or** S'udah Challah) **and one cake, called Reshikteh?**

ANSWER:

This is done to make sure everyone present would take part in the feast. The very pious would not eat food prepared in the house where a woman had given birth, because this rendered the woman and her home temporarily impure. Accordingly, the *K'vater* sent food prepared on the outside, which even the most stringent observers would be willing to eat.

(*Rebbe Sholom Kaminker*)

522. QUESTION:

Why do the pious make donations to charity whenever they are given the honor to perform a religious act (e.g. an 'aliya in the synagogue or a function in a circumcision)?

ANSWER:

It is proper that we donate money's to charity when carrying out a precept of G-d, to show that the *mitzvoth* are very dear and precious to us and not, Heaven forbid, a burden, and that we should consider ourselves greatly honored when the honor to carry them out is conferred upon us.

(*Agra dePirka*)

523. QUESTION:

Why is it customary to honor a bridegroom or a father of a new-born son with an 'aliya in the synagogue?

ANSWER:

Because taking a wife and initiating a newborn son into the Covenant of Abraham, both are Divine commandments specified in the Torah. The Rabbis say that it was for the sake of the Torah and the rite of circumcision that the world was created, and that marriage and the rearing of a family are man's one true joy in life.

(*Pachad Yitzchak*)

524. QUESTION:
What is the origin of the custom to give the name of Atler (or Alte in case of a female child) to infants in families where children have died at an early age?

ANSWER:
Alter (or *Alte*) is derived from the Judeo-German *alt*, meaning "old." The name thus implies the wish that the infant may live to a ripe old age.

Pidyon HaBen

525. QUESTION:
Why has the amount to be given to the Kohanite for the redemption of the firstborn son been set at five dollars?

ANSWER:
When the Levites were taken into Temple service in place of the firstborn, the firstborn were found to number 273 more than the Levites. This excess of firstborn Israelites therefore had to be redeemed at five shekels apiece (Numbers 3:44-51).

(*Yaavetz*)

526. QUESTION:
Why does the Kohanite go through the formality of asking the infant's father: "Which wouldst thou rather: give me thy firstborn son . . . or redeem him for five dollars?"

This statement would intimate that the father has, indeed, a choice in the matter, when, according to Rabbi Moses Isserles, "the father who desires to give the baby to the Kohen to save himself the five dollars has not really fulfilled the duty of redeeming his firstborn" (ReMa 305:10).

ANSWER:

The Kohanite goes through this formality to stress to the father the importance of the precept of Pidyon Ha-Ben.

(Piskhei T'shuvah, 305:12)

Marriage and Divorce

527. QUESTION:

Why is it customary to write the words "May He who predestines . . . **" in the pre-betrothal agreement (Tenaim)?**

ANSWER:

According to Jewish tradition, marriages are decided upon in heaven before either of the partners is born. The Rabbis said: "Forty days before the creation of a child, a voice is heard, from Heaven, saying: "The daughter of So-and-So shall marry the son of Such-and-Such" (Sotah 2a).

(Zera Kodesh)

528. QUESTION:

What is the origin of the custom that the bridegroom should be escorted to the synagogue on the Sabbath before the wedding and called up to the Torah, and again on the following Sabbath after his wedding?

ANSWER:

When Solomon built the Temple, he realized how great the virtue of loving-kindness was in the eyes of G-d. He therefore built two special gates for the Temple, one for bridegrooms and one for mourners . . .

Every Sabbath the Israelites would go and sit between these two gates, and whenever a man would pass through the "Gate of the

Bridegrooms" they would greet him with the words, "May He who dwells in this abode cause you to rejoice with sons and daughters..."

When the Temple was destroyed, the Rabbis encouraged the members of each concregation to practice loving-kindness by giving special honor to the bridegrooms in their midst.

(*Pirke de-Rabbi Eliezer*)

529. QUESTION:

What is the origin of the custom in certain localities of pelting the bridegroom with walnuts, almonds and dried fruits when he ascends the altar to read the Torah on the Sabbath before his wedding?

ANSWER:

It symbolizes the hope that the marriage about to be made should produce offspring as quickly as the almond tree produces its fruit.

530. QUESTION:

Why does the bridegroom fast on his wedding day?

ANSWERS:

1) So that all his transgressions should be forgiven. Besides, if we were to allow him to eat and drink as he pleases on his wedding day, he might become too intoxicated to go through the wedding ceremony in the proper spirit.

(*Magen Avraham, Ch.* 573)

2) The bridegroom fasts until after the Wedding Benedictions have been recited because the wedding is a religious act. Just as the pious are accustomed not to eat before they have carried out religious precepts like blessing the *Lulav* on Sukkoth or hearing the Shofar sounded on Rosh Hashanah, so the bridegroom fasts until after the wedding ceremony.

(*Rokeach*)

531. QUESTION:

If the wedding falls on Rosh Hodesh, the groom need not to fast, except if the day is Rosh Hodesh Nissan. Why must he fast in that case?

ANSWER:

It was on Rosh Hodesh Nissan that the sons of Aaron were consumed by fire. It is therefore proper for the bridegroom to fast on this day [to call to his mind the tragic consequences of unrestrained passion].

(*ReMa, Ch.* 573)

532. QUESTION:

Why is it customary for the bride, on the wedding day, to send to her bridegroom a tallith complete with tzitzith?

ANSWER:

This is in accordance with the writings of the Ari, of blessed memory, who states that "the *mitzvah* of tzitzith is a very important one, for the sight of them tends to strenghten a man in his resolve to keep his marriage vows."

(*Or HaMeir*)

533. QUESTION:

What is the origin and significance of the custom to cover the bride with a veil before she steps under the marriage canopy?

ANSWER:

To recall Rebecca's gesture of modesty when she first saw her future husband. (Cf. "And she took her veil and covered herself") (Gen. 24:65).

(*MaHaRIL, Rabbi Jacob Molin*)

It is custom for the Rabbi and the notables of the community to step up to the bride and to cover her with the veil, saying,

"Our sister! be thou the mother of thousands of myriads," as the family of Rebecca did when they sent her to Canaan to marry Isaac. [The actual covering may be done either by the Rabbi or by the bridegroom himself].

534. QUESTION:
Why are the bride and bridegroom blessed by their parents, and by the officiating Rabbi, before the ceremony?

ANSWER:
Cf. "And G-d blessed them" (Adam and Eve; Gen. 1:28).
(*Shulhan Arukh Ha-Rav, Ch.* 91)

535. QUESTION:
Why is it customary for the bridegroom to put on his Kittel (shrouds) for the marriage ceremony?

ANSWERS:
1) To make the bridegroom repent of his sins by reminding him in his hour of great happiness that he is nothing but a mere mortal.
(*Kol Bo*)

2) To symbolize the tradition that all the sins of the bride and groom are forgiven on their wedding day. Cf. "Though your sins be as scarlet, they shall be as white as snow" (Isaiah 1:18).
(*Mateh Moshe*)

536. QUESTION:
Why is it customary to have two persons, one on each side, escort the bridegroom to the marriage canopy?

ANSWER:
Cf. Genesis Rabbah, Ch. 7: "Michael and Gabriel acted as groomsmen for Adam; they led him to Eve." Also, since the bridal

couple are compared to a king and queen it is fitting that they have entourages.

(Ibid)

537. QUESTION:

Why is it customary for those escorting the bride to the marriage canopy (her parents or those two persons who act as Unterfuhrer, and in some cases also her female friends) to hold lighted candles or torches?

ANSWERS:

1) This recalls the day of the Giving of the Torah. Cf. "And all the people perceived the thunderings and the lightnings..." (Ex. 20:15).

Remember: All the customs associated with bride and groom on their wedding day are derived from the Giving of the Law when Israel was the Bride and G-d Himself was the Bridegroom.

(Tashbetz)

2) The numerical value of *ner* (light) taken twice (each *Unterfuhrer* holding one candle) is equal to that of the Hebrew for "Be fruitful and multiply." The candles held by the two persons escorting the bride thus symbolize the wish that the bride may bear many children.

(Mateh Moshe)

538. QUESTION:

Why is it customary for the bride to walk around the groom three times, in some localities it is seven times, when she joins him under the marriage canopy?

ANSWERS:

1) To imply the brides acceptance of the bridegroom as the "center of her universe."

2) To symbolize the aura of light in which marriage envelops a man.

(Karban Ani)

539. QUESTION:

Why is the presence of ten adult males required at the marriage ceremony?

ANSWER:

In the account of the marriage between Ruth and Boaz (Ruth 4:2 ff), we read that Boaz summoned ten men to witness his declaration that he was going to marry Ruth.

(Kethuboth 7b)

540. QUESTION:

Why is it customary in some localities to place a Tallith over the heads of the bridal couple as they stand under the marriage canopy?

ANSWER:

This is an allusion to Ruth 3:9, where Ruth asks her kinsman Boaz to "spread therefore thy skirt over thy handmaid." The Tallith symbolizes the robe worn by Boaz.

(Kol Bo)

541. QUESTION:

What is the purpose and significance of the marriage canopy?

ANSWER:

The marriage canopy symbolizes the home to which the bridegroom will take his bride and where she will become his wife. It should be woven from fine yarn and it should be an expensive-looking ceremonial object.

(Tolaath Yaakov)

542. QUESTION:

Why is it customary in many communities to have the marriage canopy put up out of doors or, if the ceremony is held indoors, to place the canopy under an open skylight?

ANSWER:

This is to involve the blessing of G-d on the couple so that they will be privileged to rear a large family. Cf. "Thus shall thy children be, like the stars of heaven" (Gen. 15:5).

(*K'nesseth Hagdolah*, 61:2)

543. QUESTION:

Why is the bridal canopy also referred to as Hillulah?

ANSWER:

Because the bride and groom are led to the canopy amidst rejoicing. *Hillulah* is the Hebrew word for praise.

(*Kol Bo*)

544. QUESTION:

Why do men not wear a Tallith until after they are married?

ANSWERS:

1) The man dons the Tallith for the first time only after his marriage to intimate that before his marriage, he lacked the aura of light that marriage imparts, but that now he has tken a wife, he is worthy of having 'this aura envelop him.'

(*Kithve Ha-Ari*)

2) In accordance with the following Midrash: "Why is the Biblical verse dealing with the ritual fringes ("Thou shalt make for thyself twisted cords..." Deut. 22:12) immediately followed by a verse referring to marriage ("If any man take a wife..." Deut. 22:13)?

"To teach us that man must not wear a Tallith (with ritual fringes) until he has taken a wife."

(*HaManhig*)

545. QUESTION:
Why must the wedding ring be a plain gold band, without precious stones?

ANSWER:
Because the precious stones might mislead the bride with regard to the actual value of the ring. A ring accepted under a mistaken impression would invalidate the legal "sanctification" for which the ring was intended, so that the bride under the circumstances really would not be legally married.

(*Abudraham; see Tosfoth Kiddushin* 9a, *sub voce, Vehilchetha*)

546. QUESTION:
Why is the wedding ring placed on the forefinger of the bride's right hand?

ANSWER:
It is placed on the index finger that points easily — so that she can readily display it for the two witnesses to see, as legal evidence of matrimony. The bridegroom then declares: "Behold thou art consecrated to me with this ring, according to the Law of Moses and of Israel."

547. QUESTION:
Why does the bridegroom break a glass at the end of the wedding ceremony?

ANSWERS:
1) To call to mind the incompleteness of all rejoicing as long as the Temple in Jerusalem remains in ruins.

2) It is written: "Serve the L-rd with fear, and rejoice with trembling" (Psalm 2:11). Rejoicing should always be tempered with awe and "trembling."

(Rokeach)

548. QUESTION:

Why would it not be considered proper at the end of the ceremony to break the cup over which the "Betrothal Blessings" were recited under the marriage canopy?

ANSWER:

The blessings recited with that cup consummates the marriage. To break it, therefore, would be an unlucky omen, implying a "breakup" of the marriage.

(Hupath Chassanim)

549. QUESTION:

Why is it customary in some localities to pelt the bride with leaves and small greenery as she leaves the marriage canopy?

ANSWER:

To symbolize the hope that she will bear many children and live to a ripe old age.

(Abudraham)

550. QUESTION:

What is the origin of the custom to pelt the bridal couple with wheat as they leave the marriage canopy?

ANSWERS:

1) According to Abudraham, this is to symbolize the wish that peace may reign supreme between them throughout their lives, as it is written, "He makes peace in thy borders; He satisfies thee with the *full-ripe wheat*" (Psalm 147:14).

2) To symbolize the hope that they may be fruitful and multiply like wheat.

(*Rokeach*)

551. QUESTION:
Why were the gifts presented to the newlyweds formerly known as d'rasha geshenk?

ANSWER:
Because they were given in recognition of the *d'rasha* (learned discourse) delivered by the bridegroom at the wedding dinner.

552. QUESTION:
Why, then, were the gifts always given to the bride and not to the groom?

ANSWERS:
1) To show that the bride would be the mistress of the home who, by her thrift and wise management of the home, would make it possible for her husband to go on giving his time to the study of the Law and delivering learned discourses such as the one he had held at the wedding.

2) Because this is the only way the bridal couple could be given money gifts. The bridegroom was forbidden to accept cash gifts for his learned discourse.

553. QUESTION:
Why is a prayer beginning with "Banish, O L-rd, both grief and wrath ...," recited before Grace at the wedding dinner?

ANSWER:
To bring to mind, even at the wedding feast, the destruction of the Temple in Jerusalem. The terms *devai* and *haron*, "grief" and "wrath" used in this prayer occur in the Book of Lamentations, which mourns the fall of the Temple.

(*Mateh Yehudah*)

554. QUESTION:

What is the significance of the words "in Whose abode is joy" recited before the Grace at the wedding dinner?

ANSWER:

To recall that the first to perform the *mitzvah* of making the bride and groom rejoice at their wedding was G-d Himself, for as legend tells us, "G-d Himself was "HOST" at the wedding of Adam and Eve; the angels were singing and dancing before Him."

(*Abudraham*)

555. QUESTION:

Why are the first seven days after the wedding known as "the seven days of banqueting"?

ANSWER:

The custom to continue the nuptial festivities throughout the first week after the wedding is based on statements found in the Bible.

When Jacob found himself married to Leah, his uncle Laban promised to give him Rachel in marriage, a week later, saying, "Fulfill the week of this one" (Gen. 29:27).

Samson said at his wedding, "Let me now put forth a riddle unto you; if you can declare it me within the seven days of the feast..." (Judges 14:12).

(*Yalkut Shoftim, Ch. 70*)

556. QUESTION:

Why is the Jewish bill of divorcement known as a get?

ANSWER:

It is written in the Jerusalem Talmud: "The bill of divorcement it called *get* after *gito,* a rock in one of the sea-ports that rebuffs everything that comes near it. "Get," then, implies "repulsion or severance."

(*Shiltei HaGibborim*)

557. QUESTION:
Why is the text of the Get written out in twelve lines (previously ruled out on the paper)?

ANSWER:
Because the total numerical value of the Hebrew letters in the word *Get* (גט) is twelve.

(*Levush, Laws of Divorce*, 125:11)

Visiting the Sick

558. QUESTION:
What is the significance of the term Bikur Holim (literally, "to examine the sick") commonly used in Hebrew for "visiting the sick" instead of some form of r'iya or halicha ("seeing" or "going to")?

ANSWER:
The connotation of *bikur* is that when we go to visit the sick we should gently suggest to the patient that he "examine" his past conduct and ask for forgiveness so that he may be healed.

(*Maaver Yaabok*)

559. QUESTION:
What prayer should be recited by one who is dangerously ill?

ANSWER:
"I confess before Thee, O L-rd, my G-d and the G-d of my fathers, that my healing and my death are in Thy hand.

May it be Thy will to heal me completely, but if I should die, may my death atone for all sins, wrongs and rebellious acts which I have committed before Thee. O L-rd, grant me a share in Paradise, and favor me with a portion in the World to Come which is set aside for the righteous, Amen."

(*Kol Bo*)

560. QUESTION:
Why is it forbidden to leave a patient alone once it is obvious that he is dying?

ANSWER:
At the time of death, the soul of man feels desolate and alone. Someone should therefore be present so that the soul will not be alone when it departs from the body.

(Kol Bo)

Mourning Customs

561. QUESTION:
What is the origin of the custom to pour out into the street the water contained in vessels standing near a person who has just died?

ANSWERS:
1. In order to announce the death to the neighborhood without having to spread the bad tidings by word of mouth.

(Kol Bo)

2. According to legend, the well of water which accompanied the Children of Israel through the wilderness, had been provided by G-d in recognition of the merits of Miriam, the sister of Moses. When she died, the well dried up, as it is written: "And there was no water for the congregation" (Numbers 20:1-2).

By pouring out the water that had been close to the dead person, we imply that the deceased had virtues which would make him deserving of the same honor that was done Miriam at the time of her death.

(TaSHBeTZ — Rabbi Simeon ben Zemach Duran)

562. QUESTION:
Why should the dead not be left alone?

ANSWER:

The body is guarded to prevent animals or insects touching it and in the event any sign of life appears someone should be on hand to give immediate aid. So great is the duty of guarding the body that unless the watchman is relieved by another, he is exempted from reading the *Shema* and all other religious duties.

(*Berakhoth* 18a)

563. QUESTION:

Why should the eyes of the deceased be closed?

ANSWER:

So that his eyes not behold anything else after having beheld the Divine Countenance at the moment of death.

If there is a son, it is the duty of the son to close the eyes of his father gently, as it is written of Jacob "And Joseph shall put his hand upon thy eyes" (Genesis 46:4).

If soil from the Land of Israel is available, the son should place some of it on the eyes of his dead father.

(*Maaver Yaabok*)

564. QUESTION:

Why is the dead person removed from the bed on which he died and placed directly on the ground or on a floor covered with straw?

ANSWER:

The ground, unlike a bed or table, does not become defiled by contact with the dead body.

(*Maaver Yaabok*)

A black cloth is used to cover the body of the deceased and a lighted candle placed at the head. The position of the body should be with the feet toward the exit of the room.

(*Maaver Yaabok*)

565. QUESTION:

Why is it customary to cover the face of the dead
with a sheet?

ANSWERS:

1. It is considered disrespectful to the dead to permit others to
see the ravages of death on his face.

2. Formerly, only the faces of the poor were covered, since they
had become discolored from malnutrition and the family felt ashamed
to have others see him so. In order to erase the distinction between
rich and poor in death, the Rabbis ordained that the faces of all the
dead — rich and poor alike — should be covered.

(*Mo'ed Katan* 27a)

566. QUESTION:

Why should burial take place as soon as possible
after death, preferably even on the same day?

ANSWER:

Death, Judaism teaches, atones for the sins of man. Therefore,
the body should at the earliest moment be laid to rest. Cf. "His
body shall not remain all night — but thou shalt in any wise bury
him on that day" (Deut. 21:23).

(*Zohar*)

567. QUESTION:

What is the reason for the Tahara, the Ritual
Purification of the body?

ANSWER:

When the soul departs from the body, it beholds the Divine
Countenance. It is therefore proper to cleanse and wash the body
thoroughly before it faces its Maker after it is interred. This
custom is of great antiquity.

(*TaSHBeTZ*)

568. QUESTION:

Why should linen threads be used in the sewing of the shrouds?

ANSWER:

Flax — the plant from which linen is derived, grows during the season of the early rains and is symbolic of the Tree of Life.

(*Maaver Yaabok*)

569. QUESTION:

What are the customs pertinent to K'riah, the "rending of garments" symbolic of mourning?

ANSWER:

The *K'riah* is performed on the left side of the garment for a dead parent, and on the right side for all other close relatives.

The mourner must perform the *K'riah* standing. Cf. "Then Job stood and rent his mantle" (Job 1:20). [This implies that the mourner must be able to "stand up" to the blow he has sustained].

(*Mo'ed Katan* 20b)

The rent in the garment must be one hand's breadth long. This ruling is based on (II Samuel 1:11), "Then David *took hold* on his clothes and rent them." One cannot very well "take hold" of anything less than one's hand's breadth in size.

(*Daath Zekenim*)

570. QUESTION:

What is the significance of the custom to pluck out some grass with the soil on its roots and to wash one's hands on leaving the cemetery?

ANSWERS:

1. The plucking of the grass is an allusion to the Resurrection of the Dead, as it is written, "And they of the city shall flourish *like the grass of the earth*" (Isaiah 26:19).

(*Abudraham*)

2. To symbolize the purification of one who became unclean through contact with a dead body, whose purification was by means of *water,* the ashes of the *red heifer and hyssop* (Numbers 19).

(Kol Bo)

3. It is also proper not to dry one's hands in a towel, as this would imply that one intends to "wash one's hands" completely of the dead.

It is also customary to pour out the water from the utensil in which the hands were washed.

(Maaver Yaabok)

571. QUESTION:

It is customary for neighbors to prepare the first meal to be eaten by the mourners after returning home from the funeral. Why?

ANSWERS:

1. The mourners may refuse to eat because they may feel that they, too, want to die. It is the duty of the neighbors to see that the mourners do not harm themselves by not eating.

(Chachmath Adam)

2. The Levush writes that by supplying the first meal, "the neighbors imply to the mourners that they need not worry about anything, as their needs will be taken care of."

The meal should consist of eggs and lentils. This food is symbolic of the roundness of the world and of mourning which comes to all.

(Kol Bo)

572. QUESTION:

What prohibitions apply to mourners during shiva **(the seven days of mourning), and why?**

ANSWERS:

1. They must not wear leather footgear (see Number 424).

2. They must not engage in marital intercourse. This prohibition is derived from II Samuel 12:24, "And David *comforted* Bath-Sheba,

his wife, and went in unto her," which is taken to imply that he had not been allowed to do so during his week of mourning (for his son).

(*Mo'ed Katan* 15b, 21a)

3. They must not study the Torah, for the study of Torah makes for pleasure and rejoicing, as it is written: "The precepts of the L-rd are right, rejoicing the heart" (Psalms 19:9).

(*Mo'ed Katan* 15a)

573. QUESTION:

What is the origin of the custom to keep a candle or lamp burning in the house of mourning during the seven days of shiva?

ANSWER:

It is said that the soul of the departed, derives some joy and comfort from this glowing light, "as the soul of man is the lamp of the L-rd" (Proverbs 20:27).

A candle or lamp in memory of the departed should be burning in the Synagogue throughout the first twelve months.

(*Maaver Yaabok*)

574. QUESTION:

Why is it customary to hold daily services in the house of mourning throughout the seven days of Shiva?

ANSWER:

It is told that the soul mourns over the loss of his body and comes to seek it in the place where it died. Listening to the prayers of the assembly in his own home, affords great pleasure and some compensation to the soul of the departed.

(*Shibalei Ha-Lekett*)

575. QUESTION:

Why is the Priestly Benediction recited in the Shemonah Esre, not recited during services at the house of a mourner?

ANSWER:

Because the Priestly Benediction concludes with the words "And give thee peace" (shalom), and it is forbidden to extend greetings ("shalom") to mourners.

(*Mo'ed Katan* 21b)

576. QUESTION:

Why is Tahanun not recited at daily services in the house of mourning?

ANSWER:

These penitential prayers contain the words: "I have sinned, etc." They seem inappropriate at this time since the mourner is already being chastised for his sins.

(*Levush* 131:4)

577. QUESTION:

What is the source of the prohibition against trimming one's hair while in mourning?

ANSWER:

It is deduced from the Biblical injunction to the Priests "Let not the hair of your heads go loose" (Lev. 10:6). This was taken to imply that the Priests were explicitly permitted to cut their hair even when in mourning. From this it was inferred that no non-Kohanite was permitted to trim his hair while in mourning.

(*Mo'ed Katan* 14ab)

578. QUESTION:

What is the source of the prohibition against engaging in work during the first seven days of mourning?

ANSWER:

It is deduced from Amos 8:10, "I shall turn your feasts into mourning." This is taken to imply that just as work is forbidden on a Festival, so, too, it is forbidden during the period of mourning.

(*Mo'ed Katan* 15ab; 21a)

579. QUESTION:

Why are mourners forbidden to bathe during the first seven days of mourning?

ANSWER:

The prohibition is derived from II Samuel 14:2: "And Joab sent to Tekoa and fetched thence a wise woman and said unto her, I pray thee, feign thyself to be a mourner... and anoint not thyself with oil." The "anointing" is taken to be part of the bath.

(*Mo'ed Katan* 15b)

580. QUESTION:

Why are mourners forbidden to greet others during the first seven days of mourning?

ANSWER:

This prohibition is derived from Ezekiel 24:17, where G-d said to Ezekiel, "Sigh in silence." This is interpreted to mean that the mourner should not break his silence to extend greetings to anyone.

(*Ibid.*)

581. QUESTION:

What is the significance of the Kaddish recited by mourners each day for eleven months after the death of the deceased?

ANSWER:

The Kaddish is an ancient doxological prayer composed in Aramaic (Berakhoth 3a). To it is ascribed the power of redeeming the departed soul from any suffering and the efficacy of invalidating an evil decree (Yore Deah 376:4).

By this prayer of praise to G-d, the mourner acknowledges submission to G-d's judgment and the acceptance of His justice (Sabbath 119).

The *Kaddish* recited by the children is an expression of loyalty by the mourners to the heritage of Judaism; it is regarded as a proof of the ethical life of the deceased, as remembered by affectionate survivors.

582. QUESTION:
   ## Why is Kaddish recited not throughout the year of mourning but only for eleven months?

ANSWER:

Tradition has it that the souls of the wicked are subject to judgment for twelve months. The practice of reciting Kaddish for only eleven months implies that the children do not regard their departed parent as wicked and in need of prayer.

(ReMa 376:4)

583. QUESTION:
   ## Why is the Kaddish recited in Aramaic rather than in Hebrew?

ANSWERS:

1. At one time the Gentile authorities decreed that the Kaddish should not be recited. The Rabbis therefore ruled that the Kaddish should be recited in Aramaic so that the Gentiles should not recognize it. Even after the decree was abrogated, the Rabbis retained the Aramaic version of the Kaddish, to commemorate the abolition of the evil decree passed by our foes.

(Eliyahu Rabba 56:5)

2. Originally, Kaddish was recited after the rabbi had concluded his sermon or learned discourse. Out of consideration for the many who did not understand Hebrew, the Rabbis ruled that the Kaddish

should be recited in Aramaic, the vernacular, which was understood by all.

(*Tosfoth Berakhoth* 3a, *sub voce, ve-onin*)

584. QUESTION:
Why are the first two words of the Kaddish: Yisgadal ve-Yiskadash ("Magnified and sanctified"), recited in Hebrew?

ANSWER:
Let it not be difficult in your eyes to understand why the Rabbis had [these words] recited in Hebrew. It was well nigh impossible to translate these words of extravagant praise adequately into Aramaic.

(*Abudraham*)

585. QUESTION:
Why is the Kaddish called Kaddish Derabbanan (Kaddish of the Teachers)?

ANSWERS:
1. The Kaddish contains a prayer for the welfare of our teachers, Rabbis and their disciples.

(*Eliyahu Rabba* 155:1)

2. Because it was recited after the learned Talmudic discourse which contains the teachings of the Rabbis.

(*Ibid.*)

586. QUESTION:
Why was the period of intense mourning set for seven days?

ANSWERS:
1. It is written: "I shall turn your feasts into mourning" (Amos 8:10). The feast of Sukkoth is celebrated for seven days; accordingly, mourning, should last seven days also.

(*Mo'ed Katan* 20a; *see Tosfoth, sub voce, Mah Hag*)

2. It is written in Pirkei D'Rabbi Eliezer: We derive the seven days of mourning from the story of Joseph. Cf. "And he made a mourning for his father for seven days" (Gen. 50:10).

587. QUESTION:

Why is Hallel not recited during services at the house of a mourner?

ANSWERS:

1. One of the Hallel Psalms (Ps. 115) contains the verse, "the dead do not praise the L-rd." Reciting this verse at the home of the mourner would be regarded as a mockery of the dead.

(TaZ 376:2)

2. Another verse reads: "This is the day which the L-rd hath made; we will be glad and rejoice thereon." This would not be appropriate in a house of mourning.

(Piskhei Teshuva)

However, Hallel may be recited during services at a house of mourning, if the mourners leave the room while the Hallel is being chanted.

588. QUESTION:

If the funeral takes place on the eve of a Festival and the mourners have observed a minimum of one hour's mourning, the Festival cancels the entire Shiva (seven days of mourning). Why?

ANSWER:

Because it is written in the Torah (Deut. 16:14): "And thou shalt rejoice in thy feast." This positive commandment enjoining the entire people of Israel to rejoice in their festivals, overrides the positive precept commanding individuals to mourn over their dead.

(Levush 399:1)

589. QUESTION:

Why must mourners sit on the ground or on low stools during Shiva?

ANSWER:

This is derived from the account of Job's mourning (Job 2:13): "So they sat down with him upon the ground."

(*Jerusalem Talmud*)

590. QUESTION:

Why is it customary not to offer words of comfort to the mourners until the third day of the Shiva?

ANSWER:

The first three days of mourning weigh very heavily upon the mourners, for the face of their dead is still very clear in their memories so that it almost seems to them as if he were still alive. It was, therefore, too early for them to comprehend and accept words of comfort.

(*Midrash Rabba Vayikra, Ch.* 18)

The modern practice of offering words of comfort to the family almost as soon as death has occurred is not in keeping with traditional Jewish custom.

591. QUESTION:

Why is a minor (any male child aged below thirteen years and one day, and any girl below the age of twelve) exempt from Shiva?

ANSWER:

An important reason for Shiva is to make the mourners bestir themselves, and repent all their past sins. This does not apply to a minor, since he does not become responsible for his actions until he reaches the age of thirteen years and one day (in the case of girls, the age of twelve).

(*Taanith* 13b, *Line* 1; *see Tur, Ch.* 394, *quoting Maimonides*)

[However], we do have minors perform *K'riah* (rending of garments) because he is expected to feel distress at his loss.

(*Beth Hillel, Ch.* 381)

592. QUESTION:

Shiva is followed by twenty-three days of less intensive mourning, making thirty days (Sh'loshim) in all. What is the derivation of this custom?

ANSWER:

The Bible relates that "the Children of Israel lamented after Moses thirty days" (Deut. 34:8).

593. QUESTION:

Why is it customary to visit the cemetery on Fast days?

ANSWER:

The pious dead buried there make the cemetery a holy place, and prayers recited on holy ground are considered particularly favored on High.

However, it should always be remembered that prayers recited on the cemetery are not addressed to the dead who are lying there, but to the L-rd, that He may show mercy to the living for the sake of the merits of the pious dead.

(*MaHaRIL — Rabbi Jacob Molin*)

594. QUESTION:

Why is it customary in times of personal distress, to visit the graves of one's dead and pray for help and guidance?

ANSWER:

We visit the cemetery to put us in a mood of repentance, and to ask the souls of the pious dead in the Garden of Eden to intercede on our behalf before the Almighty so that He may have mercy upon us and ease our sufferings.

(*Zohar, Leviticus*)

595. QUESTION:
When leaving a grave it is customary to pluck some grass or take some pebbles from the ground and place them on the tombstone. Why?

ANSWER:
This is done in honor of the dead and as a sign that we visited their graves.

(*Baer Hetev*)

596. QUESTION:
What is the origin of the custom of the pious to visit the grave of a righteous man on the anniversary of his death (Yahrzeit) and to offer prayers and to light candles there?

ANSWER:
This custom is derived from Rashi's comment on Yebamoth 122a, Line 1: "Each year, on the anniversary of the passing of a great man, all the learned people of the surrounding area should make a pilgrimage to his grave to pay homage to the deceased."

597. QUESTION:
It is customary to observe the yahrzeit, the anniversaries of the death of parents. Why?

ANSWER:
Says the Kitzur Shulhan Arukh: "It is meritorious to fast on the death anniversary of one's father or mother as a means of repentance and self-examination, which in turn will help his departed parent to reach a higher sphere in Gan Eden (Paradise) ... It is customary to light a *Yahrzeit* candle ..."

598. QUESTION:

What is the meaning of the Hebrew word P'tira, which is used as a euphemism for the death of a righteous person?

ANSWER:

The word is derived from *patur,* the Hebrew for "free." It is meant to imply that the deceased has freed himself from the bonds of the world of falsehood and is entering the True World of joy and happiness.

(Toldoth Yaakov Yosef)

In this connection, the author of Divre David quotes the Tzaddik of Czortov as follows: "It is for this reason that the children of the Tzaddik and his disciples make a feast each year on the anniversary of his passing, for with each passing year, the Tzaddik is raised to a higher sphere on this very day."

HE WILL SWALLOW UP DEATH FOREVER,
AND THE L-RD G-D WILL WIPE AWAY
TEARS FROM ALL FACES (ISAIAH 25:8).

Concluded with the
help of G-d,
may He be blessed
and exalted.

תם ונשלם שבח לאל בורא עולם

מנהג

הבנתה בספרות התלמודית ובפי העם היא, התנהגות איש או של
צבור, כמו: מנהג גדול היה בירושלים מפה פרוסה ע"ג הפתח, כל זמן
שמפה פרוסה אורחין נכנסים (ב"ב צ"ג:) או מנהג אבותינו תורה הוא
(ש"ע יו"ד סי' שע"ו ד'). אמרו במקום שנוהגין עושין כך וכך ובמקום
שאין נוהגין אין עושין, ולעולם אל ישנה אדם מן המנהג (ב"מ פ"ו:)
שהרי משה עלה למרום ולא אכל לחם, מלאכי השרת ירדו למטה ואכלו
לחם. כן אין משנין מנהג שכבר נתקבל משום דרך ארץ, ור' יוחנן אמר
לבני ביישן, דאמרי אבהתן אפשר להו אנן לא אפשר לן, כבר קיבלו
אבותיכם עליהם ונאמר שמע בני מוסר אביך ואל תטוש תורת אמך (פסחים
נ':). ויש מנהג אשר מבטל גם ההלכה מפורשת. עי' ירושלמי ב"מ פ"ז א',
אמר רב הושעיא זאת אומרת המנהג מבטל את ההלכה (ועי' פ"מ שם).
ובפרט אין לשנות מנהג אפילו הוא שלא כדין אם על ידי השינוי יצא לעז
על הראשונים. מטעם זה אמרו (ירושלמי יבמות ריש פי"ב): חולצין
בסנדל שכך נהגו רבים ואפילו אם יבא אליהו ויאמר אין חולצין בו אין
שומעין לו. ולפעמים עת ההלכה רופפת בידי החכמים סמכו על המנהג
(ירושלמי פאה פ"ז, ה"ה). כן עשה הלל עת נעלמה ממנו ההלכה ע"ד הבאת
סכין בערב פסח שחל להיות בשבת, ורבא כשנשאל הלכה מאי, אם לברך
שהכל בתחילה ולבסוף בורא נפשות, ענה, פוק חזי מה עמא דבר, איך
נוהגים (ברכות מ"ה, פסחים ס"ו).

ישנם מנהגים הנעשים מפני שאדם גדול היה נוהג לעשות כן, כן
אנו כורכים מצה ומרור ואוכלים ביחד מפני שכן עשה הלל. וישנם כמה
איסורים הנוהגים מפני שרבנים גדולים החמירו בעצמם וקבלו עליהם העם
להחמיר על פיהם, למשל כתב הרמ"א (יו"ד סי' פ"ט, א') שהמנהג הפשוט
היה להמתין שעה אחת אחר אכילת הבשר והיו אוכלין אחר כך גבינה.
הש"ך החמיר שעכ"פ בני תורה לא יקילו בעצמם פחות משש שעות,
ונוהגים כל העם במדינות רוסיה ופולין להמתין שש שעות. ומנהגים כאלה
בכל חיי היהודי רבו עד לאין מספר (אוצר ישראל ערך מנהג).

305

Bibliography and Index

A

Abudraham (Rabbi David ben Joseph), 32, 33, 37, 39, 56, 58, 59, 63, 67, 72, 86, 110, 111, 122, 126, 127, 129, 130, 138, 139, 155, 161, 169, 171, 181, 184, 187, 191, 192, 193, 201, 208, 218, 227, 228, 231, 248, 250, 251, 255, 261, 262, 264, 267, 269, 272, 274, 285, 286

Adei Zahav, 19

Agra D'Kallah (Rebbe T'zvi Elimelekh Shapiro of Dinov), 76, 177

Agra D'Pirka, 14, 28, 82, 235, 272, 276

Ahavath Jonathan, 229

Ahavat Shalom (Menachem Mendel, Rebbe of Kassov, 59, 156, 202

Alfasi (Isaac), 54

Ari (Rabbi Yitzhak Luria Ashkenazi), 21, 37, 60, 77, 160, 211, 223, 284

Arvei Nahal, 33, 141

Atereth T'Zevi, 157

Atereth Z'kenim (Rabbi Menahem Mendel Auerbach), 13, 21, 22, 253, 262

Avkath Rocheil, 167

Avodat HaKodesh, 14

Avodath Yisrael (Rebbe Yisrael of Koznitz), 180

B

Baal HaTurim (Rabbenu Jacob ben Asher), 65

Baal Shem Tov (BESHT; Israel ben Eliezer), 18, 60

Baal Torath Hayim, 148

Bachya ibn Pakuda, 81, 119, 142

Baer Hetev (Rabbi Zechariah Mendel of Cracow), 19, 69, 83, 105, 108, 211, 243, 260, 266, 303

BaH (Beth Hadash; Rabbi Joel Sirkes), 173

Beth Aaron (Rebbe Aaron of Karlin), 17

Beth Yosef (Rabbi Yosef Caro), 13, 19, 23, 37, 38, 39, 48, 58, 65, 71, 92, 105, 121, 145, 177, 178, 206, 207, 239

Bigdei Yeshah, 107

Bikoreth Ha-Talmud, 257

Binath Moshe (Menahem Mendel, Rebbe of Koznitz), 176

Binyan Ariel, 204, 224

Birke Yosef (Rabbi Hayim Yosef David Azulay), 13, 14, 83

B'Nei Yisashar (Rabbi T'Zevi Elimelekh Shapiro of Dinov), 51, 93, 101, 201, 204, 270

C

Chachmath Adam, 294

Chayei Adam (Rabbi Abraham Danzig of Vilna), 104

D

Daath Moshe (Maggid of Koznitz), 54, 119, 176

Daath Z'kenim mi-Baalei Ha-Tosfoth, 189, 293

Dagul Mervavah (Rabbi Ezekiel Landau of Prague), 210

Darke Moshe (Rabbi Moses Isserles, 180, 268

Degel Machnei Ephraim, 18

Derekh Emuna, 157

Derekh Pikudekah, 272

Devir Hamutzna, 206

Divrei Emeth, 82, 156

Divrei Shaul, 120

Divrei Yehezkel (Rabbi Yehezkel Shrage Halberstam), 60, 166

D'vash L'fi (Rabbi Hayim Yosef David Azulay, 81

E

Elijah, Gaon of Vilna, 136, 196

Eliyahu Rabbah, 15, 19, 21, 29, 98, 102, 113, 118, 137, 140, 298, 299
Emek Beracha (Rabbi Abraham ben Shabsi Sheftel Ha-Levi Horovitz of Prague), 174
Eshel Avraham (Rabbi Avraham David, Gaon of Buczacz), 101, 104, 105, 106, 118, 143, 160, 174, 250, 257

G
Genesis Rabbah, 42
Geullath Israel, 84, 85, 146, 245
Gevurath HaShem, 192

H
Hadrath Kodesh, 27
Hagaoth Maimonides (Rabbi Meir Ha-Cohen of Toledo), 98
Hagaoth Minhagim, 135, 169, 205, 238
Haham T'zvi (Rabbi T'zvi Hirsh Ashkenazi), 84
Halakhot Ketanoth (Rabbi Jacob Hagiz), 134
HaManhig (see Sefer HaManhig).
HaMaor HaGadol, 107
Hasde Avoth, 212
Hatham Sofer (Rabbi Moses Schreiber), 31, 259
Hayim of Tzanz (Rebbe), 188
Hayim Yosef David Azulay (HIDA), 116
Hechal Ha-Kodesh, 15
Hessed le-Avraham (Rabbi Abraham Azulai), 175, 186
Ho-il Moshe, 188
Hok Yaakov, 179, 190, 191, 197, 201
Hok Yosef, 193
Hupath Chassanim, 286

I
Igeret HaTiyul (Brother of Rabbi Lowe of Prague), 53
Imrei Tzaddikim (Rebbe Dov Ber of Meziritch), 208
Imrot Tehorot, 142
Israel ben Eliezer (see Baal Shem Tov).
Isaac Luria (see Ari).
Iyun Tefillah, 101

J
Jerusalem Talmud, 169, 204, 234, 301

K
Kad HaKemach (Rabbi Bachye ben Asher), 72, 86, 133, 254, 264
Karban Ani, 283
Kav Ha-Yashar (Rebbe T'Zevi Hirsch Kaidenover), 14, 90
Kedushath Levi (Rabbi Levi Yitzhak of Bardichev), 112, 183, 208
Kerem S'hlomo (Rabbi Solomon Haas of Dresnitz), 43, 107, 153
Kitzur SHeLaH (Rabbi Yechiel Michael Epstein), 15, 22, 27, 28, 30, 37, 48, 52, 87
Kitzur Shulhan Arukh (Rabbi Solomon Ganzfried), 76, 214, 303
K'nesseth Hagdolah, 284
Kol Bo, 62, 66, 70, 95, 102, 107, 124, 132, 154, 162, 163, 165, 172, 204, 205, 213, 215, 240, 244, 245, 255, 259, 261, 281, 283, 284, 289, 290, 294
K'tav Yosher, 21

L
Lehem Hamudoth, 102
Lev David (Rabbi Hayim Yosef David Azulay), 176, 205
Levi Yitzchak of Bardichev (see Kedushath Levi).
Levush (Rabbi Mordecai Jaffe; Baal Ha-Levushim), 17, 25, 28, 35, 41, 43, 48, 63, 68, 71, 73, 74, 77, 81, 91, 96, 103, 104, 123, 126, 134, 139, 140, 149, 155, 163, 178, 180, 181, 182, 185, 188, 191, 194, 196, 199, 203, 208, 209, 210, 217, 221, 222, 225, 227, 229, 232, 235, 238, 240, 242, 243, 246, 247, 252, 253, 256, 260, 261, 262, 265, 289, 296, 300
Likhutei Hilkoth Shabbat, 117

M
Maasei HaShem, 190
Maaver Yaabok, 289, 291, 293, 294, 295

Machze Avraham, 108, 229, 252
Magen Avraham (Rabbi Avraham Gumbiner), 15, 16, 19, 27, 54, 57, 64, 81, 91, 93, 95, 98, 103, 111, 119, 136, 143, 158, 167, 168, 170, 173, 181, 186, 188, 195, 203, 204, 210, 215, 237, 240, 248, 262, 279
Maggid of Mezhirich (Rebbe Abraham ben Dov Ber), 149, 166
Maggid of Zlochuv (Rebbe Yechiel Michel), 107
Magid Taalumah (Rebbe T'zevi Elimelekh Shapiro of Dinov), 82
MaHaRaM (Rabbi Meir of Rothenburg), 77, 177
MaHaRIT (Rabbi Joseph Trani), 233
MaHaRIL (Rabbi Jacob Molin), 55, 164, 173, 212, 228, 268, 270, 275, 280, 302
MaHaRSHaL (Rabbi Solomon Luria), 53, 235
Maimonides (Rabbi Moses ben Maimon), 124, 142, 169, 199
Makhtzith Ha-Shekel (Rabbi Samuel HaLevi), 33, 113, 126, 141, 179
Ma'or Va-Shamesh, 30, 106
Masok Midvash, 148
Mateh Aaron, 192
Mateh Ephraim (Rabbi Ephraim Zalman Margolius), 116, 120, 233, 237, 240
Mateh Moshe (Rabbi Moses Abraham of Premsla), 60, 80, 144, 154, 191, 201, 209, 239, 241, 252, 254, 260, 281, 282
Mateh Yehudah, 287
Mayim Rabim, 31
Meir of Rothenburg (see MaHaRaM).
Menahem Mendel (Rebbe of Kassov), 41
Menahem Tziyon (Rebbe of Rimanov), 195, 202, 239
Mesorat HaBrith, 25
Midrash Echa Rabthi, 97

Midrash Rabbah, 178, 234, 301
Midrash Rabbah Esther, 270
Midrash Shir Ha-Shirim, 257
Midrash Talpiyoth (Rabbi Elijah Ha-Cohen of Izmir), 66, 169, 275
Midrash Tanhuma, 71, 258
Minhath Yaakov, 130
Mishkenoth Ha Ro'im, 147
Mishna Berura (Rabbi Israel Meir Kagan; Hafetz Hayim), 106
Mordekhai (in Arve Pesahim), 187

N

Nachlath Yaakov (Rabbi Yaakov of Lisa), 222
Natrunai Gaon, 31
Noam Elimelekh (Elimelekh, Rebbe of Lizensk), 61
Notzer Hessed (Rebbe of Komorn), 60

O

Orakh Hayim (Shulhan Arukh; Rabbi Yosef Caro), 15, 24, 49, 67, 77, 123, 206, 211, 224
Orchoth Hayim (Rabbi Nachman Kahana of Spinka), 83, 105, 106, 153, 154
Or HaHayim (Rabbi Hayim Atar), 41, 203
Or HaMeir, 280
Or LeShamayim (Rebbe Meir of Stovnitz), 117
Or Tzaddikim (Rabbi Meir Papirsh), 33, 36, 75

P

Pachad Yitzchak, 276
Pinhas, Rebbe of Karetz, 205, 224
Pirkei deRabbi Eliezer, 65, 168, 207, 216, 274, 279, 300
Piskhei Teshuva (Rabbi Abraham T'zevi Hirsch Eisenstadt), 83, 278, 300
P'ri Etz Hayim, 173
P'ri Hadash (Rabbi Hezekiah Silva), 135, 168, 178, 235
P'ri Megaddim (Rabbi Joseph Teumim), 23, 40, 137, 141, 143, 185, 244, 252

R

Rabbenu T'zevi Ha-Kohen of Rimanov, 22
Rabbenu Yonah, 50
Rabbenu Nissim, 145
Rabbi Eliezer of Kamarna, 175
Rabbi Feibish of Dobritch, 231
Rabbi Hayim Vital, 173
Rabbi Judah the Pious, 30
Rabbi Judah the Prince, 258
Rabbi Moses Cordovero, 168
Rabbi Moses Schreiber (see Hatham Sofer).
Rabbi Samson Ostropoler, 205
Rabbi Yechiel Michel (Maggid of Zlochuv), 107
Rabbi Yehudah T'zevi of Razdil, 231
Rachmei Ha-Av, 18, 105, 106, 231
RaN (Rabbi Nissim Gerandi), 226
RaSHBA (Rabbi Solomon ben Abraham Adereth), 16, 108
RaSHBaM (Rabbi Samuel ben Meir), 129
Rashi (Rabbi Solomon Yitzhaki), 23   44, 81, 107, 126, 183, 190, 242
Rav Hai Gaon, 30
RAVeD (Rabbi Abraham ibn Daud), 213
Rebbe Ber of Nadvorno, 104
Rebbe of Apt (Rabbi Abraham Joshua Heshel), 29
Rebbe of Lublin (Jacob Isaac), 166
Rebbe of Rimanov (Menahem Mendel), 150, 155, 231, 239
Rebbe of Rimanov (T'zevi Ha-Cohen), 156
Rebbe of Sassov (Moses Leib), 106
Rebbe Shlomo Kaminker, 276
Rebbe Shlomo Karlin, 272
Rebbe Shlomo of Skol, 166
Redak (Rabbi David Kimchi), 130
ReMa (Rabbi Moses Isserles), 27, 67, 86, 119, 147, 244, 266, 267, 280, 298

Responsas of MaHaRaM (Rabbi Meir of Rothenburg), 141
Responsas of MAHARAYE of Bruna, 29
Responsas Panim Me'Iroth (Rabbi Meir Ashkenazi of Eisenstadt), 50
Responsa Yaavetz (Rabbi Jacob Emden), 131
Rokeach (Rabbi Eliezer ben Judah), 31, 101, 124, 143, 266, 279, 286, 287
Rosh Ephraim, 109

S

Seder HaYom (RaSHBA; Rabbi Solomon ben Abraham Adreth), 15, 26, 128, 165, 246
Sefer HaBrith, 78
Sefer HaGan VeDerekh Moshe, 49, 85
Sefer HaHayim, 161
Sefer HaManhig (Rabbi Avraham ben Nathan Hayarchi of Lunel), 114, 211, 248, 285
Sefer HaOlamoth, 78
Sefer Hassidim (Rabbi Judah the Pious), 30, 51
Sefer Ho-Orah, 77
Sefer Mussar, 234
Shaarei Ephraim (Rabbi Ephraim Zalman Margolies of Brody), 77, 198
Shaarei Teshuva (Rabbi Hayim Mordecai Margulies), 13, 15, 22, 116, 197, 209
Shaddai Hemed, 83
Shalom (Rebbe of Belz), 27, 41, 106, 149
SHeLaH (Shenei Luhoth Ha-Berith; Rabbi Isaiah Horovitz), 22, 104, 220
Shibalei Ha-Lekett (Rabbi Zedekiah ben Abraham De Pietosi of Rome), 47, 64, 128, 271, 273, 295
Shiyurei Beracha (Rabbi Hayim Yosef David Azulay), 108
Shiltei HaGibborim, 288
Shulhan Arba, 90

Shulhan Arukh Ha-Rav (Rabbi Schneur Zalman of Liadi-Lubavitch), 14, 73, 95, 113, 139, 149, 151, 158, 238, 244, 245, 253, 281
Shulhan Arukh Ha-Ari (see Ari).
Siddur Lev Sameakh (Rebbe of Alesk), 27, 41
Sifte Emeth (Rebbe of Brezan), 99
Sodei Razi, 140

T

TaSHBeTZ (Rabbi Simon ben Zemach Duran), 20, 52, 210, 282, 290, 292
TaZ (Turei Zahav; Rabbi David Ha-Levy), 20, 56, 77, 91, 92, 103, 139, 170, 184, 194, 198, 202, 219, 221, 224, 225, 230, 242, 243, 268, 300
Terumath HaDeshen, 114
Tolaath Yaakov (Rabbi Meir ibn Gabbai), 125, 161, 254, 283
Toldoth Aaron (Rebbe Aaron of Zhitomer), 117
Toldoth Esther, 196
Toldoth Menahem, 121
Toldoth Yaakov Yosef (the Pulnaer), 142, 304
Torath Ha-Adam, 54
Tosfoth, 39, 51, 53, 137, 147, 161, 204, 227, 242, 244, 250, 299
Totzoath Hayyim, 28
Tur (Baal Ha-Turim; Rabbi Jacob ben Asher), 31, 34, 36, 37, 38, 39, 43, 44, 48, 59, 64, 96, 115, 118, 122, 123, 125, 131, 150, 164, 172, 181, 184, 185, 187, 216, 222, 225, 239, 301
Tzemach David (Rebbe David of Dinov), 148, 164

T'zevi Hirsh (Rebbe of Zidichov), 144

V

Vavei Ha-Amudim, 223
Vital, Rabbi Hayim, 173

Y

Yaaroth D'Vash (Rabbi Jonathan Eibeschutz), 83
Yaavetz (Rabbi Jacob ben T'zevi Emden), 84, 120, 152, 159, 188, 271, 275, 277
Yad Aaron (Rebbe Aaron Leib of Nadvorno), 146
Yad Ephraim, 84
Yaakov Yitzchak (Rebbe of Lublin), 30
Yalkut Shoftim, 288
Yesh Nochlin, 57
Yeshuoth Yaakov (Rabbi Yaakov Yehoshua Orenstein of Levuv), 81
Yesod HaTeshuvah, 220
Yesod Ve-Shoresh Ha-Avodah (Rabbi Alexander Susskind of Grodno), 171
Yismach Moshe (Rabbi Moses Teitelbaum), 235
Yom Tov Lipman Heller (Tosfoth Yom Tov), 83
Yosef Ometz (Rabbi Hayim Yosef David Azulay), 109

Z

Zerah Kodesh (Rebbe of Ropshitz), 17, 52, 60, 150, 233, 249, 251, 278
Zichron Tov (Rebbe of Neschitz), 56, 132, 166
Zohar, 13, 14, 15, 17, 19, 28, 33, 57, 64, 90, 200, 292, 303
Zohar Hai (Rebbe Yitzhak Eizik of Kamarno), 114
Zusia, (Rebbe of Anipol), 54